AF531579

# Information Security in a Networked World

# Information Security in a Networked World

Sahibjeet Singh

RANDOM PUBLICATIONS
NEW DELHI (INDIA)

**Information Security in a Networked World**

---

ISBN 978-93-5111-468-0


Published in 2015 in India by

**RANDOM PUBLICATIONS**

4376-A/4B, Gali Murari Lal, Ansari Road
New Delhi-110 002
Phone : +9111-43580356, 011-23289044, 011-43142548
e-mail: sales@randompublications.com,
info@randompublications.com, randomexports@gmail.com

Reprint 2021

*Type Setting by* : Friends Media, Delhi-110089
*Digitally Printed at:* Replika Press Pvt. Ltd.

# Preface

Information security is the process of protecting the availability, privacy, and integrity of data. While the term often describes measures and methods of increasing computer security, it also refers to the protection of any type of important data, such as personal diaries or the classified plot details of an upcoming book. No security system is foolproof, but taking basic and practical steps to protect data is critical for good information security.

Governments, military, corporations, financial institutions, hospitals, and private businesses amass a great deal of confidential information about their employees, customers, products, research, and financial status. Most of this information is now collected, processed and stored on electronic computers and transmitted across networks to other computers.

If confidential information about a business' customers or finances or new product line fall into the hands of a competitor, such a breach of security could lead to negative consequences. Protecting confidential information is a business requirement, and in many cases also an ethical and legal requirement. For the individual, information security has a significant effect on privacy, which is viewed very differently in different cultures.

The field of information security has grown and evolved significantly in recent years. There are many ways of gaining entry into the field as a career. It offers many areas for specialization including: securing network(s) and allied infrastructure, securing applications and databases, security testing, information systems auditing, business continuity planning and digital forensics science, etc.

This book presents a general overview of information security and its core concepts. It is designed for students and instructors in information technology, computer science, and engineering, as well as for professionals working in these fields.

**Author**

# Contents

# 1

# The Digital Revolution

The digital revolution is the change from analog mechanical and electronic technology to digital technology that has taken place since about 1980 and continues to the present day. Implicitly, the term also refers to the sweeping changes brought about by digital computing and communication technology during the latter half of the 20th century. Analogous to the Agricultural Revolution and Industrial Revolution, the Digital Revolution marked the beginning of the Information Age.

Central to this revolution is the mass production and widespread use of digital logic circuits, and its derived technologies, including the computer, digital cellular phone, and fax machine.

The underlying technology was invented in the later half of the 20th century and became economical for widespread adoption after the invention of the personal computer. Claude Shannon, a Bell Labs mathematician, is credited for having laid out the foundations of digitalization in his pioneering 1948 article, A Mathematical Theory of Communication. The digital revolution converted technology that previously was analog into a digital format. By doing this, it became possible to make multiple generation copies that were identical to the original. In digital communications, for example, repeating hardware was able to amplify the digital signal and pass it on with no loss of information in the signal. Of equal importance to the revolution was the ability to easily move the digital information between media, and to access or distribute it remotely.

A major landmark in the revolution was the transition from analog to digital recorded music. In the 1980s, the digital format of optical compact discs supplanted analog formats, such as vinyl records and cassette tapes, as the popular medium of choice.

Underlying the digital revolution was the development of the digital electronic computer, the personal computer, and particularly the microprocessor with its steadily increasing performance (as described by Moore's law), which enabled computer technology to be embedded into a huge range of objects from cameras to personal music players. Equally important was the development of transmission technologies including computer networking, the Internet and digital broadcasting. 3G phones, whose social penetration grew exponentially in the 2000s, also played a very large role in the digital revolution as they simultaneously provide ubiquitous entertainment, communications, and online connectivity.

## The Information Age

The Information Age, also commonly known as the Computer Age or Digital Age, is a period in human history characterized by the shift from traditional industry that the industrial revolution brought through industrialization, to an economy based on the manipulation of information, i.e., an information society. The onset of the Information Age is associated with Digital Revolution, just as the Industrial Revolution marked the onset of the Industrial Age.

During the information age individuals gained the ability to transfer information freely, and to have instant access to information that would have been difficult or impossible to find previously.

The Information Age formed by capitalizing on the computer microminiaturization advances, with a transition spanning from the advent of the personal computer in the late 1970s to the internet's reaching a critical mass in the early 1990s, and the adoption of such technology by the public in the two decades after 1990. Bringing about a fast evolution of technology in daily life, as well as of educational life style, the Information Age has allowed rapid global communications and networking to shape modern society.

### The Internet

The Internet was conceived as a fail-proof network that could connect computers together and be resistant to any single point of failure. It's said that the Internet cannot be totally destroyed in one event, and if large areas are disabled, the information is easily rerouted. It was created mainly by DARPA; its initial software applications were e-mail and computer file transfer.

Though the Internet itself has existed since 1969, it was with the invention of the World Wide Web in 1989 by British scientist Tim Berners-Lee and Belgian Robert Cailliau and its implementation in 1991 that the Internet truly became a global network. Today the Internet is a global platform for accelerating the flow of information and is pushing many, if not most, older forms of media into obsolescence.

## Progression

Library expansion was calculated in 1945 by Fremont Rider to double in capacity every 16 years, if sufficient space were made available. He advocated replacing bulky, decaying printed works with miniaturized microform analog photographs, which could be duplicated on-demand for library patrons or other institutions. He did not foresee the digital technology that would follow decades later to replace analog microform with digital imaging, storage, and transmission mediums. Automated, potentially lossless digital technologies allowed vast increases in the rapidity of information growth. Moore's law was formulated around 1970.

The proliferation of the smaller and less expensive personal computers and improvements in computing power by the early 1980s resulted in a sudden access to and ability to share and store information for more and more workers. Connectivity between computers within companies led to the ability of workers at different levels to access greater amounts of information.

### *Information storage*

The world's technological capacity to store information grew from 2.6 (optimally compressed) exabytes in 1986 to 15.8 in 1993, over 54.5 in 2000, and to 295 (optimally compressed) exabytes in 2007. This is the informational equivalent to less than one 730-MB CD-ROM per person in 1986 (539 MB per person), roughly 4 CD-ROM per person of 1993, 12 CD-ROM per person in the year 2000, and almost 61 CD-ROM per person in 2007. Piling up the imagined 404 billion CD-ROM from 2007 would create a stack from the earth to the moon and a quarter of this distance beyond (with 1.2 mm thickness per CD).

### *Information transmission*

The world's technological capacity to receive information through one-way broadcast networks was 432 exabytes of (optimally compressed) information in 1986, 715 (optimally compressed) exabytes in 1993, 1.2 (optimally compressed) zettabytes in 2000, and 1.9 zettabytes in 2007 (this is the information equivalent of 174 newspapers per person per day). The world's effective capacity to exchange information through two-way telecommunication networks was 281 petabytes of (optimally compressed) information in 1986, 471 petabytes in 1993, 2.2 (optimally compressed) exabytes in 2000, and 65 (optimally compressed) exabytes in 2007 (this is the information equivalent of 6 newspapers per person per day). In the 1990s, the spread of the Internet caused a sudden leap in access to and ability to share information in businesses, at home and around the globe. Technology was developing so quickly that a computer costing $3,000.00 in 1997 would cost $2,000.00 two years later and only $1000.00 the following year.

### *Computation*

The world's technological capacity to compute information with humanly guided general-purpose computers grew from 3.0 × 108 MIPS in 1986, to 4.4 × 109 MIPS in 1993, 2.9 × 1011 MIPS in 2000 to 6.4 × 1012 MIPS in 2007.

## Relation to Economics

Eventually, Information and Communication Technology—computers, computerized machinery, fiber optics, communication satellites, Internet, and other ICT tools—became a significant part of the economy. Microcomputers were developed and many business and industries were greatly changed by ICT. Nicholas Negroponte captured the essence of these changes in his 1995 book, Being Digital. His book discusses similarities and differences between products made of atoms and products made of bits. In essence, one can very cheaply and quickly make a copy of a product made of bits, and ship it across the country or around the world both quickly and at very low cost.

## The Impact on Jobs and Income Distribution

The Information Age has impacted the workforce in several ways. First, it has created a situation in which workers who perform tasks which are easily automated are being forced to find work which involves tasks that are not easily automated. Second, workers are being forced to compete in a global job market. Lastly workers are being replaced by computers that can do the job more effectively and faster. This poses problems for workers in industrial societies, which are still to be solved. However, solutions that involve lowering the working time usually find high resistance.

Jobs traditionally associated with the middle class (assembly line workers, data processors, foremen, and supervisors) are beginning to disappear, either through outsourcing or automation. Individuals who lose their jobs must either move up, joining a group of "mind workers" (engineers, doctors, attorneys, teachers, scientists, professors, executives, journalists, consultants), or settle for low-skill, low-wage service jobs.

The "mind workers" are able to compete successfully in the world market and command high wages. Conversely, production workers and service workers in industrialized nations are unable to compete with workers in developing countries and either lose their jobs through outsourcing or are forced to accept wage cuts. In addition, the internet makes it possible for workers in developing countries to provide in-person services and compete directly with their counterparts in other nations.

This has had several major consequences:

- *Increased opportunity in developing countries.* Workers in developing countries have a competitive advantage which translates into increased opportunities and higher wages. The full impact on the workforce in developing countries is complex; there are downsides.
- *The globalization of the workforce.* In the past, the economic fate of workers was tied to the fate of national economies. For example, workers in the United States were once well paid in comparison to the workers in other countries. With the advent of the Information Age and improvements in communication, this is no longer the case. Because workers are forced to compete in a global job market, wages are less dependent on the success or failure of individual economies.

## Automation, Productivity, and Job Loss

There is another way in which the Information Age has impacted the workforce: automation and computerization have resulted in higher productivity coupled with net job loss. In the United States for example, from Jan 1972 to August 2010, the number of people employed in manufacturing jobs fell from 17,500,001 to 11,500,000 while manufacturing value rose 270%.

It initially appeared that job loss in the industrial sector might be partially offset by the rapid growth of jobs in the IT sector. However after the recession of March 2001, the number of jobs in the IT sector dropped sharply and continued to drop until 2003. Even the IT sector is not immune to this problem. As such, modern society still has to solve this social problem.

### The Rise of Information-intensive Industry

Industry is becoming more information-intensive and less labor and capital-intensive. This trend has important implications for the workforce; workers are becoming increasingly productive as the value of their labor decreases. However, there are also important implications for capitalism itself; not only is the value of labor decreased, the value of capital is also diminished. In the classical model, investments in human capital and financial capital are important predictors of the performance of a new venture. However, as demonstrated by Mark Zuckerberg and Facebook, it now seems possible for a group of relatively inexperienced people with limited capital to succeed on a large scale.

## Socio-Economic Impact of Digital Revolution

### Positive Effects

Positive aspects include greater interconnectedness, easier communication, and the exposure of information that in the past could have more easily been suppressed by totalitarian regimes.

The economic impact of the digital revolution has been large. Without the World Wide Web (WWW), for example, globalization and outsourcing would not be nearly as viable as they are today. The digital revolution radically changed the way individuals and companies interact. Small regional companies were suddenly given access to much larger markets. Concepts such as On-demand services and manufacturing and rapidly dropping technology costs made possible innovations in all aspects of industry and everyday life.

After initial concerns of an IT productivity paradox, evidence is mounting that digital technologies have significantly increased the productivity and performance of businesses.

### Negative Effects

Negative effects include information overload, Internet predators, forms of social isolation, and media saturation.

In some cases, company employees' pervasive use of portable digital devices and work related computers for personal use — email, instant messaging, computer games — were often found to, or perceived to, reduce those companies' productivity. Personal computing and other non-work related digital activities in the workplace thus helped lead to stronger forms of privacy invasion, such as keystroke recording and information filtering applications (spyware and content-control software).

### Information Sharing and Privacy

Privacy in general became a concern during the digital revolution. The ability to store and utilize such large amounts of diverse information opened possibilities for tracking of individual activities and interests. Social libertarians and privacy rights advocates feared the possibility of an Orwellian future where centralized power structures control the populace via automatic surveillance and monitoring of personal information in such programs as the CIA's Information Awareness Office. Consumer and labor advocates opposed the ability to direct market to individuals, discriminate in hiring and lending decisions, invasively monitor employee behavior and communications and generally profit from involuntarily shared personal information.

The Internet, especially the WWW in the 1990s, opened whole new avenues for communication and information sharing. The ability to easily and rapidly share information on a global scale brought with it a whole new level of freedom of speech. Individuals and organizations were suddenly given the ability to publish on any topic, to a global audience, at a negligible cost, particularly in comparison to any previous communication technology.

Large cooperative projects could be endeavored (e.g. Open-source software projects, SETI@home). Communities of like-minded individuals were formed (e.g. MySpace, Tribe.net). Small regional companies were suddenly given access to a larger marketplace.

In other cases, special interest groups as well as social and religious institutions found much of the content objectionable, even dangerous. Many parents and religious organizations, especially in the United States, became alarmed by pornography being more readily available to minors. In other circumstances the proliferation of information on such topics as child pornography, building bombs, committing acts of terrorism, and other violent activities were alarming to many different groups of people. Such concerns contributed to arguments for censorship and regulation on the WWW.

### Copyright and Trademark Issues

Copyright and trademark issues also found new life in the digital revolution. The widespread ability of consumers to produce and distribute exact reproductions of protected works dramatically changed the intellectual property landscape, especially in the music, film, and television industries.

The digital revolution, especially regarding privacy, copyright, censorship and information sharing, remains a controversial topic. As the digital revolution progresses it remains unclear to what extent society has been impacted and will be altered in the future.

## Technological Revolutions: Future Concerns

The Agricultural revolution lead to agricultural cities in the ancient world, such as the ancient egyptian and ancient chinese cities. Then the Industrial revolution lead to industrial cities in the 19th century, such as New York City. Thus there is evidence of a trend, that follows that the digital revolution may lead to digital cities sometime in the future. Perhaps some sort of virtual immersion technology may lead to immersion within these virtual cities of the future.

While there have been huge benefits to society from the digital revolution, especially in terms of the accessibility of information, there are a number of concerns. Expanded powers of communication and information sharing, increased capabilities for existing technologies, and the advent of new technology brought with it many potential opportunities for exploitation. The digital revolution helped usher in a new age of mass surveillance, generating a range of new civil and human rights issues. Reliability of data became an issue as information could easily be replicated, but not easily verified. The digital revolution made it possible to store and track facts, articles, statistics, as well as minutia hitherto unfeasible.

From the perspective of the historian, a large part of human history is known through physical objects from the past that have been found or preserved, particularly in written documents. Digital records are easy to create but also easy to delete and modify. Changes in storage formats can make recovery of data difficult or near impossible, as can the storage of information on obsolete media for which reproduction equipment is unavailable, and even identifying what such data is and whether it is of interest can be near impossible if it is no longer easily readable, or if there is a large number of such files to identify. Information passed off as authentic research or study must be scrutinized and verified. With such massive proliferation of information it became possible to write an article citing wholly false sources, also based on false sources.

These problems are further compounded by the use of digital rights management and other copy prevention technologies which, being designed to only allow the data to be read on specific machines, may well make future data recovery impossible. Interestingly, the Voyager Golden Record, which is intended to be read by an intelligent extraterrestrial (perhaps a suitable parallel to a human from the distant future), is recorded in analog rather than digital format specifically for easy interpretation and analysis.

## References

Bhagwati, Jagdish N. (2005). *In defense of Globalization.* New York: Oxford University Press

Cooke, Sandra D. (2003). "Information Technology Workers in the Digital Economy", in Digital Economy 2003. 2003: Economics and Statistics Administration, Department of Commerce.

Peltier, Thomas R. (2001). *Information Security Risk Analysis.* Boca Raton, FL: Auerbach publications.

Rider (1944). *The Scholar and the Future of the Research Library.* New York City: Hadham Press.

# 2

# Networked World: Risks and Opportunities

Technology is not inherently good or bad -the outcome depends on how it is used. Some people argue that technology is a reward of development, making it inevitable that the digital divide follows the income divide. True, as incomes rise, people gain access to the benefits of technological advance. But many technologies are tools of human development that enable people to increase their incomes, live longer, be healthier, enjoy a better standard of living, participate more in their communities and lead more creative lives. From the earliest times, people have fashioned tools to address the challenges of existence, from war to health care to crop production. Technology is like education -it enables people to lift themselves out of poverty. Thus technology is a tool for, not just a reward of, growth and development.

Technology has been at the heart of human progress since earliest times. Our prehuman ancestors fashioned sticks to reach for food, used leaves to sop up water and hurled stones in anger, just as chimpanzees do today. The first human species is named Homo habilis -the "handy man ". Its fossils from some 2.5 million years ago lie with chipped pebbles, the first unequivocal stone tools. Early Homo may have used the perishable technologies of gourds to drink water and leather slings to carry infants. About half a million years ago, Homo erectus fashioned elegant leaf-shaped hand axes throughout Africa, Asia and Europe and was apparently using fire. Our own species, Homo sapiens -the "wise man "from some 40,000 years ago in Europe, the Middle East and Australia -made tools of stone, bone and antler as well as necklaces for adornment, and drew symbolic art on rock walls -technology in the service of ideas and communication.

Technological innovation is essential for human progress. From the printing press to the computer, from the first use of penicillin to the widespread use of vaccines, people have devised tools for improving health, raising productivity and facilitating learning and communication.

Human health and survival began to improve dramatically in both regions in the 1930s. By the 1970s life expectancy at birth had climbed to more than 60 years, achieving in four decades an increase that took Europe a century and a half starting in the early 1800s. The 1980s saw the impact of two new breakthroughs -oral rehydration therapy and vaccines better adapted to conditions in developing countries.These technologies, diffused through a major global campaign, enabled major reductions in child mortality. In developing countries deaths from major childhood diseases and from diarrhoea-related illnesses were cut by about 3 million between 1980 and 1990 -an especially impressive achievement given that it came during that "lost decade "of economic growth, when income growth was stagnant or negative

The importance of technology is quantified in a recent World Bank study showing that technical progress accounted for 40 -50% of mortality reductions between 1960 and 1990 - making technology a more important source of gains than higher incomes or higher education levels among women. Food production and nutrition. Technological progress has played a similar role in accelerating food production. It took nearly 1,000 years for wheat yields in England to increase from 0.5 tonnes per hectare to 2, but only 40 years to go from 2 tonnes per hectare to 6.4 Starting in 1960 a green revolution of plant breeding, fertilizer use, better seeds and water control transformed land and labour productivity around the world. This had dynamic effects on human development: increased food production and reduced food prices eliminated much of the undernutrition and chronic famine in Asia, Latin America and the Arab States. Because the poorest families rely on agriculture for their livelihood and spend half their incomes on food, this also contributed to huge declines in income poverty.

Like the printing press of earlier centuries, the telephone, radio, television and fax of the 20th century opened up communications, reducing isolation and enabling people to be better informed and to participate in decisions that affect their lives. Tied to these technologies is the free media, a pillar of all functioning democracies. The advent of the fax machine in the 1980s enabled much more rapid popular mobilization both nationally and globally. In the 1970s the acquisition and adaptation of manufacturing technology brought rapid gains in employment and incomes to the Republic of Korea, Malaysia and Singapore.

The industrial revolution was triggered by technological change, and economists argue that technological progress plays a pivotal role in sustained long-term economic growth. Cross-country studies suggest that technological change accounts for a large portion of differences in growth rates.

Information and communications technology involves innovations in microelectronics, computing (hardware and software), telecommunications and opto-electronics -microprocessors, semiconductors, fibre optics.These innovations enable the processing and storage of enormous amounts of information, along with rapid distribution of information through communication networks.

Moore's law predicts the doubling of computing power every 18 -24 months due to the rapid evolution of microprocessor technology. Gilder's law predicts the doubling of communications power every six months -a bandwidth explosion -due to advances in fibre-optic network technologies. Both are accompanied by huge reductions in costs and massive increases in speed and quantity. In 2001 more information can be sent over a single cable in a second than in 1997 was sent over the entire Internet in a month. The cost of transmitting a trillion bits of information from Boston to Los Angeles has fallen from $150,000 in 1970 to 12 cents today. A three-minute phone call from New York to London that in 1930 cost more than $300 costs less than 20 cents today.

E-mailing a 40-page document from Chile to Kenya costs less than 10 cents, faxing it about $10, sending it by courier $50. Linking computing devices and allowing them to communicate with each other creates networked information systems based on a common protocol. Individuals, households and institutions are linked in processing and executing a huge number of instructions in imperceptible time spans.This radically alters access to information and the structure of communication -extending the networked reach to all corners of the world.

## From the Industrial to the Network Age

Structures of production and other activities have been reorganized into networks that span the world. In the industrial age -with its high costs of information access, communications and transportation -businesses and organizations were vertically integrated. In the network age, with the costs of communications and information down to almost zero, horizontal networks make sense. Production is increasingly organized among separate players -subcontractors, suppliers, laboratories, management consultants, education and research institutes, marketing research firms, distributors.Their complex interactions, with each playing a niche role, create the value chains that drive the technology-based global economy.

The new age is giving rise to global networks in many areas of activity. When these networks reach a critical mass of members and interactions, they become an important new force in shaping the path and spread of technology. Scientific research and innovation -the original networked communication between universities that breathed life into the Internet -is increasingly collaborative between institutions and countries.

From 1995 -97, scientists in the United States coauthored articles with scientists from 173 other countries; scientists in Brazil with 114, in Kenya with 81, in Algeria 59.

Production -global corporations, often headquartered in North America, Europe or Japan, but with research facilities in several countries and outsourced production worldwide, drawing many new countries into creating their global value chains.

E-business -only now emerging as a future commerce network, business-to-business e-commerce is projected to rise.

Diaspora -skyrocketing demand for information and communications technology personnel makes top scientists and technologists globally mobile. When they come from developing countries, their global dispersal creates diaspora that can become valuable networks of finance, business contacts and skill transfer for their home country.

Rapid advances in two technologies -digital storage and processing of information (information) and satellite and optical fibre transmission of information (communications)-are creating new and faster ways of storing, handling, distributing and accessing information. More than that, these advances are dramatically lowering costs.

These new technologies dramatically increase access to information and communications, breaking barriers to knowledge and participation. The potential is only beginning to be explored. Initiatives are mushrooming and hint at tremendous possibilities. Political participation is being redefined by the creative use of two-way communications.

In the Philippines an electronic advocacy network was set up in early 2001 in response to the impeachment trial of former President Joseph Estrada, collecting more than 150,000 petition signatures and coordinating a letter-writing campaign that targeted senators to vote with their consciences, not with their vested interests. In Honduras an organization of small-scale fishermen has sent Congress a video of the illegal destruction of their mangroves by politically powerful commercial farmers, raising awareness of and protesting against the loss of their livelihoods and habitat. In the future, virtual committee rooms could allow citizens to testify on various issues, further expanding the Internet's possibilities for enhancing participation.

Greater transparency in planning and transactions is making markets and institutions work better. In Morocco the ministries of finance and planning have used information and communications technology to make the budget process more efficient, creating a common platform to share data on tax revenue, auditing and spending management. The time required to prepare a budget has been halved, and budgets better reflect actual revenue and spending.

In the Indian state of Gujurat, dairy farmers are paid based on the weight and fat content of their milk, which can be tested instantly using low-cost equipment. Such transparent and accurate measures reduce the risk of underpayment, and farmers 'accounts are matched with databases of their cattle, keeping a record of inoculation requirements -helping co-operatives to better manage input requirements and veterinary services.

Income Inventive use of the Internet is increasing incomes in developing countries. In Pondicherry, India the MS Swaminathan Research Foundation has set up rural information centres for local communication and Internet access using solar and electric power and wired and wireless communications. Farmers are getting information such as market prices, enabling them to negotiate better with intermediaries.

Fishermen can download satellite images that indicate where fish shoals are. Internet connections with other villages have encouraged local dialogue on farming techniques, microcredit management, business and education opportunities, traditional medicine and religious events. About one-third of the users are from assetless households, and about 18% are women.

Grameen Telecom provides telephones throughout Bangladesh, allowing individuals, schools and health centres to get the information they need easily and cheaply. Studies suggest that a single call provides real savings of 3 -10% of the average family's monthly income, benefiting poor households that use village phones for calls that replace the need to collect information through more expensive channels.

Health Where health problems are rooted in lack of information, new solutions are emerging. In Ginnack, a remote island on the Gambia river, nurses use a digital camera to record patients 'symptoms. The pictures are sent electronically to a nearby town to be diagnosed by a local doctor, or sent to the United Kingdom if a specialist's opinion is required.

The Healthnet Project is a network of networks launched in 1989 for health care professionals -especially in remote areas -in Africa, Asia and Latin America. It enables them to procure equipment efficiently, cooperate with medical institutions worldwide and provide information on emerging outbreaks. Nepal's Healthnet has 150 user points around the country, reaching 500 health professionals and getting 300 hits a day on its Website.

These examples are just the beginning. Tapping the potential of these new technologies will depend on adaptations to the conditions in developing countries, especially for poor users. Much will depend on innovations - technological, institutional and entrepreneurial -to create low-cost, easy to use devices and to set up access through public or market centres with affordable products.

In health ,pharmaceutical companies are moving from drug discovery and development based on medicinal chemistry to designing and developing drugs based on information provided by genomics and related technologies. Nearly 300 biopharmaceuticals have been approved for use or are being reviewed by the US Food and Drug Administration.

The genomics-based pharmaceutical market is projected to grow from $2.2 billion in 1999 to $8.2 billion in 2004. These products offer treatment for diseases that was not possible be- fore. Insulin as a tool to fight diabetes was made possible through recombinant DNA technology, as was a vaccine for hepatitis B. But that is just the beginning. Biotechnological knowledge has the potential to develop better treatment and vaccines for AIDS, malaria, cancer, heart disease and nervous disorders.

Gene therapy and antisense technologies will forever change the treatment of disease by actually curing diseases rather than treating symptoms. Five gene therapy drugs for various forms of cancer are expected to hit the market by 2005. Researchers at Cornell University in the United States have created transgenic tomatoes and bananas that contain a hepatitis B vaccine. Just one dried banana chip or one portion of tomato paste inside a wafer contains enough of the needed medication to act as a dose -costing less that one cent to make, in contrast to the usual $15. PowderJect Pharmaceuticals, a British company, has created DNA-based vaccines with a needle-free way to deliver them. The handheld device pumps a microscopic powdered vaccine painlessly into the skin in a jet of gas, making it far easier and safer to use than syringes and eliminating the need for refrigeration.

Biotechnical knowledge could also be used to modify organisms that transmit diseases -for example, creating the "perfect " mosquito, unable to carry malaria. In agriculture ,plant breeding promises to generate higher yields and resistance to drought, pests and disease. Traditional crossbreeding takes a long time, typically 8 -12 years.

Biotechnology speeds the process of producing crops with altered traits by using a specific genetic trait from any plant and moving it into the genetic code of any other plant. More significantly, the modification of plants is no longer restricted by the characteristics of that species. Cacti genes responsible for tolerating drought can be used to help food crops survive drought. Dwarfing genes used to increase cereal yields have been shown to have the same effect on other crops, so dwarfing could increase yields in crops previously unable to benefit from these genes. Genetic control of the rice yellow mottle virus shows what transgenics can do where conventional approaches failed. And farmers in China have been able to control the cotton bollworm, which can no longer be controlled by chemicals or host plant protection, by growing cotton expressing the Bacillus thuringiensis toxin.

New treatment for livestock diseases appears to be the most significant area for product development. Diagnostic tests and recombinant DNA vaccines for rinderpest, cowdriosis (heartwater), theileriosis (East coast fever) and foot-and-mouth disease are reportedly ready for large-scale testing or product development. Technology concerns are likewise addressed with countervailing pressure and alternative opinions, from access to HIV/AIDS drugs and intellectual property rules to the risks of genetically modified foods.

## New Possibilities

Today's technological advances can accelerate human development in many areas. Biotechnology provides a way forward in medicine and agriculture where earlier methods were less successful. Designing new drugs and treatments based on genomics and related technologies offers potential for tackling the major health challenges facing poor countries and people - possibly leading, for example, to vaccines for malaria and HIV/AIDS.

Genomics can speed up plant breeding and drive the development of new crop varieties with greater drought and disease resistance, less environmental stress and more nutritional value. Biotechnology offers the only or the best 'tool of choice 'for marginal ecological zones -left behind by the green revolution but home to more than half of the world's poorest people, dependent on agriculture and livestock.

There is a long way to go before biotechnology's potential is mobilized. Transgenic crops increased from 2 million hectares planted in 1996 to 44 million hectares in 2000. But 98% of that is in just three countries - Argentina, Canada and the United States. Moreover, all governments must devise new institutional and scientific policies to manage the health, environmental and social risks of this new innovation.

Applications in information and communications technology are farther ahead of those in biotechnology. The Internet has grown exponentially, from 16 million users in 1995 to more than 400 million users in 2000 -and to an expected 1 billion users in 2005.15 Connectivity is rising at spectacular rates in Europe, Japan, the United States and many developing countries.

In Latin America Internet use is growing by more than 30% a year - though that still means that only 12% of individuals will be connected by 2005. Broader expansion is limited by low household incomes. Connecting a major portion of the population will be a challenge in developing regions. But the digital divide need not be permanent if technological adaptations and institutional innovations expand access.Creativity and entrepreneurship in Brazil, India, Thailand, Niger and elsewhere have already developed software for illiterate users and low-cost, solar-powered wireless devices.

Community access -public and private -is proliferating in urban and rural settings. From South Africa to Bangladesh, innovations like prepaid phone cards are expanding access to information and communications technology.

Multiple uses are made from health to education to political participation, not to mention raising the incomes of poor families.

Access to information is as central as education to building human capabilities. While education develops cognitive skills, information gives content to knowledge. The Internet and the World Wide Web can deliver information to the poor and the rich alike.

Poor people and communities are often isolated and lack means to take collective action. Global Internet communications have powered many global civil society movements in recent years: the agreement to ban land mines, initiatives to provide debt relief to poor countries and efforts to provide HIV/ AIDS drugs in poor countries. The Internet is just as powerful in mobilizing people locally. E-mail campaigns against corruption influenced Korea 's 1999 elections and gave rise to the recent movement that deposed Philippine President Joseph Estrada. The world over, citizens are increasingly able to use the Internet to hold governments more accountable.

Breaking barriers to economic opportunity. Despite the recent drops in technology stocks and the demise of many dot-coms, information and communications technology and related industries are among the most dynamic sectors of the global economy. They offer the potential for developing countries to expand exports, create good jobs and diversify their economies.

The information and communications technology sector requires less initial investment in capital and infrastructure than do more traditional sectors -which may explain why high-tech industries are growing faster than medium-tech industries in developing countries. Moreover, such industries are labour-intensive, providing new jobs and wages for educated workers. Wages are high for Indian software professionals, but competitive in the global market.

Global spending on information and communications technology is projected to grow from $2.2 trillion in 1999 to $3 trillion by 2003 -providing many niche opportunities for service providers in developing countries. There are now about 2.5 billion unique, publicly accessible Web pages on the Internet, and 7.3 million new ones are added every day.

The World Wide Web is too expensive for millions of people in developing countries, partly because of the cost of computers that are the standard entry point to the Web: in January 2001 the cheapest Pentium III computer was $700 -hardly affordable for low-income community access points. Further, the text-based interface of the Internet puts it out of reach for illiterate people.

To overcome these barriers, academics at the Indian Institute of Science and engineers at the Bangalore-based design company Encore Software designed a handheld Internet appliance for less than $200. Based on the Linux open source operating system, the first version of the Simputer will provide Internet and email access in local languages, with touch-screen functions and mi-crobanking applications.Future versions promise speech recognition and text-to-speech software for illiterate users.

The intellectual property rights have been transferred for free to the non-profit Simputer Trust, which is licensing the technology to manufacturers at a nominal fee -and the device is soon to be launched.

With Internet access through wireless devices, including mobile phones, expected to outstrip personal computer access by 2005, people and businesses in developing countries will become increasingly able to access valuable Internet-based information. Global business to consumer e-commerce is projected to grow from $25 billion in 1999 to $233 billion by 2004; business to business e-commerce projections range from $1.2 to $10 trillion by 2003.

Developing countries that can develop the requisite infrastructure can participate in new global business models of intermediation, business process outsourcing and value chain integration. In developing countries, as the user base expands, costs fall and technologies are adapted to local needs, the potential of information and communications technology will be limited only by human imagination and political will.

Proponents of the new economy claim that today 's technological revolution has created a new growth paradigm that will allow US GDP to keep expanding at well over 4%a year -a new engine of higher long-term growth comparable to the railway or electricity. But a dismissive contingent, bolstered by the downturn in dot-coms and NASDAQ share prices, claims that increases in productivity have been confined to the computer sector, helped along by the economic cycle -and that computers and the Internet do not rate with the industrial revolution.

Several contours of this new age must be understood if poor countries and poor people are to take advantage of the new opportunities. First, skills matter more than ever in today 's more competitive global market. Technology transfer and diffusion are not easy. Developing countries cannot simply import and apply knowledge from outside by obtaining equipment, seeds and pills.

Not every country needs to develop cutting-edge technologies, but every country needs domestic capacity to identify technology 's potential benefits and to adapt new technology to its needs and constraints. To use a new technology, firms and farmers must be able to learn and develop new skills with ease.

In Thailand four years of education triples the chance that a farmer will use fertilizer effectively. In India educated farmers are more likely to use irrigation and improved seeds. In this era of rapid technological advance, mastering new technology is a continuous process. Without continuous upgrading of skills, countries cannot stay competitive. Second, new global rules giving value to technology also matter more.

New rules endorsed by almost all countries have brought tighter intellectual property protection worldwide. These raise the market value of technology, increasing incentives to invest in research and development. But they also imply new choices for developing countries in accessing technology and shifts in costs for consumers.

Third, the private sector is leading global research and development, and has much of the finance, knowledge and personnel for technological innovation. Among most OECD countries the private sector finances 50 - 60% of research and development. Firms play an even bigger role in research and development in Ireland, Japan, Korea and Sweden. In most countries corporations implement more research than they fund, indicating that there is some government funding of corporate research and development.

Universities typically undertake 15 -20% of national research and development, while public research institutions account for about 10% in North America and the Nordic countries, slightly more than 15% in the European Union. New forms of private financing of high-risk research are part of the story.

Small, technology-based startups carry high risks, making them unlikely candidates for conventional financing.Venture capital, central to the technology boom in the United States and backing new technology companies in Europe and Japan, allows the market to pick a winner. It is emerging elsewhere -including China, India, Israel and Singapore.

Corporations dominate research and development in the information and communications technology and biotechnology that matter so much for human development. Worldwide, the pharmaceutical and biotechnology industries spent $39 billion on research and development in 1998.

Research-based pharmaceutical companies in the United States invested $24 billion in 1999, increasing to $26.4 billion in 2000. Since the mid-1990s the top 20 pharmaceutical companies have doubled their spending on research and development. If that trend continues, average spending per company could rise to $2.5 billion by 2005.

Fourth, a global labour market has emerged for top technology professionals. Propelled by skill shortages in Europe, Japan and the United States, such workers are increasingly mobile across countries. In 2000 the United States approved legislation allowing 195,000 more work visas each year for skilled professionals.

Of the 81,000 visas approved between October 1999 and February 2000, 40% were for individuals from India and more than half were for computer-related occupations, a sixth for sciences and engineering. A secondary effect has emerged: a new kind of business or brain diaspora. A strong link between Silicon Valley and Bangalore is built on the Indian diaspora in economic networks as they invest at home, but is also facilitating contacts for market access.

Fifth, startup companies, research labs, and financiers and corporations are converging in new global hubs of innovation, creating a dynamic environment that brings together know-how, finance and opportunity.

What real promises does the new economy hold for developing countries? The explosive expansion of global information and communications technology has triggered new opportunities for niche activities. In India the industry generated 330 billion rupiah ($7.7 billion) in 1999,15 times the level in 1990, and exports rose from $150 million in 1990 to nearly $4 billion in 1999. One study estimates that this could rise to $50 billion by 2008, leading information technology to account for 30% of India 's exports and 7.5% of its GDP. Employment in the software industry is projected to rise from 180,000 in 1998 to 2.2 million in 2008, to account for 8% of India 's formal employment.

Information and communications technology has created new outsourcing opportunities by enabling services to be provided in one country and delivered in another. Delivered by telecommunication or data networks, the services include credit card administration, insurance claims, business payrolls and customer, financial and human resource management. The global outsourcing market is worth more than $100 billion, with 185 Fortune 500 companies outsourcing their software requirements in India alone. India now has 1,250 companies exporting software.

India shows why public policy is important. By providing education for information technology -India 's English-language technical colleges turn out more than 73,000 graduates a year -and investing in infrastructure, the government has ensured India 's place in the new economy. These efforts will deliver long-term benefits for human development and equitable economic growth.

## Technology Achievement Index (TAI)

The uneven diffusion of information and communications technology -the digital divide -has caught the attention of world leaders. Bridging this divide is now a global objective. But the uneven diffusion of technology is nothing new. There have long been huge differences among countries. As a result the world 's 200 or so countries face the challenges of human development in the network age starting from very different points. In addition to the differences across countries, the index reveals considerable disparities within countries. Consider India, home to one of the most dynamic global hubs - Bangalore, which Wired rated 11th among the 46 hubs.

Yet India ranks 63rd in the technology achievement index, falling among the lower end of dynamic adopters. Because of huge variations in technological achievement among Indian states. The country has the world 's seventh largest number of scientists and engineers, some 140,000 in 1994. Yet in 1999 mean years of schooling were only 5.1 years and adult illiteracy was 44%.

The technology achievement index focusses on three dimensions at the country level:

— Creating new products and processes through research and development.

— Using new technologies -and old -in production and consumption.

— Having the skills for technological learning and innovation.

New invention and product development, mostly the result of systematic investments in research and development, are carried out almost exclusively in high-income OECD countries and a handful of developing countries in Asia and Latin America. OECD countries, with 14% of the world 's people, accounted for 86% of the 836,000 patent applications filed in 1998 and 85% of the 437,000 scientific and technical journal articles published worldwide. These countries also invest more in both absolute and relative terms -an average of 2.4% of their GDP in research and development, compared with 0.6%, in South Asia.

Innovation also means ownership. Of worldwide royalty and license fees in 1999,54% went to the United States and 12% went to Japan. Still, this picture of concentration in OECD countries masks developments and dynamism in many developing countries. There are hubs of innovation in Brazil, India, South Africa, Tunisia and elsewhere, and several other Asian and Latin American countries are increasingly engaged in technology creation.

Brazil is developing low-cost computers, Thailand has developed treatments for dengue fever and malaria and Viet Nam has developed treatment for malaria using traditional knowledge. Argentina, China, Korea, Mexico and Thailand are filing substantial numbers of patents. In Korea spending on research and development amounts to 2.8% of GDP, more than in any other country except Sweden.

The use of new and old technologies is, not surprisingly, uneven -an obvious function, among other things, of income. What is surprising is the rapid diffusion of new technologies in some countries and the diverse trends among them.

In Hong Kong (China, SAR), Iceland, Norway, Sweden and the United States the Internet Viet Nam has dramatically reduced malaria deaths and cases using locally produced, high-quality drugs. Between 1992 and 1997 the death toll from malaria was slashed 97%, and the number of cases fell almost 60%.

In the early 1990s the Vietnamese government took advantage of an upturn in the economy, increasing its investment in malaria control and identifying the drive against malaria as a national priority. The first major breakthrough was the development and manufacture of a new drug has reached more than half the population, and in other OECD countries close to one-third.

In the rest of the world the shares are much smaller, reaching only 0.4% of Sub-Saharan Africans. Even in India, home to a major global hub of innovation, only 0.4% of people use the Internet. From these levels it will take years for the digital divide to be bridged.

Today 79% of Internet users live in OECD countries, which contain only 14% of the world 's people. Still, Internet use is exploding in many countries -in OECD countries excluding the United States the share of Internet users quadrupled from 7% to 28% between 1998 and 2000. Even in developing countries the increase was dramatic: from 1.7 million to 9.8 million users in Brazil, from 3.8 million to 16.9 million in China and from 2,500 to 25,000 in Uganda. Yet because they are starting from very low bases, the portion of the population reached remains small.

The diffusion of the Internet has also been uneven within countries, concentrated in urban areas, among young men and among people with higher incomes and more education. In a positive sign, the gender gap seems to be closing in several countries, while the spread of access sites such as Internet cafes and community information centres is increasing use by lower-income groups.

Many countries are using the latest technology competitively in manufacturing industries, as shown by their success with high-tech exports. Of the 30 top exporters, 11 are in the developing world -including Korea, Malaysia and Mexico. But in Sub-Saharan Africa, the Arab States and South Asia high-tech exports still account for less than 5% of the total.

Yet many inventions that are decades old have not been adopted around the world despite their enormous value as tools of human progress. With many of these old technologies, diffusion has stagnated or stalled, apparently hitting the limits of income, infrastructure and institutions.

Electricity has not reached some 2 billion people, a third of the world 's population. In 1998 average electricity consumption in South Asia and Sub-Saharan Africa was less than one-tenth that in OECD countries.

The telephone has been around for more than a hundred years. While there is more than 1 mainline connection for every 2 people in OECD countries, there is just 1 for every 15 in developing countries -and 1 for every 200 in the least developed countries. Such disparities impede Internet access and hinder connections to the network age.

Recently, however, infrastructure investments, institutional reforms, innovations in marketing and technological progress have accelerated the spread of telephone connections. Between 1990 and 1999 mainline density increased from 22 to 69 per 1,000 people in developing countries.

Mobile telephones have overcome infrastructure constraints, spreading as widely as mainlines in some countries. South Africa has 132 cellular subscribers compared with 138 phone lines per 1,000 people, and Venezuela has 143 cellular subscribers and 109 mainlines per 1,000 people. Until recently, though, mobile phones have actually widened the gap because they have been diffused more rapidly in OECD countries.

Agrotechnical transformations of plant breeding, better seeds, fertilizer, water control and mechanization started in Europe in the mid-18th century and spread to the rest of the world. With the green revolution, world cereal yields doubled between the early 1960s and late 1990s, growing especially fast in Asia and Latin America. But Sub-Saharan Africa lags far behind in the use of modern seed varieties, tractors and fertilizer. Climate and soils help explain such differences, but lower yields also reflect lower technological inputs.

Developing countries that rank high in the technology achievement index have made spectacular gains in human skills in the past few decades. Tertiary gross enrolment rates in Korea rose from 15% to 28% between 1980 and 1997, and 34% of that enrolment is in science and mathematics -well ahead of 28%,the OECD average. But most developing countries lag far behind OECD countries in school enrolment.

At the end of the 19th century the application of science to manufacturing techniques or to agricultural practices became a basis of production systems, eventually increasing most workers 'incomes.

In the 20th century investments in research and development transformed knowledge into a critical factor of production, and industrial laboratories began producing inventions that soon found their way to the shop floor.

Entrepreneurship and market incentives accelerated technological progress to meet consumer demand. In just the past 10 years the store of indigenous knowledge has begun to reach people more widely. Its value can be enhanced when developed with modern methods, diffused and marketed.

But the market is not enough to channel technological development to human needs. The market may produce video games and palliatives for baldness, but it will not necessarily eliminate the ill health, malnutrition, isolation and lack of knowledge that afflict poor people.

Many 20th century successes required deliberate efforts to develop technological solutions to human problems, adapt them to developing countries and diffuse them widely to poor people. The green revolution required mobilizing the international community in a massive programme of agricultural research to prevent global famine, along with scientific research and adaptation at local levels.

Oral rehydration therapy emerged from state-of-the-art research, but its dissemination required a major public effort. And though penicillin was discovered in 1928, it was not marketed until 15 years later. The untapped demand for antibiotics was undoubtedly huge, but pharmaceutical companies were not interested. It took a war to crystallize this demand into a viable market.

So, turning technology into a tool for human development often requires purposive effort and public investment to create and diffuse innovations widely. Investment in creating, adapting and marketing products that poor people can afford or need is inadequate because their incomes are too low and do not present a market opportunity for the private sector. In developing countries national capacities are also limited.

Intellectual property rights can stimulate innovation, but in today 's world of very uneven demand and capacity, they are not enough to stimulate innovation in many developing coun- tries. At the global level, potentially huge benefits require difficult coordination. Yet public investment in technology development can have enormous returns.

The technology achievement index (TAI), which aims to capture how well a country is creating and diffusing technology and building a human skill base -reflecting capacity to participate in the technological innovations of the network age.

This composite index measures achievements, not potential, effort or inputs. It is not a measure of which country is leading in global technology development, but focuses on how well the country as a whole is participating in creating and using technology.

Take the United States -a global technology powerhouse -and Finland. The United States has far more inventions and Internet hosts in total than does Finland, but it does not rank as highly in the index because in Finland the Internet is more widely diffused and more is being done to develop a technological skill base throughout the population.

A nation 's technological achievements are larger and more complex than what this or any other index can capture. It is impossible to reflect the full range of technologies -from agriculture to medicine to manufacturing. Many aspects of technology creation, diffusion and human skills are hard to quantify. And even if they could be quantified, a lack of reliable data makes it impossible to fully reflect them.

For example, important technological innovations occur in the informal sector and in indigenous knowledge systems. But these are not recorded and cannot be quantified. Thus the TAI is constructed using indicators, not direct measures, of a country 's achievements in four dimensions. It provides a rough summary -not a comprehensive measure -of a society 's technological achievements.

The TAI is intended to help policy-makers define technology strategies. The development strategies need to be redefined in the network age. It calls on policy-makers to take a new look at their current technology achievements as a first step. A composite index helps a country situate itself relative to others, especially those farther ahead.

Many elements make up a country 's technological achievement, but an overall assessment is more easily made based on a single composite measure than on dozens of different measures. Like other composite indices in Human Development Reports (such as the human development index), the TAI is intended to be used as a starting point to make an overall assessment, to be followed by examining different indicators in greater detail.

The design of the index reflects two particular concerns. First, to focus on indicators that reflect policy concerns for all countries, regardless of the level of technological development. Second, to be useful for developing countries. To accomplish this the index must be able to discriminate between countries at the lower end of the range.

The TAI focuses on four dimensions of technological capacity that are important for reaping the benefits of the network age. The indicators selected relate to important technology policy objectives for all countries, regardless of their level of development:

— *Creation of technology*: Not all countries need to be at the leading edge of global technological development, but the capacity to innovate is relevant for all countries and constitutes the highest level of technological capacity.The global economy gives big rewards to the leaders and owners of technological innovation. All countries need to have capacity to innovate because the ability to innovate in the use of technology cannot be fully developed without the capacity to create - especially to adapt products and processes to local conditions.

Innovation occurs throughout society, in formal and informal settings, though the current trend is towards increasing commercialization and formalization of the process of innovation. In the absence of perfect indicators and data series the TAI uses two indicators to capture the level of innovation in a society. The first is the number of patents granted per capita, to reflect the current level of invention activities. The second is receipts of royalty and license fees from abroad per capita, to reflect the stock of successful innovations of the past that are still useful and hence have market value.

— *Diffusion of recent innovations:* All countries must adopt innovations to benefit from the opportunities of the network age. This is measured by diffusion of the Internet -indispensable to participation -and by exports of high-and medium-technology products as a share of all exports.

— *Diffusion of old innovations*: Participation in the network age requires diffusion of many old innovations. Although leapfrogging is sometimes possible, technological advance is a cumulative process, and widespread diffusion of older innovations is necessary for adoption of later innovations. Two indicators used here -telephones and electricity -are especially important because they are needed to use newer technologies and are also pervasive inputs to a multitude of human activities. Both indicators are expressed as logarithms and capped at the average OECD level, however, because they are important at the earlier stages of technological advance but not at the most advanced stages. Thus while it is important for India to focus on diffusing electricity and telephones so that all its people can participate in the technological revolution, Japan and Sweden have passed that stage. Expressing the measure in logarithms ensures that as the level increases, it contributes less to the index.

— *Human skills: A* critical mass of skills is indispensable to technological dynamism. Both creators and users of new technology need skills. Today 's technology requires adaptability -skills to master the constant flow of new innovations. The foundations of such ability are basic education to develop cognitive skills and skills in science and mathematics. Two indicators are used to reflect the human skills needed to create and absorb innovations: mean years of schooling and gross enrolment ratio of tertiary students enrolled in science, mathematics and engineering.

The data used to construct the TAI are from international series that are the most widely used in analyses of technology trends, and so are considered the most reliable of available sets, as shown below. The range of appropriate indicators is limited to those with reasonable coverage. Limitations in data series must be taken into account in interpreting TAI values and rankings. Some countries will have undervalued innovations because patent records and royalty payments are the only systematically collected data on technological innovation and leave out valuable but non-commercialized innovations such as those occurring in the informal sector and in indigenous knowledge systems.

Moreover, national systems and traditions differ in scope and criteria. High numbers of patents may reflect liberal intellectual property systems. Diffusion of new technologies may be understated in many developing countries. Internet access is measured by Internet hosts because these data are more reliable and have better coverage than Internet user data at the country level.

## The Risks of Digital Revolution

The digital revolution combined with the setting up of open, interconnected, interactive networks has fostered a number of radical changes, the most important of which have resulted in the dematerialization of products, growing concentration in cultural sectors and the globalization of communication networks. The overall trend, associated with the free circulation of products around the world, raises a number of questions of a statutory, cultural and political nature. Over and above the issues raised by the progress in technological convergence and industrial conflicts, there remain a number of problems: those concerning the place of copyright and neighbouring rights in the future information society, those with respect to national cultures and their diversity in the general trend towards globalization, and finally those of the new information and communication technology in economic, social and cultural development.

All these areas are both significant and strategic in the quest for enhanced democracy in the information society - the only factor that might induce the participation of all political, cultural and linguistic viewpoints around the world.

The scale of the technological upheavals that go hand in hand with the dematerialization of products has confused the judicial concepts on which intellectual property rights were based, and has sparked wide-ranging debate about the ways in which copyright should be applied and complied with in a digital environment.

Copyright and neighbouring rights form one of the very first areas of international cooperation. International structures for the protection of copyright were set up from the end of the nineteenth century onwards. The 1886 Berne Convention was the first multilateral agreement instituting the international protection of literary and artistic works. Since then, the convention has been revised several times, most recently in 1971. It guarantees creators a high level of protection of their rights (moral rights, economic rights relating to the reproduction, representation or public performance, broadcasting, adaptation and translation of their work).

The Universal Copyright Convention, adopted under the aegis of UNESCO in 1952 in Geneva and revised in Paris in 1971, obliges signatory states to ensure effective and adequate protection of copyright, leaving them free to adapt that protection to the requirements of their socioeconomic reality. It was this convention that introduced the a symbol followed by the name of the copyright holder and the year of first publication, to replace the registration formalities required by certain legislations. Finally, the Rome Convention, signed in 1961, provided a flexible, international legal framework for the protection of performers, producers of phonograms and broadcasting organizations. All these texts were drafted well before the digital revolution, and cannot directly take into account the developments that have occurred in this area since 1961. The enormous advantages of digital technology compared with analog systems.

Digital technology also provides a major opportunity for intellectual and creative works in that they can be disseminated an infinite number of times. That selfsame power of dissemination, however, can also lead to the violation of copyright, notably through piracy and other forms of computer crime. Around the world can be seen an increasing number of flourishing unauthorized businesses manufacturing and marketing illegal 'smart card' decoders for the reception of telecasts without the payment of any licence fee. Piracy and the other forms of counterfeiting are a major problem whose economic consequences cost tens of billions of dollars every year. All these risks are a cause for concern among creators and have led states to examine the usefulness of creating a special legal system for the new digital environment. At the international level and as part of the work carried out by the World Intellectual Property Organization (WIPO), most participants consider it unnecessary to draft new special legislation.

Two basic viewpoints have emerged on the subject, however. The first consists in applying distribution rights together with reproduction rights to works transmitted via digital means. This is, for the most part, the position defended by the United States, which proposes to consider transmission as a form of distribution, whether it involves 'on-line' transmission or the dissemination of the reproduction of a work recorded on a material medium. The American position requires that international transmission be considered as a form of import. The second viewpoint regards the act of digital transmission as an act of public communication. This is the position of Argentina, Australia, Canada, Japan, the member states of the European Union, and Uruguay, a point of view backed by several non-governmental organizations. Public communication rights would be combined with reproduction rights when the end-user makes a copy of the work transmitted.

The WIPO treaties on copyright and neighbouring rights adopted on 20 December 1996 in Geneva contain no provision with respect to reproduction rights in the digital environment for lack of agreement on this sensitive point. The adoption of this article, however, was linked to an interpretative statement to the effect that 'it is understood that the mere provision of physical facilities for enabling or making a communication does not in itself amount to communication within the meaning of this Treaty or the Berne Convention'. The declaration further indicates that the provisions of the treaty with regard to limitations and exceptions do not prevent a signatory from applying of the Berne Convention. The statement seems to suggest that the provision of the physical facilities for enabling or making a digital communication is not a sufficient stage in the digital communication of works to warrant protection under copyright laws. It leaves a number of questions unanswered with respect to the liability of providers of wide-area networking servers in the process of digital transmission.

At regional and national levels, the issue has become particularly acute with the publication of the US White Paper of September 1995. Drafted by the Working Group on Intellectual Property Rights of the White House Information Infrastructure Task Force set up by President Clinton in 1993, the document contains detailed proposals for adaptation of the US Copyright Act to cyberspace. Their concern has also been echoed in Canada with the report of the Information Highway Advisory Council, which was published the same year. The importance of protecting intellectual property also led the European Community in 1988 to present a Green Paper containing an economic and judicial analysis of the various problems raised by the new information technology in legal terms. Multilateral discussions held during the drafting of the paper resulted in the adoption in 1995 of the Green Paper on Copyright and Related Rights in the Information Society. It lists a catalogue of fifty-five problems concerning future copyright.

The protection of intellectual property to be a crucial element in the development of a European multimedia market. The European Commission has announced another Green Paper specially devoted to the legal protection of encrypted signals, and has raised the possibility of intervention by the Union to make technical protection systems mandatory when the former have been sufficiently developed and accepted by industry. Finally, also worthy of note is the CITED project (Copyright in Transmitted Electronic Documents) developed under the ESPRIT programme.

UNESCO, which initiated the Universal Copyright Convention (1952), was an active participant in the Diplomatic Conference organized by WIPO in December 1996 with a view to adopting a new protocol to be appended to the Berne Convention. The presence of UNESCO at the conference, as well as at those organized by the European Commission on Copyright and Related Rights on the Threshold of the Twenty-first Century (June 1995) and at the Intellectual Property Conference of the Americas (July 1996), was intended primarily as a means of achieving a consensus on an arrangement reconciling the respective rights of authors, producers, copyright holders and the general public, as well as those of exporters and importers of protected works. UNESCO also launched a wide-ranging consultation with specialists in the field of communication, publishing and development. In that connection, worthy of note was the organization in co-operation with the Spanish Government of an International UNESCO Symposium on Copyright and Communication in the Information Society (Madrid, March 1996). Discussions at the symposium focused on three major subjects:

— The outlines of a national policy to set up the basic infrastructures for the digital transmission and broadcasting of information (the role of the state and of private operators), and the norms that should govern the operation of those infrastructures, as well as the principles for regional and international co-operation in the area.

— The guidelines to follow in order to adapt national legislations so as to ensure that they protect the legitimate rights of authors and others right-holders in the digital and multimedia environment and enhance harmonization of those rights at the international and regional levels.

— Strategies for national policies aimed at fostering the creation and development of cultural economic sectors, the digital broadcasting of works and performances, and distance learning, with a view to international and regional co-operation in this area.

The Member States of the Organization, especially those from developing countries, to acquire up-to-the-minute legal and technological data in the field of intellectual property rights. The symposium was followed by a series of regional meetings of Committees of Experts on copyright in the information society (basic infrastructures, the protection of rights and their social and cultural impact). The first of these, for Latin America, the Caribbean and Canada, was held in Bogotá in September 1996. The second, for Asia, the Pacific and the Arab States, was organized in New Delhi in November 1996. The Committee of Experts of Europe is scheduled to meet in Monaco in March 1997 and that of Africa in 1998. On the whole, the various meetings have agreed on the need to simplify legal rules at the international level, in order to maintain a three-way balance of:

a) the rights of authors in relation to those of the traditional cultural economic sectors and of information highway service providers,

b) the rights of right-holders in relation to the public interest (both of which are contained in the Declaration of Human Rights), and

c) the interests of countries exporting 'copyright' in relation to those of importer countries, notably the developing nations.

The issue of the access to information and to new communication technology and contrasts the views of three groups of thinkers: those that relate network access to a fundamental right on the same grounds as other rights; those that consider access must be modulated in relation to the varying contexts and types of information in question (information which is access-free, in the public domain or restricted); and finally, those that would make all network access part of a commercial service. The problem is complex and multidimensional.

The absence of legal protection is not supportive of creativity worldwide, and it is equally obvious that overprotection is not conducive to access to the networks by research workers and academics of developing countries. The correct balance therefore remains to be found between the right of creators to benefit from the use of their work and the needs of users to access those works and use them freely. One further suggestion, developed by a number of non-governmental organizations in particular, militates in favour of a political alternative, based on non-market mechanisms ensuring right-free access for underprivileged countries to digital productions connected with social and economic development.

Other ideas, based for example on consumer initiative or on codes of ethics developed ad hoc by information professionals, may suit the complexity of the problem and ultimately be more effective. This only underlines, however, the vital role of dialogue and co-operation among the various parties concerned, which, alone, may enable the right balance to be found between the interests of some, the duties of others and the solidarity of all.

## Economic Obstacles

The development of the information society raises the issue of the inequalities which are a feature of both the industrialized and the developing countries, and which at the same time come between the rich and poor within the same society.

The developing nations are confronted with the challenges of the new technology, the production and distribution of which take place outside their frontiers. A large majority of these countries feel excluded from that progress and some continue to denounce the aggravation of the obvious imbalances in the flow of information exchange between the North and the South. The debate began as long ago as the 1980s within UNESCO and in other international circles, about the idea of the New World Information and Communication Order (NWICO).

The talks have at least brought to the attention of international opinion the extent of the disparities and distortions that exist in the area of communication and new technology, imbalances suggesting that the vision of a global village which so many have held for so long will basically be attained by the richest or most recently industrialized countries in which the data banks, software systems and programs are gathered and stored. The gap is particularly wide in Africa, which has only 1 per cent of the telephone lines available in the world, but 12 per cent of its population. In 1994, there were more telephone lines in the city of Tokyo alone than in the whole of Africa, when the population of the continent is thirty times greater than that of the Japanese capital. Inside Africa there are also remarkable differences in development. Over the last decade, the number of telephone lines per 100 inhabitants—known as teledensity—has doubled in the Maghreb. In South Africa, the number has increased by more than 200 per cent and is now close to 10. Teledensity in sub-Saharan Africa has stagnated, emphasizing the disparity between the affluent and the underprivileged countries. The same observation holds true of information and communication. The inequalities are just as pronounced in terms of audiovisual equipment as for the production and content of their programmes.

The same applies to the consumption of the written press, of radio and television programmes, and to the flow of programmes from producer to consumer countries. This imbalance has been still further highlighted with the emergence of digital technology and the broadcasting of programming streams. Market globalization favours communications between developed or newly industrialized countries or within such countries, or links between major cities and rural zones. In the economic sphere, the imbalances reflect both the highly unequal economic development of nations, the diversity of their political systems and the specific character of each society. They can be explained as much by the past as by certain current effects of globalization.

These somewhat pessimistic observations must, however, be tempered by the emergence of a number of Asian and Latin American countries that have worked wonders where telecommunications and audiovisual technology are concerned. Some even form the driving force behind economic growth rates that contradict the climate of recession in the rest of the world. Others have begun policies for technology transfer and adaptation by offering attractive subcontracting capabilities and thereby off shoring communication multinationals.

**Cultural and Linguistic Obstacles**

The imbalances between nations and within them, together with the acceleration in the globalization of the contents of programmes, also arouse concern about the dangers of cultural and linguistic standardization. Developing countries are at risk from standardization of local cultures through a form of planetary brainwashing caused by the white noise of poor programme content. These dangers may have grave consequences, such as the marginalization and possible disappearance of fragile community cultures, the weakening of cultural foundations, the temptation to withdraw into an identity coinciding with religious beliefs, and the threat of violent inter-ethnic conflict. While the existence of these dangers raises questions of ethics and political sovereignty, they have also been used by some states and their single parties as a convenient alibi to justify their stranglehold on the media and the use of the media.

The member states of the European Community also appear to be jealous of their cultural identity and make it a fundamental factor in their national sovereignty. They are striving to protect their audiovisual production by a policy of broadcasting quotas adopted within the framework of the directives of the 'Television without Frontiers' programme. The economic issues implicit in quotas became a subject of confrontation with the United States during the GATT trade talks in 1993 (now the World Trade Organization). There are two contradictory viewpoints on the subject. The United States is pushing for the free circulation of programmes, while Europe and Canada intend to protect their cultures and their film industries by arranging programming rules.

The Americans wish to encourage a form of total market internationalization and the globalization of trade, whereas Europe and Canada consider the audiovisual field to be a service whose cultural purpose justifies its treatment as a special case in relation to the overall GATT agreements. Hence the importance for the European Union to have an audiovisual and cinema policy designed to preserve cultural identities, to strengthen economic development and to create jobs in the audiovisual sector. However, according to the European specialists, the results of the

GATT trade talks (in December 1993) hardly changed anything, either in terms of the current market situation, which favours American programmes, or with respect to the risks of furthering their market domination with the arrival of digital clusters of TV programming streams.

As digital technology rapidly develops, however, the scope of deregulation is widening in Europe to include the private telecommunications sector. The latter is to become a competitive market from 1998 onwards, and should facilitate the circulation of images. In addition, the future prospects outlined in the European Commission's Green Paper on the audiovisual policy of the European Union are already those of a demand focus on 'profitability in an open, dynamic global market' based on a largely free trade attitude. On top of this, the renegotiations of the 'Television without Frontiers' directive reached a compromise with some difficulty as a result of strong reluctance on the part of countries such as Germany, the United Kingdom and Italy, all of which demanded the straightforward abolition of the quota policy. Together, these new trends have led the European Union to think about implementing a different policy basically aimed at strengthening the broadcasting industry.

The other major issue is the risk of linguistic standardization. An example frequently quoted is the fact that the vast majority of programmes circulating on the Internet are in English and that the main navigation software systems are not capable of reading characters other than those of the Latin alphabet.

These fears apparently are being allayed by the market trend towards linguistic diversification throughout the system. With the stupendous growth of the Internet, English-speaking countries owned only 70 per cent of sites in January 1997 as against 90 per cent a few months before. Today three language groups are extending their reach throughout the network: Germanic (German, Dutch and the Scandinavian languages) with 11 per cent; Romance (French, Italian, Portuguese and Spanish) with 9 per cent, and Japanese with 5 per cent. The world's other languages are used on only 5 per cent of the sites. This is a poor showing if the Internet is to be multilingual and sensitive to the whole family of cultures. Yet the latest technological progress in automatic translation makes data processing possible in a number of languages. Moreover, for exponential growth of network navigating and surfing tools, the setting of common standards adapted to the various non-roman scripts, and public and private investments in on-line services, could transform the network fundamentally in the medium term by giving every user access to a huge amount of data in foreign languages using non-roman scripts.

**Crisis in Public Service Broadcasting**

Media globalization together with the arrival of competition from international and national private television channels raises the issue of the status, role and future of the public service in the new audiovisual fields around the world. For many years, public television channels enjoyed a period of stability based on a monopoly. There are three main reasons for their domination. The first of these is technical, and concerns the use and distribution of frequency spectra considered to be a collectively owned, rare resource. In this area, the state played the role of a microwave 'regulator', to prevent frequencies from being used in a disorganized and anarchic manner. This function is generally performed today by an authority independent of the government, its role being to enforce conditions of fair competition. The second reason concerns the public service role which is conferred on all the broadcasting services. The power of radio and of television seems truly vast from the political, social or cultural viewpoints, since it provides the general public with access to cultural information programmes that they would not be able to receive elsewhere or otherwise. The third and final reason is linked to the traditional distrust of public authorities with respect to the market's capacity to perform the public service assignments imposed on the broadcasting industry.

The arrival in the 1980s of private operators and distributors on the market had as its consequence the end of the supremacy of public television channels, a setback which then depleted their audience ratings and advertising market share. Technological innovations in the satellite area also led to the development of new markets, accompanied by an increase in private capital and publicity investments in television.

Since then, the growth in private channels has taken place to the detriment of advertising revenue for public television, undermining the traditional balance between the public and private sectors. These various reversals have occurred in an environment of increasing internationalisation and worldwide televisual exchange. All around the world, clusters of private, general-interest or specialized digital television channels are springing up in audiovisual marketplaces which are becoming increasingly turbulent.

Against this backdrop, the public channels have had to face stagnating or diminishing public subsidies, forcing them to reduce their expenses or seek other sources of revenue such as the introduction of TV commercials. Reduced government involvement in public service channels in several countries, notably those in Europe, has accelerated the rate of change in the audiovisual marketplace and thrown the public television sector into disarray.

The future of public service broadcasting depends on a clearer distinction between public service and public sector, which are two very different concepts altogether. Privately owned television operators exist that provide educational or cultural programmes, traditionally classified as being the role of the public service. In the United States, for example, the major networks such as CBS, ABC or NBC also provide programmes of an educational and cultural nature, as does the federal CBC-Radio Canada network. These programmes are all part of a complementary, diversified offer. The assignments and obligations of the public service are not necessarily incompatible with the ownership of corporate capital, and the difference between private and public as diametrically opposed sectors is no longer pertinent.

The concept of public service seems nevertheless to be gaining ground in Europe, and is even moving towards that of universal service, notably where the texts of the European Union are concerned. Universal service is relatively far removed from the Canadian or French concept of public service, and lies somewhere between the Latin and Anglo-Saxon definitions. Generally speaking, a universal service is seen as a compensatory factor within a market-controlled regulation system. The future of the public service also depends on a clearer distinction between public service and commercial television, which obeys market laws first and foremost.

The public service should be free of economic and financial considerations dictated by audience ratings and market share, to carry out its role as a social link. In a world open to the internationalization of data flow and image exchange, a public service should provide basic landmarks of a historical, cultural and political nature for a nation. It should embody, among other things, the relationship that a people has with both its image and its imagination - hence the importance of the provision by public television of true diversity and pluralism to its viewers. These are the two concepts which are the key both to the identity of the public service and indeed to that of democracy. It is no doubt through a form of television in keeping with the tradition of the BBC, far removed from political or economic power, that the public service will really accomplish its mission of informing the general public.

## Managing Technological Change

The benefits of technologies can be far greater than what their creators foresaw. When Guglielmo Marconi invented the radio in 1895, he intended it for two-way private communication, not for broadcasting.

Today the transistor is heralded as one of the most significant inventions ever -but on its invention in 1947 foreseers could think of few uses beyond developing better hearing aids for deaf people. In the 1940s IBM thought that the market for computers would never amount to more than a few unit sales a year.

At the same time, the hidden costs of technologies can be devastating. Bovine spongi-form encephalitis -mad cow disease -almost certainly owes its origin and spread to cost-cutting techniques used to make cattle feed. Nuclear power, once believed to be a limitless source of energy, came to be seen as a dangerous threat to health and the environment after the accidents at Three Mile Island (United States) and Chernobyl (Ukraine). Some harms are revealed quickly and removed.

Thalidomide, first marketed in 1957 to treat morning sickness in pregnant women, resulted in horrific birth defects in thousands of children around the world and was banned by the early 1960s. But other harms are hidden for decades.

Chlorofluorocarbons (CFCs), invented in 1928, were widely used in refrigerators, aerosol cans and air conditioners. Only in 1984 -more than 50 years later -came conclusive evidence of their connection with the depletion of the ozone layer and increased skin cancer for people in countries exposed to more ultraviolet light. Still used in many countries, CFCs are to be phased out by 2010.

Societies respond to these uncertainties by seeking to maximize the benefits and minimize the risks of technological change. Doing so is not easy: managing such change can be complex and politically controversial. Though the agricultural technology of the green revolution more than doubled cereal production in Asia between 1970 and 1995, the impacts on farm workers 'income and on the environment are still hotly debated.

As in previous eras of change, today's technological transformations raise concerns about their possible ecological, health and socioeconomic impacts. Genetically modified plants are suspected of introducing new sources of allergens, of creating "super weeds "and of harming species such as monarch butterflies.

Cutting-edge biotechnological research has raised ethical concerns about the possibility of human cloning and the easy manufacture of devastating biological weapons. Information and communications technology facilitates international crime, supports drug trade networks and assists the dissemination of child pornography. There are three reasons for adopting new technologies:

— *Potential benefits*: The possibilities for promoting human development through today's technological transformations are tremendous in developing countries. In some cases the expected benefits are at least as great as the risks.

— *Costs of inertia versus costs of change*: New technologies often improve on the ones they replace: the modern jet, for example, is safer and faster than the propeller aeroplane. Had the Luddites succeeded in prohibiting the adoption of spinning jennies, Britain would have forgone the productivity growth that allowed employment and incomes to increase so dramatically.

— *Means of managing risks*: Many potential harms can be managed and their likelihood reduced through systematic scientific research, regulation and institutional capacity. When these capacities are strong, countries are far more able to ensure that technological change becomes a positive force for development.

Yet out of these reasons for embracing change comes a dilemma for many developing countries: the potential benefits of change may be great and the costs of inertia significant -but the institutional and regulatory capacity needed to manage the concurrent risks may be too demanding. The trade-offs of technological change vary from country to country and use to use: societies expect different benefits, face different risks and have widely varying capacities to handle those risks safely. From this perspective, most developing countries are at a disadvantage in the face of technological change because they lack the regulatory institutions needed to manage the risks well. But there can be advantages to being technological followers.

Unlike frontrunners, followers do not incur the first-mover risks of using new technologies: they can instead observe how those risks play out in other countries. They can also learn from others in designing their regulations and institutions.

Moreover, for some technologies they may be able to establish low-cost regulatory systems that build on, or even rely on, the regulatory standards of early adopters. Societies ultimately face choices in the timing and extent of embracing technological change. Given the importance of getting it right, and the risks of getting it wrong, developing countries need to build national policies, and need international support, to create the capacity that will enable them to embrace new opportunities.

## References

Manuel Castells (2000) *The Rise of the Network Society. The Information Age: Economy, Society and Culture*. Volume 1. Malden: Blackwell. Second Edition.

Michael Dawson/John Bellamy Foster (1998) Virtual Capitalism. In: Robert W. McChesney/Ellen Meiksins Wood/John Bellamy Foster (Eds.) (1998) *Capitalism and the Information Age.* New York: Monthly Review Press. pp. 51–67.

Alistair Duff (2000) *Information Society Studies.* London: Routledge.

Esther Dyson/George Gilder/George Keyworth/Alvin Toffler (1994) Cyberspace and the American Dream: A Magna Carta for the Knowledge Age. In: *Future Insight 1.2.* The Progress & Freedom Foundation.

Tony Fitzpatrick (2002) Critical Theory, Information Society and Surveillance Technologies. In: *Information, Communication and Society*. Vol. 5. No. 3. pp. 357–378.

# 3

# The Information Society

Information Society is a term for a society in which the creation, distribution, and manipulation of information has become the most significant economic and cultural activity. An Information Society may be contrasted with societies in which the economic underpinning is primarily Industrial or Agrarian. The machine tools of the Information Society are computers and telecommunications, rather than lathes or ploughs.

Progress in information technologies and communication is changing the way we live: how we work and do business, how we educate our children, study and do research, train ourselves, and how we are entertained. The information society is not only affecting the way people interact but it is also requiring the traditional organisational structures to be more flexible, more participatory and more decentralised.

The idea of a global Information Society can be viewed in relation to Marshall McLuhan's prediction that the communications media would transform the world into a "global village."

## Networked World

New media is the concept that new methods of communicating in the digital world allow smaller groups of people to congregate online and share, sell and swap goods and information. It also allows more people to have a voice in their community and in the world in general. The most important structural characteristic of new media is the integration of telecommunications technologies. The second structural new media characteristic of the current communications revolution is the rise of interactive media. Interactivity is a sequence of action and reaction. The downloaded link or the supply side of web sites, interactive television and computer programs is much wider that the uplink or retrieval made by their users. The third, technical, characteristic of new media is digital code. The new media are defined by all three characteristics simultaneously: "they are media which are both integrated and interactive and also use digital code at the turn of the 20th and 21st centuries."

The network society is a social structure based on networks operated by information and communication technologies based on microelectronics and digital computer networks that generate, process and distribute information via the nodes of the networks. The network society can be defined as a social formation with an infrastructure of social and media networks enabling its prime mode of organization at all levels (individual, group, organizational and societal). Increasingly, these networks link all units or parts of this formation. In western societies, the individual linked by networks is becoming the basic unit of the network society. In eastern societies, this might still be the group (family, community, work team) linked by networks.In the contemporary process of individualisation, the basic unit of the network society has become the individual who is linked by networks. This is caused by simultaneous scale extension (nationalisation and internationalisation) and scale reduction (smaller living and working environments) Other kinds of communities arise. Daily living and working environments are getting smaller and more heterogenous, while the range of the division of labour, interpersonal communications and mass media extends. So, the scale of the network society is both extended and reduced as compared to the mass society. The scope of the network society is both global and local, sometimes indicated as "glocal". The organization of its components (individuals, groups, organizations) is no longer tied to particular times and places. Aided by information and communication technology, these coordinates of existence can be transcended to create virtual times and places and to simultaneously act, perceive and think in global and local terms.

A network can be defined as a collection of links between elements of a unit. The elements are called nodes, units are often called systems. The smallest number of elements is three and the smallest number of links is two. A single link of two elements called relationship. Networks are mode of organization of complex systems in nature and society. They are relatively complicated ways of organizing matter and living systems. The characteristic of units and elements, among them human individuals, and the way they are made up, are not the focus of attention. So, networks occur both in complicated matter and in living systems at all levels. Networks are selective according to their specific programs, because they can simultaneously communicate and incommunicate, the network society diffuses in the entire world, but does not include all people. In fact, in this early 21st century, it excludes most of humankind, although all of humankind is affected by its logic and by the power relationships that interact in the global networks of social organization.

Networks are not new. What is new is the microelectronics-based, networking technologies that provide new capabilities to an old form of social organization: networks. Networks throughout history had a major problem vis-a-vis other forms of social organization. Thus, in the historical record, networks were the domains of the private life. Digital networking technologies enable networks to overcome their historical limits. They can, at the same time, be flexible and adaptive thanks to their capacity to decentralize performance along a network of autonomous components, while still being able to coordinate all this decentralized activity on a shared purpose of decision making. Networks are not determined by the industrial technologies but unthinkable without these technologies. In the early years of the 21st century, the network society is not the emerging social structure of the Information Age: it already configures the nucleus of our societies.

There is an explosion of horizontal networks of communication, quite independent from media business and governments, that allows the emergence of what I call self-directed mass communication. It is mass communication because it is diffused throughout the Internet, so it potentially reaches the whole planet. It is self-directed because it is often initiated by individuals or groups by themselves bypassing the media system. The explosion of blogs, vlogs, podding, streamin and other forms of interactive, computer to computer communication set sup a new system of global, horizontal communication Networks that, for the first time in history, allow people to communicate with each other without going through the channels set up by the institutions of society for socialized communication.

The network society constitutes socialized communication beyond the mass media system that characterized the industrial society. But it does not represent the world of freedom sung by the libertarian ideology of Internet prophets. It is made up both of an oligopolistic business multimedia system controlling an increasingly inclusive hypertext, and of an explosion of horizontal Networks of autonomous local/global communication-and, naturally, of the interaction between the two systems in a complex pattern of connections and disconnections in different contexts. The network society is also manifested in the transformation of sociability. Yet, what we observe is not the fading away of face-to-face interaction or the increasing isolation of people in front of their computers. We know, from studies in different societies, that are most instances Internet users are more social have more friends and contacts and re more socially politically active than non users. Moreover, the more they use the Internet, the more they also engage in face to-face interaction in all domains of their lives. Similarly, new forms of wireless communication, from mobile phone voice communication to SMSs, WiFi and WiMax, substantially increase sociability, particularly for the younger groups of the population. The network society is a hyper social society, not a society of isolation. People, by and large, do not face their identity in the Internet, except for some teenagers experimenting with their lives. People fold the technology into their lives, link up virtual reality and real virtuality; they live in various technological forms of communication, articulating them as they need it. However, there is a major change in sociability, not a consequence of Internet or new communication technologies but a change that is fully supported by the logic embedded in the communication networks. This is the emergence of networked individualism, as social structure and historical evolution induce the emergence of individualism as the dominant culture of our societies, and the new communication Technologies perfectly fit into the mode of building sociability along self-selected communication networks, on or off depending on the needs and moods of each individual. So, the network society is a society of networked individuals.

What results from this evolution is that the culture of the network society is largely shaped by the messages exchanged in the composite electronic hypertext made by the technologically linked networks of different communication modes. In the network society, virtuality is the foundation of reality through the new forms of socialized communication. Society shapes technology according to the needs, values an interests of people who use the technology. Furthermore, information and communication technologies are particularly sensitive to the effects of social uses on technology itself. The history of the internet provides ample evidence that the users, particularly the first thousands of users, were, to a large extent, the producers of the technology. However, technology is a necessary, albeit not sufficient condition for the emergence of a new form of social organization based on networking, that is on the diffusion of networking in all realms of activity on the basis of digital communication networks.

## Evolution of Networked Digital Information

Two decades ago, computerized information was still an arcane art limited to those in the computer and database production profession and to those users called then information retrieval specialists whose task was to search the computerized records for the data pertinent to their business activities. Information was still more of an art than a business. This is not to say that the existence of such computerized information technologies and search capabilities was unknown to the rest of the professional communities it was just that it did not yet touch them directly, it was still something that somebody else did.

The moment the personal computer began its inexorable conquest of every working desk is when " Information " reached society at large and can be said to have acquired an awareness of its own. Information awareness created the need to communicate it, to exchange it, information in fact developed an irresistible urge to travel the rapidly expanding digital highways. The personal computer became a repository of information and every PC user became a de facto information specialist, society now knows the consequential problems and benefits associated with storing retrieving and transmitting information .

Digital information in the newly acquired societal awareness encompasses all aspect of daily life from speech to images and created a new term to define it " Multimedia ". The advent of the PC distorted the regular linear progression of the modus vivendi between science, information and society, there exist now a kind of symbiotic relation between the use that society at large makes of the technological development of computer science and information science. This new relationship appears to have speeded up the intellectual capacity in our everyday working life by increasing our ability to do more complex things in a shorter time and more efficiently. If this revolution was put on trial the defense would claim that everybody in the whole world is benefiting from it, while the prosecution would claim that in effect the defense is confusing between the part of society being exposed to it or having knowledge of its existence and the other part who actually benefits from it and that this division is applicable in varying proportion to all nations, developing and developed alike.

The benefits of the digital revolution can additionally be classified as direct for those earning a living and making a profit from producing and delivering " Information " and indirect for those who, in a position to pay, use it in their daily professional and private lives. Then there is the rest of society who has a remote vision of this revolution in as much as it is limited to see only its results and its use in the availability of public information and some consumer products.

There is no such thing as free digital information as there in no such thing as free communication, digital or otherwise. The most significant emerging parameter however is the spectacular growth in information traffic and the communications networks to carry it, this has lead to an equally spectacular growth on the part of communications carriers and owners of large " private " network of mergers, acquisitions and cooperative ventures to consolidate their relative positions in the global marketplace and to be thus better able to exploit the universally predicted Multimedia revolution. In the same manner and for the same objectives the publishing industry and the online information services are slowly gravitating toward a small number of large conglomerates. The domination of the market place will then be monopolized by few and it is not difficult to predict that the divide between those who can afford to be in the information society and those who cannot will get wider and wider. Unless minority interests both in term of information content and social groups are openly debated, considered and protected.

In theory networked digital information knows no borders or boundaries. It travels free and it is available to everybody . In practice it is more controllable than any other media. Nations can create filtered entry and exit points, monitor its traffic and identify content sources and so can the network providers, corporations and institutions. The fact that it has not been widely done so far does not mean it cannot be done, the tools are all there. When we talk about applying ethical considerations to digital information we imply control, of the content, its access and of its dissemination. This in turn impacts directly on the freedom of information argument and who controls the application of ethical rules, will this monitoring be done nationally or internationally , by the application of legislation or through semivoluntary rules by the three principal groups in this game, the network controller, the information dissemination services and content providers any of whom can veto information content they consider unethical.

At present, the industrialized countries have an overwhelming lead in development over most developing nations. However, modern information and communication technologies offer a significant window of opportunity for developing countries to accelerate their development in all spheres of economic and social activity and to narrow the gap between countries. The world stands today on the threshold of a Global Information Society. This position has been arrived at through the truly remarkable advances that have been made in recent years in the development of ICT as well as the construction and development of national and global information infrastructure.

Through these developments it is now both technically and economically feasible to bring modern information and communications technologies to any part of the entire world. Equally as important, people around the world, including those in developing countries, are increasingly demanding access to the emerging global information network. Hence, communities in Mexico, for example, have installed personal computers and built microwave towers to communicate with the rest of the world, allowing school children to interact with other students all over the world and keeping farmers apprised of both local and world crop prices. Also, India launched a programme to link its biggest cities with a nationwide network that will facilitate the dissemination of government information and provide an infrastructure for commercial applications.The present Global Information Infrastructure (GII) has evolved from a research and development programme in networking that was initiated and funded by United States government in the 1960s. This programme, which sought to establish a decentralized telecommunications system in which an assortment of variously located computers could communicate with each other even when one or more parts of the system had been seriously damaged, was primarily designed to satisfy the military requirements of the United States. From these origins, the Internet has since developed into a global network of computer networks with many different types of users.

The Internet today is a fast-growing, global network that enables people from all over the world to provide and access a variety of content, communicate with one another, purchase goods and services, and even co-ordinate complex, far flung worldwide activities at relatively low cost. The Net is estimated to be growing at a rate of 10-15% per month, with numbers rising from about 56 million Internet users worldwide in 1995 to about 200 million people in 1999. Also, its American origin notwithstanding, more than 50 per cent of current Net users at present are outside the United States and that percentage is rising; by 2000, less than 20 per cent of all Internet users are projected to be in the US. At present, citizens and residents of industrialized countries enjoy good access to the Internet. For example, Finland and Iceland - first and second among countries with the most Internet hosts per capita - had 62 and 42 Internet hosts per 1,000 population, respectively, in 1997. At the other end of the scale, the information revolution has hardly arrived in Africa - the world's least developed region - where fewer than 15 countries had full Internet access in 1996.

As a result of this situation, most developing countries have yet to assume a serious role in discussions on setting goals and standards for the GII. This should not deter them from seeking ways to ensure that their concerns and interests are included in the design, delivery, regulation and content of the world's information expansion. Clearly, a partnership between rich and poor countries is necessary in such an endeavour. The potential benefits of the Internet for developing countries are well-known: namely that it presents exciting new opportunities to reinvigorate and accelerate the rate of economic and social development.

However, the changes engendered by the Internet have been generally to the exclusion of the very poor people in developing countries that the Internet can particularly benefit. At present, the proliferation of the technology is restricted by the lack of appropriate infrastructure and the expense of computing technology. Hence, the dilemma for the average farmer in a developing country, say, would be to choose between spending about $3000 on the technology and approximately $20 - 50 per month on subscription fees or investing that money on farming tools, fertilizers or irrigation systems to produce a good harvest and an adequate income.

Unfortunately, in nearly all cases in most developing countries, the question simply does not arise because the farmer lacks the necessary financial resources or access to them to enable him (or her) to use the

Internet. Under these conditions, the race to effectively deploy the technology to increase productivity and promote social change and development may be over before it starts.While it cannot be denied that top-level decision makers in some developing countries are not always convinced that investing in ICT should be accorded topmost priority, there is now at least a political will in many developing countries to support and encourage these processes.

Much of this new spirit has been encouraged by industrialized donor countries and organisations such as the United States, Denmark, UNDP and the World Bank which have provided much financial and technical support to developing countries to strengthen and develop their national information infrastructure technologies.

As a result, new legal frameworks and standards are being set up to promote the development and interconnection of national information infrastructures. In Ghana, for example, the basic policy instruments to encourage private investment and entrepreneurial activities to expand and enhance information technology has been put in place and the country has three licensed Internet Service Providers as well as five network services that provide mainly e-mail services. Major challenges that confront developing countries in embracing modern ICT include the formulation and implementation of effective and practical strategies to enhance the capabilities of their populations to make the best possible use of information technology.

Obviously, any country that wants to take full advantage of the opportunities provided by ICT will have to prepare its population to use the technology effectively. An obvious strategy to achieve this objective is to establish computer literacy courses. This may not be sufficient, however. Consequently, it will be necessary to ensure that these courses are complemented by teaching people - from primary school pupils, secondary school and university students as well as adult learners - skills to find information, critically evaluate it and also how to use it creatively to solve their problems. A related objective is to ensure the effective application of information technologies to reduce, rather than widen and deepen social inequities or worsen inequality across the technological divide.

Mechanisms to achieve this objective include, for example, public telecentres that have been promoted by the ITU as well as information service centres which are promoted by a coalition of private and public sector interests in the United States. These centres provide people with access to development-oriented applications and content as well as ICT-based facilities with associated training. Further, these centres can serve as the community libraries of the future and major instruments to achieve the goal of wide public access to the Internet. Regardless of the sophistication of the technology or services being offered, a simple strategy to achieve these objectives could include the provision of assurances to potential users that they can allow the GII entry into their homes, workplaces and lives to access and share information safely and without forfeiting any of their rights.

Governments, businesses and public-interest groups working together on information policy and content issues, must address these concerns. Equally as important, governments and the private sector must continuously seek to demonstrate in imaginative and practical ways the potential benefits of the GII to citizens, especially the more disadvantaged in society, for example, through tele-medicine or access to information on market prices for their crops. After all, it is only when people are exposed to, and see, tangible results of applications that they can begin to appreciate how the ICT can be used to improve their lives. This appreciation is the key to stimulating demand for the services and content of the GII, which in turn will provide the impetus to remove institutional and regulatory barriers to its full utilisation. It should be noted that most young people, regardless of whether they live in rich or poor countries, will feel strongly motivated to learn and use ICT, from portable phones to the Internet. As a consequence all governments should place emphasis on educational programmes as a lever to increase the competence of the population at large.

Decentralisation is an important characteristic of the Internet's culture and technology. Another important feature is that many Internet users view themselves as part of an "Internet community" that has its own culture, ethics and rules. We are all aware of "netiquette" as well as the existence of Internet jargon that has been developed by Internet users. As this community grows, many challenges concerning access and use as well as issues such as regulation, ethics and content on the Internet will confront policy makers. There is a general consensus around the world that development of the GII and realisation of the goals of a Global Information Society will require concerted action and co-operation to develop a global information policy framework that will ensure, among other things, that:

1) the privacy of individuals and organisations using the GII is protected;

2) the security and reliability of the networks the information passes over are preserved;
3) the intellectual property rights of those who create the information, education, and entertainment content are protected;
4) that the content of information (particularly that of an intolerant, racist or pornographic nature) circulating on the Internet and access to it, especially by children, is regulated.

Deliberations and action on all these issues must involve all countries represented by their governments, private sectors, labour, academia and the general public. Wide consultation involving all the major stakeholders should foster the formulation of a constructive regulatory framework that will be attractive to all and safeguard the interests of individual countries or groups of countries. In these deliberations, the stakeholders must seek to avoid or iron out potential discrepancies. For example, an impending EU law that aims to safeguard the privacy rights of European citizens by setting common rules for the export and use of many kinds of personal data has an unintended consequence: a chance of trade conflict with the US.

More generally, if exercised, the data protection directive could play havoc with global trade flows by cutting off companies' international communications networks. Another concern involves the potential of ICT to have a negative effect on the social behaviour of users. For example, the range of services that can be accessed on the Internet is so comprehensive that it can, as stated by UNESCO, "unduly privilege the 'man-machine' relationship" to the detriment, on the one hand, of social intercourse and, on the other, the development of self-reliance. At present, however, many of the risks associated with some of these phenomena are poorly understood and more detailed study and research is needed to enable policy-makers adequately consider the necessary actions, if any, that will be required to address the problems. There is also considerable concern in many quarters about the maintenance of linguistic and cultural diversity. Given its origins in the United States as well as the dominance of the English language as a medium of international communication, 90% of the databases on the Internet at present are in English.

Consequently, non-English speakers do not have effective access to the content available on the Internet. However, there are few technical constraints on the development of databases in other languages that can serve the interests of a variety of local communities. Nonetheless, technology-induced globalisation is seen by many as a threat to local customs, values and beliefs. This is therefore an area in which further research. Promotion of the growth and development of the Global Information Infrastructure and its use presents several challenges to all countries, perhaps most especially for developing countries. Developing countries will, in particular, have to develop cheap, simple and robust technologies for coping with increasing numbers of users and traffic. In pursuit of this objective, research and development is required on the development of means for promoting equal access to cyberspace.

## Global Information Infrastructure

The new technologies are inherently democratic, provide the public and individuals with access to information and sources and enable all to participate actively in the communication process. Action by states to impose excessive regulations on the use of these technologies and, again, particularly the Internet, on the grounds that control, regulation and denial of access are necessary to preserve the moral fabric and cultural identity of societies is paternalistic. These regulations presume to protect people from themselves and, as such are inherently incompatible with the principles of the worth and dignity of each individual. Internet connectivity is of special significance to civil society.

Computer networks fill a "media gap" between interpersonal communication facilitated by telephone, telegram, and letters, and mass communication facilitated by radio, television, and print media. Computer networks can greatly facilitate small-group participation--within groups, between groups, and between groups and their constituencies--and thus help to strengthen the forces of civil society. Many human rights organizations have embraced the Internet as a means of exchanging information quickly and cheaply. Groups in the Middle East and North Africa have proved no exception to this trend.

Governments around the world, claiming they want to protect children,thwart terrorists and silence racists and hate mongers, are rushing toeradicate freedom of expression on the Internet, the international "network ofnetworks," touted as the Information Superhighway. It is particularly crucialnow, in the early stages of vast technological change, that governmentsreaffirm their commitment to respect the rights of citizens to communicatefreely.

Restrictions on Internet access and content are increasing worldwide,under all forms of government. Censorship legislation was recently enacted inthe United States, the birthplace of the Bill of Rights as well as of this newcommunications medium and, for better or worse, a model for other nations'Internet policies. The Clinton administration claims the law will protectminors from "indecent" material and appears unconcerned that it will reduceon-line expression between adults to what may be deemed suitable for a child.Other democratic countries are following suit. The German phone company cutoff access to all the sites hosted by an American Internet service provider(ISP) in an effort to bar Germans from gaining access to neo-Nazi propagandaon one of the sites it hosted. The governments of France and Australia havealso indicated they may enact legislation to control Internet content. Authoritarian regimes are attempting to reconcile their eagerness to reap the economic benefits of Internet access with maintaining control over the flow of information inside their borders. Censorship efforts in the U.S. and Germany lend support to those in China, Singapore, and Iran, where censors target not only sexually explicit material and hate speech but also pro-democracy discussions and human rights education.

Proposals to censor the Internet wherever they originate violate the free speech guarantees enshrined in democratic constitutions and international law. In the attempt to enforce them, open societies will become increasingly repressive and closed societies will find new opportunity to chill political expression. Because the Internet knows no national boundaries, on-line censorship laws, in addition to trampling on the free expression rights of a nation's own citizens, threaten to chill expression globally and to impede the development of the Global Information Infrastructure (GII) before it becomes a truly global phenomenon.

Democratic countries, including the U.S. and Germany, that are pushing for the development of the GII will lack legitimacy in criticizing efforts by China to eliminate information that "hinders public order" or by Vietnam, where the "the cultural aspect" is cited as a reason to censor connections to pro-democracy discussions abroad. An issue closely related to censorship is that of access, which is to a large extent determined by the existing telecommunications system. According to a 1995 report by the Panos Institute, a London-based international non-profit organization specializing in development issues.

Forty-nine countries have fewer than one telephone per 100 people, 35 of which are in Africa. India, for example, has 8 million telephone lines for 900 million people. At a global level at least 80% of the world's population still lacks the most basic telecommunications. Opportunities to promote access have never been greater, however. New communications technologies are providing developing countries with an unprecedented means to leapfrog antiquated communication networks. Limits on access are imposed by governments for a variety of reasons, including economic gain and political control. Some governments, including India and Saudi Arabia, have chosen to control the liberalizing effect of the Internet by denying access to entire segments of their populations, either through exorbitant charges or by confining access to select populations, such as universities.

Rather than attempting to extend the Internet to a diverse group of citizens, these governments are striving to reap the economic benefits of Internet access without making it available to economically, socially, and politically disadvantaged groups, for whom it has the greatest potential for positive change. In some countries, such as Saudi Arabia, individuals who have Internet connections through foreign-owned corporations are able to elude these restrictions.

On-line communications are particularly susceptible to unauthorized scrutiny. Encryption technology is needed to ensure that individuals and groups may communicate without fear of eavesdropping. The Internet has the potential to be a tremendous force for development by providing quick and inexpensive information, by encouraging discussion rather than violence, and by empowering citizens, to cite but a few examples. But this potential can be realized only if it becomes a truly global effort. Policy makers must make every effort to ensure that internationally guaranteed rights to free expression are extended to on-line communication and call for the repeal of censorship legislation. Without such commitments, individuals face the danger of seeing their rights eroded by the very technologies they are embracing.

The Internet is composed of a number of different ways of organizing, transmitting and accessing data. Because of this multiplicity of systems, it is unlike any other single medium. Rather, it incorporates characteristics of several other media and communications systems, including print, broadcast, and postal systems. Electronic mail (e-mail) allows for one-to-one or one-to-many communication. Gopher sites provide text-only information arranged according to menus. The World Wide Web allows for the display of many types of information, including text, images, sound and video, as well as interactive communication. A recognition by world leaders of the need to formulate policy for this powerful new medium prompted members of the G7 to hold a "Ministerial Conference on the Information Society" in Brussels in February 1995. At that conference, a number of principles were agreed to, including encouraging competition and private investment, defining an adaptable regulatory framework, providing open access to networks, ensuring universal access, and promoting equality of opportunity and diversity of content. Although freedom of expression was not highlighted in specific terms, to the disappointment of Human Rights Watch and other groups that had urged such an emphasis, it is implied in the final goal promoting diversity of content which can be achieved only by encouraging free expression for people all over the world.

Governments around the globe are anxious to control this new medium. Every communications advance in history has been seen by self-appointed moral guardians as something to be controlled and regulated. By 1558, a century after the invention of the printing press, a Papal index barred the works of more than 500 authors.

In 1915, the same year that the D. W. Griffith film "Birth of a Nation" changed the U.S. cultural landscape, the U.S. Supreme Court upheld the constitutionality of an Ohio state censorship board created two years earlier, thus exempting motion pictures from free speech protection on the grounds that their exhibition "is a business, pure and simple, originated and conducted for profit...." The same view was applied in the early days of radio entertainment programs were thought to be exempt from freedom of speech guarantees. The Internet, as the first truly "mass" medium, is even more threatening than these earlier media. While few individuals and groups can publish books or newspapers, make a film, or produce a radio or television program, any person with a personal computer and a modem can communicate with a huge international audience.

The implications of a real GII for the advancement of human rights and democracy are vast. When traditional means of communication broke down and the war in Sarajevo made it impossible for civilians to leave their homes without risking their lives, many citizens used on-line technology to communicate with family members, the international press, and humanitarian relief agencies.

Human rights groups, political organizations, and builders of burgeoning democracies are using the Internet to communicate, educate, and organize. During the United Nations Fourth World Conference on Women, held in Beijing in 1995, women all over the world were able to feel a sense of participation because of regular postings on the proceedings. It is precisely because of the Internet's potential for increasing the political participation of the disenfranchised that governments are seeking to control it. These initial achievements could easily disappear if the censors are allowed to have their way. Governments and other institutions that support freedom of expression must ensure that the Internet is granted the same guarantees that are given to other forms of individual expression.

International law is clear on what electronic rights of expression must entail. Although international law does not address such communication specifically, the Universal Declaration on Human Rights and the International Covenant on Civil and Political Rights enshrine rights to freedom of expression, access, and privacy, which are relevant to the new medium. Article 19 of the Universal Declaration of Human Rights proclaims: Everyone has the right to freedom of opinion and expression; this right includes freedom to hold opinions without interference and to seek, receive and impart information and ideas through any media and regardless of frontiers.

In response to the debate about cyberspace, the Canadian government formed the Information Highway Advisory Council (IHAC) in 1994 to study and prepare an official statement on what directions the Internet should take in Canada. In September 1995, the council released its first report, which contained only vague recommendations.

On the issue of content, it concluded that there should be controls on two primary targets: obscenity and racist/hate material. It is illegal to spread "hate propaganda" and "obscenity" in Canada. Sexually explicit material is legal as long as it is not deemed obscene, that is, characterized by "undue exploitation of sex," meaning sex plus violence or degrading sex. Under a new law on child pornography that has not been tested by the Supreme Court, mere possession is illegal. According to David Jones, president ofElectronic Frontiers Canada, "There are no new laws being proposed that apply specifically to the Internet." That could change, however. On April 2, 1996, Justice Minister Allan Rock released a discussion paper inviting Canadians to present their views on regulating excessive violence in the media, including the Internet.

Asia now has over 1.5 million users, two-thirds of them in Japan. Among the region's authoritarian nations, only North Korea and Myanmar are without any Internet connection. Currently, most countries in Asia are connected directly to the U.S., rather than to each other, but new initiatives have proposed establishing an intra-Asia connection. Some Asian governments, including Pakistan, are choosing to control the Internet's effects mainly by limiting its availability.

A senior scientist at Pakistan's state-owned National Institute of Electronics has noted that Internet access would be limited by the small number of nodes and hosts available to users and by the intervention of service providers who could stop undesirable discussion groups and electronic messages.24

In India, where commercial Internet access was launched in mid-1995, only the state-owned phone company, VSNL, has been allowed to provide international Internet services, in order to maintain the government's monopoly on long-distance phone services.According to guidelines issued by the Department of Telecommunications (DoT) based on the antiquated Indian Telegraph Act of 1885, an ISP must ensure that nothing objectionable or obscene is carried on the network, but it is not clear that these have been enforced. In late January 1996, the DoT decided to allow commercial access, but all companies will have to route their services through VSNL.

Thailand's National Electronics and Computer Technology Center (Nectec), an official agency responsible for information technology policy, recently called upon local ISPs to police their own sites for sexually explicit material. It also said that subscribers and operators are required to agree not to show anything considered indecent or they will face criminal prosecution.

In the Philippines, Internet censorship measures have been introduced in the legislature. In early March 1996, member nations of the Association of Southeast Asian Nations (ASEAN) said they planned to set up a regulatory body to deal with the flood of information technology; they also voiced concern about pornography and disinformation.Commercial Internet accounts became available in China in mid-1995, but at prices far beyond the means of all but the wealthiest.

In June 1995, China's telecommunications minister stated that "as a sovereign state, China will exercise control on the information" entering China from the Internet. "By linking with the Internet, we do not mean the absolute freedom of information." Many Usenet newsgroups, including those classified as alt, rec and soc, were reportedly not allowed on Chinese Internet host computers, but the comp and sci hierarchies were apparently provided.

The Hong Kong-based China Internet Corporation (CIC), principally owned by China's state-run Xinhua News Agency, offers Chinese business subscribers only limited access to business-related information. Users have access to information generated outside China, but only after it has been screened in Hong Kong. According to James Chu, CEO of CIC, customers can be assured their e-mail will not be screened or bugged by mainland "unless you have broken the law."ChinaNet, based in Beijing and Shanghai, which became available in May 1995, provided commercial Internet access. Control of Internet access accounts was extremely tight, and people wishing to open them were required to register at the Postal Ministry. Fairly quickly, black market permits became available. On January 1, 1996, several days after CompuServe cut off access to 200 Usenet newsgroups, Xinhua News Agency, China's official medium, reported that the government had called for a crackdown on the Internet to rid the country of unwanted pornography and "detrimental information."

A joint statement issued by the State Council and the Communist Party Central Committee said effective measures had to be adopted to solve the problem of uncontrolled information. The leadership also reportedly summoned the Chinese suppliers of Internet connections, and on January 15, the biggest supplier announced a "moratorium" on new subscribers. According to press reports, officials said that as many as 70,000 people were using the Internet through 7,000 accounts, and that the high volume was more than the current system could handle. On January 23, a cabinet session chaired by Premier Li Peng adopted draft rules governing links to the Internet. The cabinet reiterated its provisional approval for global computer links but declared it "imperative" to formulate rules to govern China's use of the new technology. On February 4, Xinhua announced that the new Internet regulations required existing computer networks to "liquidate" and "re-register," and to use only international channels provided by the Ministry of Posts and Telecommunications, the Ministry of Electronics Industry, the State Education Commission and the Chinese Academy of Sciences.

Hong Kong has not drafted any policy or released any official statements regarding Internet censorship. The 1987 Obscene and Indecent Articles Ordinance does not specifically discuss on-line communication, but the ordinance reportedly applies to communication on the Internet.

The Hong Kong government's Recreation and Culture Branch, which oversees on-line media, recently commissioned a study of on-line communication. Its secretary said that developments in other countries, including the United States, would be taken into account. There are currently more than fifty Hong Kong ISPs, and some censor content, including Hong Kong SuperNet, one of the largest Hong Kong ISPs, which voluntarily ended access to sexually explicit material on Usenet in March 1995. Star Internet followed suit in November, by blocking about twenty newsgroups with erotic text and pictures. In March 1996, Commissioner of the Television and Entertainment Licensing Authority Peter Cheung Po-tak said that controls on the Internet should ensure a "minimum degree of decency" to protect children and said the best solution would be for ISPs to regulate themselves.

In Singapore the Internet is treated as a broadcast medium, regulated under the Singapore Broadcasting Authority Act of 1995, which established the Singapore Broadcasting Authority (SBA). Singapore allows three service providers: Singnet, which is part of Singapore Telecom, Pacific Internet and Cyberway. The government claims that it does not currently censor e-mail, but in 1994 it disclosed that it had searched individual accounts to try to identify those who had downloaded sexually explicit material. After businesses expressed alarmed about the security of their information, authorities said they would refrain from conducting such searches in the future. The main means of censorship up to now has been to control access. In addition, sexually explicit material and news have been censored by the Ministry of Information and the Arts, the government body in charge of media censorship.

Fewer than half of Usenet newsgroups are available through Singnet. Currently there are no widespread uniform guidelines or procedures for restricting use of any Internet services, and local administrators have to make arbitrary decision on access. Although authorities initially stated that they would not heavily censor political criticism, they have reportedly shifted from watching for sex-related material to watching for "misinformation."

Indonesia's first commercial provider, Indonet, began operation in late 1994. A number of others soon followed, and the country now has numerous

ISPs. The more established electronic bulletin board networks also draw extensively from the Internet.

The Internet is more free than any other mass medium in Indonesia, and there are no laws, regulations or ministerial decrees concerning its use. Tempo, a news weekly that was closed by the government two years ago, recently established a site on the Web, with the blessing of the minister of information who agreed "there are no regulations against it," but warned that "maybe the House [of Representatives] will want to discuss legislating the Internet." At this stage, however, the government has chosen to compete with opposing views by establishing its own Web sites. Armed Forces spokesman Brig.-Gen. Surwarno Adiwijoyo told Reuters news agency that the military had suggested to the Communications Ministry the need for some sort of "toll gate" to "black out" news that could damage culture or affect security. It has also suggested registering uses and users, he said.

At present, private ISPs do not carry all Usenet groups, but this is reportedly done in the interests of conserving disk space and because of the language barrier.

The Malaysian Institute of Microelectronic Systems (Mimos), the nation's sole Internet provider, has experienced a huge demand, with an average monthly increase of 22 percent since it began service in late 1994. As of October 1995, there were some 30,000 users. In April 1996, Mimos announced that it would appoint eight new ISPs to help ease congestion.Usenet newsgroups are heavily censored. The "acceptable use" policy at Jaring, the main Malaysian Internet line, states that "members shall not use Jaring network for any activities not allowed under any Law of Malaysia." The government reportedly realizes that on-line censorship may not be effective. In reaction to Malaysian students abroad criticizing Malaysia on the Internet, the government has considered various ways to curb such dissent, according to the information and education ministers, and the education minister proposed cutting scholarships of offending students.

In South Korea, about half of all Internet users are affiliated with universities or the government. The nationally run telephone corporation, Korea Telecom, started service in June 1994, and there are a number of other commercial providers. The government has decided to censor computer networks, according to statements by communications officials in October 1995. The decision was reportedly made out of growing concern regarding children's access to sexually explicit and other undesirable material. Local computer networks will be asked to prohibit access by local subscribers to banned sites, according to the Information and Communications Ethics Committee of the Data and Communications Ministry. Sexually explicit material will be banned, along with information deemed "subversive," such as instructions on making bombs and drugs. Computer games and other software are already censored. Details, such as punishments, have reportedly yet to be worked out.

The state-owned telecommunications company Vietnam Datacommunications Company (VDC) had planned to launch Internet service earlier this year, but it reportedly put off the opening day because officials decided to first draft regulations on allowable Internet links and users.

Internet regulations will reportedly comply with the government's existing censorship regulations. Pham Dao, director of VDC, said that an Internet firewall would be installed to screen out transmissions from specified senders or news resources cutting out much of the anti-government commentary. carried by dissident groups, including support for jailed Buddhists and dissidents.56

It appears likely that the Ministry of Culture and Information will monitor on-line content and that Interior Ministry will be in charge of monitoring Internet national security issues. Nguyen Ngoc Canh of the General Directorate of Posts and Telecommunications, which sets communication policy, said competing domestic services likely will be allowed as long as Vietnam Datacommunications Company monitors a single outside link. Until recently, Vietnam's Internet service was made available through the Institute of Information Technology, which exists mostly for the benefit of academics and nongovernmental organizations. A VDC official told the press that the organization's effort to control the Internet "is the requirement from our leaders, our government. The Internet must be controlled, not only for technical and security reasons but from the cultural aspect." The government is reportedly worried about sexually explicit material from foreign countries and about "foreign organizations" transmitting information. Some overseas Vietnamese groups have distributed anti-government tracts in Hanoi.

Australia has been considering regulating the Internet since 1993. In August 1994, the Department of Communications and the Arts released a report, "Regulation of Computer Bulletin Board Systems," which called for regulations. A year later, the recommendations in that report were updated and released in the "Consultation Paper on the Regulation of On-line Information Services." One of the goals elucidated in the consultation paper was "to protect freedom of expression, especially with regard to private communication between adults, while at the same time limiting children's exposure to harmful or unsuitable material." It proposed a system of self-regulation reinforced by legislative sanctions. Objectionable material was defined in the consultation paper as material that "depicts, expresses, or otherwise deals with matters of sex, drug misuse or addiction, crime, cruelty, violence or revolting or abhorrent phenomena in such a way that it offends against the standards of morality, decency and proprietary generally accepted by reasonable adults to the extent that the material should be refused classification."

In August 1995, the minister for communications and the arts directed the Australian Broadcasting Authority (ABA), an independent federal authority responsible for the regulation of the broadcasting industry, to investigate the content of on-line information and entertainment services and report to him by June 30, 1996. The resulting ABA "issues paper" became available in December 1995, with an invitation for comments to be submitted by the public until mid-February. The paper discusses various issues involved in the development of a code of practice, the adoption of a classification scheme, enforcement of a code, and blocking offensive sites. Electronic Frontiers Australia, a nongovernmental organization working for rights of Internet users in Australia, submitted a response to the issues paper, arguing a number of points, including that the Internet, because of its interactivity, significantly differs from broadcast media. "Classification of content is unnecessary and in most instances impossible to police," it pointed out. The EFA also urged the government to consult with the industry and "develop a grasp of the realities of the on-line service industry."

Some state governments, including those of New South Wales, Queensland, Victoria, Western Australia, Northern Territory, and Tasmania, have already passed or are planning to introduce on-line censorship legislation. In early October 1995, eighteen people were being questioned and fifteen computers seized across the state of Queensland for alleged involvement with child pornography, based on the state's Classification of Computer Games and Images Act.

In Victoria state, the Classification. Bill, which has passed two houses of Parliament and awaits enactment, makes it an offense to use an on-line network to transmit "objectionable" material to minors. Victoria's bill has passed two houses of Parliament. A similar law in Western Australia went into effect on January 1, 1996. Both leave primary censorship in the hands of service providers, and seek to punish senders of information deemed "objectionable" and senders of information classified as "restricted" to minors according to broad definitions contained in the legislation. ISPs are liable only if they knowingly permit objectionable material to be transmitted on their network. An even more extreme bill now before the parliament in New South Wales will hold individuals and ISPs responsible for objectionable material, which includes not only sexually explicit information but also drug- and crime-related material. All state laws are subject to change when new federal laws are adopted.

Restrictive Internet legislation was proposed in Parliament in 1994, but, according to Stephen Bell, an Internet activist in New Zealand, it "is widely perceived as more or less dead" at present because of unrelated political developments. Under the legislation, the New Zealand Technology and Crimes Reform Bill, all users would be cut off from any site that transmitted a single piece of objectionable material to a single user. Those found in violation of the law could be fined thousands and lose the use of a telephone for up to five years. Under current law, computer disks are treated as "publications," and may be censored as such under the Films, Videos and Publications Classification Act of 1993. If authorities find one example of the more serious grade of "objectionable" material, as defined by the Act, they may arrest and shut down an ISP. Apparently fearing possible liability, several universities and Internet providers have been blocking access to newsgroups dealing with erotica.

The Middle East is coming on-line in increasing numbers, but many governments are hoping to control access to sensitive political and religious discussion as well as sex-related material. Bahrain went on-line in December 1995 through Batelco, the government-run phone company, after installing an expensive system to block access to certain Internet-related sites.

GlobeNet, a U.S. firm, won a contract to provide Internet service in Jordan in 1995 and was asked by authorities to install a special screening facility to control sexually explicit material. Kuwait is planning to launch a new Internet service soon, but a Communications Ministry official told the press that the new ISP "must ensure that no pornography or politically subversive' commentary is available in Kuwait." There is no new content-related legislation planned at present. In Abu Dhabi, an Internet club "ha[s] agreed to ban sex, religion and politics on the Internet to respect the local laws." Police in the United Arab Emirates recently held a seminar on combatting political dissent and sexually explicit material. In Morocco, the state Office National des Postes et Telecommunications (ONPT) brought the Internet to the nation on November 16, 1995. ONPT has secured an agreement with the commercial companies that will provide the service. Charges will be fixed, and a convention has been signed to govern all aspects of the Internet's operation. The service has been targeted at the banking and insurance sectors, universities, and multinational corporations.

The first Iranian Internet line was opened in 1992 by the Institute for Studies in Theoretical Physics and Mathematics through a link to Vienna. The government helped with funds. Internet users, still mostly at universities, now number around 30,000. The government also sponsors a network whose chat rooms allow on-line dialogue between only two subscribers at a time, and private ISPs also exist. Access to the Internet is relatively unregulated, but its increasing popularity will likely result in greater government control. One private network had its lines cut by the Telecommunications Company (TCI) of Iran in August 1995. TCI may have been reacting to reports that the network was being used by young people for sex chats, or it may have been trying to reduce competition to its own network service.

In Saudi Arabia, Internet access has been confined to universities and hospitals. All local accounts, which automatically note the material accessed, are open to inspection by the Ministry of the Interior. Government officials have justified their reluctance to permit large-scale access on the grounds that there is a need to protect people from pornographic and other harmful effects. Existing pornography laws apply to the Internet, but loopholes are available: large foreign companies are increasingly offering their unmonitored Internet access to Saudi business acquaintances, and commercial members of the GulfNet are also free from scrutiny. Internet access will reportedly be made available to businesses in 1996, but reportedly with strict controls. Mohammed Benten, a dean at King Fahd University for Petroleum and Minerals in Dhahran, told a local newspaper, "Here in the kingdom, with our strict rules and regulations, we will see the Internet being accessed only for constructive objectives." Minister of Posts,

Telephones and Telegraphs Dr. Ali Al-Johani said in February 1996 that, although the Internet was beyond government control, authorities were investigating how it could be regulated.

The European Union is considering adopting some Internet-related controls. In late January 1996, a European Union Consultative Commission on Racism and Xenophobia said it "hope[d] the EU [would] take all needed measures to prevent Internet from becoming a vehicle for the incitement of racist hatred." It also called for the "creation of protective judicial measures." It urged all member states to follow the example of Germany, which has been trying to censor racist and pornographic messages.

France joined the call for regulation in early February, when the French minister for information technology announced that France would request members of the EU to draft new legislation to cope with legal issues posed by the Internet. It is believed that France's reaction has to do with the recent posting on the Internet of the banned book, Le Grand Secret, by Claude Gubler, the late President Mitterand's physician.

EU culture and telecommunications ministers met informally in Bologna, Italy in late April 1996, to discuss Internet regulation. At the meeting, France proposed the drafting of a global convention on Internet regulation. The ministers agreed to ask the European Commission, the executive body of the EU, to draw up a report on the question. The Commission is reportedly supposed to determine whether the EU should deal with this issue, or whether the issue should proceed directly to international negotiations. That same week in Strasbourg, Irish Minister of State for European Affairs Gay Mitchell called on the EU to investigate controls on the transmission of child pornography on the Internet at a joint meeting organized by UNICEF and the Council of Europe, to discuss the commercial exploitation of children.

The European Commission reportedly plans to draft a discussion paper on interactive services, including the Internet, which may lead to a directive that may include content regulation. The European Commission is considering a regulation requiring EU member states to send draft national legislation affecting the Internet to the EU in order for member states to vet the laws before they are adopted. The European Commission is reportedly divided over how to standardize Internet policies of its member states. The European Parliament has introduced changes to the EU's broadcasting law to extend its scope to the Internet, but that approach is strongly opposed by many in the computer industry.

The UK has not yet enacted any Internet-specific censorship legislation but has relied, instead, on existing laws banning obscenity. Gay groups, however, reportedly feel they are being victimized. An organizer for the London-based group, S&M; Gays, for example, told the press that "The police seem to have great difficulty in distinguishing between gay men and pedophiles." The group closed down its computer bulletin board, fearing that it might become a police target. In its recent proposals for media ownership, the UK government suggested that the media industry regulator could have some influence over the content of the Internet.

An inter-departmental group was set up in March 1995 to examine tackling such issues as sexually explicit material on the Internet. A new defamation bill extending libel to computer networks was introduced in February 1996; it provides a defense for ISPs as long as they are do not knowingly permit a defamatory statement to be made over their networks. On-line service providers have asked the government for further clarification on their responsibilities under the legislation. In March 1996, British Trade and Industry Minister Ian Taylor said the UK was seeking a voluntary approach to regulation of content on the Internet.

The Internet Service Providers Association (ISPA), a voluntary grouping of service providers to be formally launched in May 1996, is drawing up a code of practice that will cover fair trading issues, and Taylor said that he expected the code to cover "both illegal and undesirable material." He added, "The only alternative to voluntary action ... is increased political pressure for legislation in various areas. That pressure may get increasingly hard to resist."

On March 15, 1996, French ISPs were subpoenaed after a French Jewish student organization brought charges against them for alleged "complicity" in making available propaganda that denies the Holocaust; such propaganda is illegal in France. A decision was to be reached in April, as this report went to press.

Germany and CompuServe have both been criticized for their roles in the CompuServe censorship episode. CompuServe and the German officials involved have made conflicting statements regarding who actually made the decision to censor Usenet newsgroups. As far as Human Rights Watch has been able to determine, a task force was set up by the Bavarian minister of the interior at police headquarters in Munich in 1994 to search for on-line child pornography. The task force obtained a search warrant to investigate the Munich CompuServe office on November 22, 1995. The search was reportedly more like a visit, in which the authorities told the company of their concerns and CompuServe agreed to comply. Two days later, CompuServe's German managers reportedly stated that they would support German authorities' fight against pornography in cyberspace. On December 8, the authorities gave them a list of more than 200 suggested newsgroups with a letter saying "...it is left to CompuServe to take the necessary steps to avoid possible liabilities to punishment." CompuServe then made the decision to take all the groups off its servers, apparently without making the effort to look at them. Among the groups it "banned" were discussion groups for homosexuals and the news service Clarinet, which was not even on its servers.As with other instances of Internet censorship, the ban was an ineffective effort to comply with the demands of an ill-informed authority.

CompuServe users still of course had access to the Internet and could therefore connect to other host computers that carried the forbidden newsgroups. In February, CompuServe again provided access to the 200 formerly censored newsgroups, except for five groups. The Bavarian minister of justice recently claimed that CompuServe's new Cyber Patrol software does not meet the company's obligations under German law because the company has an obligation not to supply illegal material to German citizens. Moving from sexually explicit material to hate speech, in January 1996, Deutsche Telekom (DT), the national telephone company, blocked users of its T-Online computer network from accessing Internet sites used to spread anti-Semitic propaganda, which is a crime in Germany.

Authorities also announced that they were expanding their investigation to America Online and Deutsche Forschungsnetz, the national scientific research network. The company was responding to demands by Mannheim prosecutors who were investigating Ernst Zuendel, a German-born neo-Nazi living in Toronto. DT also blocked access to a Santa Cruz, California computer service, Web Communications, that also provides access to Zuendel's site. Web Communications stated that although it did not agree with Zuendel, it was not the company's policy to censor its users. A DT spokesman said that access to certain providers was blocked while government prosecutors investigated on-line neo-Nazi material. The lack of organized monitoring by DT is reflected in the fact that Zuendel's Web site was still available through CompuServe at the same time as it was "banned" through Web Communications. Rita Suessmuth, president of the Bundestag, the German parliament, was recently quoted in German newspapers as saying, "The information superhighway must not be allowed to become a forum for those who defile children." She added, "Freedom of expression reaches its limit when human dignity is violated and violence is promoted."The government reportedly disagrees with her assessment, however. Justice Minister Edzard Schmidt-Jortzig said in late March 1996 that the government would introduce Internet censorship legislation before the summer recess. The legislation will seek to punish an ISP only if it knowingly permits illegal material on its service, but will not expect ISPs to be responsible for all the content on their servers. The legislation is expected to face opposition from the regional states, who plan to contest the measure on constitutional grounds and may propose a more restrictive law.

Internet censorship has not become a major issue in Latin America. Latin America is fully connected, except for Paraguay, Haiti, Belize and Cuba. In May 1996, Cuba, which at present has only e-mail service, will hold its first national telecommunications and informatics conference, Ariadna, to discuss the Internet. Jesus Martinez, director of the Center for Automated Information Exchange, the server for Cuba's largest e-mail network, says that regulations affecting electronic information connections and security are being studied "that do not anticipate including individuals." He also told the press that Cuba was "studying regulations about connections and security." Rosa Elena Simeon, the minister of science, technology and environment, said in January that Cuba must learn how to "use the Internet's capabilities and advantages while reducing its risks and disadvantages as much as possible." Guyanese officials also reportedly announced that the government "would move to prevent any unauthorized installation' of Internet services and added that they were studying ways of regulating links."

South Africa's Deputy President Thabo Mbeki pointed out to the G7 conference of wealthy countries that there were more telephone lines in Manhattan, New York than in the whole of sub-Saharan Africa." In Africa, access, technology and training are the huge hurdles to cross before censorship will be a major issue. As of late 1995, fewer than ten countries were directly connected to the Internet. In those countries, however, government control and censorship have already asserted themselves. As in Asia and the Middle East, some countries, such as Botswana, that have Internet access do not allow private ISPs to operate. The reason is reportedly not so much one of content control, but of money. The government is anxious not to lose the revenue from its monopoly on telecommunications services.

In the southern African country of Zambia, where Internet access is limited, the February 5 Internet edition of The Post, a daily and one of Zambia's most important opposition voices, was banned by President Chiluba under the State Security Act. The charges relate to a report based on leaked documents, revealing secret government plans to hold a referendum on the adoption of a new constitution. It remained on the Web site for two days until the police warned the ISP, Zamnet Communications, that it would be liable. Rather than striving to control content on the Internet, democratic governments should be working to ensure that the GII becomes truly global, and to motivate citizens to become more involved in decision making as they organize, debate, and share information unrestricted by geographic distances or national borders. Although the extraordinary potential for a GII has been suggested by existing on-line communications networks, the present on-line community is still quite limited. Only countries with a sophisticated telecommunications infrastructure are able to take full advantage of on-line technology. Even in countries with advanced telecommunications infrastructures, only persons with access to equipment and training can take advantage of new information resources. General illiteracy remains the primary obstacle to computer literacy.

## Information Economy

An economy does not have to be at the frontier of technology to get gains from the process and progress of reforms that underpin e-commerce. Since both technology capital and the environment in which it is used matter, at least some aspects of e-commerce could be driven by "low-tech" cell phones or faxes in one country, weekly visits to an Internet café in another, or widespread use of broadband in a third.

For policymakers in emerging and transition economies, this implies that each economy can enjoy at least some of the benefits of the e-commerce by following its own path, with its own resources. Economies with superior resources as well as a superior policy environment reap the greatest gains. For example, in Sri Lanka, fisherman use cell phones to call associates in the fish market in Colombo to get information about what is selling and 'real-time' prices for their fish, which increases their power in negotiations. In Morocco, a micro-credit enterprise businesses with 36 offices around the country is linking the computers into those offices rather than fax the daily credit reports to the head office, making account consolidation quicker and less error-prone.

The global potential inherent in the Internet and e-commerce has strong implications for trade competitiveness and participation in the global value chain of production. Creating a more facilitating environment confers an advantage for global participation and trade competitiveness. For example, Dell computer's web-site sends information about a new on-line order to plants all over the world that produce components, which significantly reduces time to build and costs of inventory. Plants that cannot keep up with this real-time technique cannot be part of Dell's highest value chain.

Creating a facilitating environment also may enable superior delivery of health and education services. For example, in Vietnam, a web-site for a health clinic started by providing information, but soon began taking appointments and filling orders, leading to both an expanded business and happier clients. There is not conflict between e-commerce objectives and development goals: A commitment to e-commerce is a commitment to growth, trade, and economic development.

There are two complementary approaches to e-commerce policy. Some economies have focused on specific projects or technology parks, for example. There are benefits to these approaches by building awareness and islands of success. However, to gain the full potential of e-commerce, it should transform the activities of business, consumer, and government activities. Transformation is best assisted through the package of structural policies, networked ICTs, and human resources. The package creates an environment where technology is diffused and used more effectively to raise productivity growth throughout the whole economy. Of course, why do we care about productivity growth at all? Labor productivity growth is the foundation for gains in real wages. An economy with higher overall productivity growth can support faster GDP growth without generating inflation.

In many countries, the growth of the Internet and of electronic commerce is being stymied by problems with key infrastructures. In many cases, the root of these problems is with the policy environment. However, the sense of urgency that policymakers are feeling to get on the Internet bandwagon is initiating new approaches to reform to create a facilitating environment. The private sector, both domestic and foreign, is playing a bigger role.

In many countries the telecommunications system remains a monopoly controlled by the government. Service is poor and costs are high. However, policymakers find it politically difficult to take "head-on" the powerful telecommunications ministry. Privatization alone may not yield a better outcome. For example, in Morocco, the state-run telecom authority was privatized, but without any independent regulator in place. The country traded a public monopoly for a private monopoly, which is no more responsive to market demand than was its predecessor.

Policymakers are looking to technological solutions to increase competition and provide superior service at lower costs. For example, in Singapore, the Information Development Authority is considering award a value-added-services license to a well-know firm to conduct broadband trading. However, ultimately, the authority would need to award a facilities-based license to this firm, something that has so far not been allowed. Vietnam offers another example of how policymakers are inviting in new technology to help create competition.

As it stands now, the monopoly provider charges independent ISPs at a higher rate than they change their own ISP. And, the single international gateway for Vietnam is slow and costly. To generate some increased competition, the government is building two software parks which will have satellite links; the government expects to regulate these prices at a lower level and they expect that most ISPs will reside in one of these parks in order to get the benefit of the lower pricing.

Access is a second area where countries offer important business opportunities. For a variety of reasons, ranging from financial to cultural, most countries will not follow the US model of the home-based or work-based PC as the means of access. Instead a community oriented access point, such as kiosks in gas-stations in El Salvador or after-school community sessions in schools in Japan are examples.

Access via a non-PC device is another opportunity; Linux-based hand-held units are being used in Honduras to help farmers negotiate better prices for their produce and to connect them to information at the agricultural extension station. Access in the language that is not English has already created profitable businesses- Spanish and Chinese content is the fastest growth. Once customers can use the Internet, they will want content and business transactions to be done in their own language.

Problems in the financial system are a huge impediment to the development of electronic commerce. Policymakers play a very big role in determining the playing field for financial institutions. Technological solutions offered by the private sector seem to offer excellent prospects for business as well as for improving the environment for business to do business. For example, in many countries, policymakers simply do not want a credit culture to develop. And, whether because of fraud or foreign exchange volatility, the actual rates for international credit card usage are too high--5 to 7 percent of each transactions in Taiwan and Bulgaria for example-for this to be a viable approach to electronic commerce transactions. Devising alternative approaches to on-line payment is a huge opportunity that would be welcomed by policymakers and business alike.

On-line security is a major factor affecting the development of electronic commerce and secure financial products is a large and underserved market in many countries. For example, unlike US law, in many countries, including Taiwan and China, holders of credit or debit cards are liable for the full amount of any charges on their cards, regardless of whether the card or number is stolen. Holders of cards often don't use them because of the fear of insecure transactions. In some countries, such as in Thailand and Bangladesh, they are right to worry-there are few to no secure servers so that indeed everyone on the Internet can have access to the numbers!

Private sector approaches to on-line security, on-line payments are desperately needed to jump-start the development of e-commerce in many countries. The key is for policymakers to encourage these innovations rather than discourage them. Finally, Central Bank authorities in some countries are quite concerned that allowing international purchases over the Internet will undermine their ability to track and control the use of foreign exchange. Because countries are concerned that they might "run out" of foreign exchange (as for example happened with Thailand, Korea, and Russia several years ago), Central Banks need a greater ability to, at minimum, track transactions on a real-time basis. No longer is over-night clearing sufficient.

Distribution, including customs, is an area that can trip-up e-commerce transactions, and slow the process from real-time to a long-time. Countries are coming to realize that bad roads can be just as damaging to e-commerce as are bad telecommunications.

The sense of urgency is propelling policymakers to attract private businesses to help them create an environment more conducive to Internet business development. A good example is Sri Lanka, where textiles and apparel are a very important export market. The private sector invested in the necessary technology to move up the value-chain from underwear to fashion garments, which requires a fast information links to the buyer and a much quicker turn-around in the production of the garments. While the producers were able to perform on the faster basis, they were stymied when faced with getting their product to the airport, through customs, and onto an airplane.

Legal systems in many countries offer tremendous opportunities. Not only are necessary laws governing electronic contracts and signatures necessary, but more broadly a culture of law and a rule of law are necessary. Simply writing new laws will do little to support the development of e-commerce if the culture is one of corruption and evasion.

The globalization of production and trade in goods and services is associated with increased use of information technologies and transformation of economic activities. Some industry sectors in the leading economies are using e-commerce particularly intensively. Production partners who do not or cannot effectively use these technologies run the risk of losing their position in the global value chain. Notice that many of the developing countries in this example have export sectors that are more demanding in their use of e-commerce as compared to some of the industrial countries.

"The New Economy and APEC" provides a tool for policymakers to assess the extent to which the trade of their economy is concentrated in the goods or services that are the heaviest users of technology. If their trade is so concentrated, then shaping the proper policy environment through structural reforms is that much more important.

Structural reform and policies to shape a policy environment conducive to transformation and effective use of information and technology are necessary but may not be sufficient for e-commerce to diffuse throughout an economy. Fostering entrepreneurship is necessary, but this is a policy area that requires a different approach to the top-down, or government initiated, policy reforms in services infrastructures.

Entrepreneurs are leaders—in whatever region, forum, or community they populate. Even in the most destitute areas, there are trusted, respected risk-taking visionaries. Innovation, ideas of how to use effectively information and technology for the benefit of a local community will only come from that local community. Innovation and entrepreneurship cannot be forced down from top and in general, 'fly-by' consultants also will not really know how the locals might best apply the tools of e-commerce.

Government and NGOs can still play an important role in fostering these entrepreneurs: Building awareness of the possibilities is key. Pilot projects with community input may give shape to local vision, and show success. Technology parks can incubate. While the temptation is to be very directed, government assistance in this process needs to be light-handed in order to preserve local incentives and interests, to avoid permanent subsidy projects, and to ensure diffusion out of "technology parks" into the real world of the local economy. Government's role principally is in shaping the environment, not determining how to best to do business in that environment.

Government is a big business in many countries. It should be an exemplar in using e-commerce, both to show the way, as well as act as a test of the policy environment that is being created for private e-commerce. If government cannot do e-commerce because of poor infrastructures, then likely private firms cannot do it either, appoint a "Domestic Champion." This Senior Policy Figure should have the highest charisma, stature, and authority. This person must have the vision of what electronic commerce can offer a country and will emphasize the cross-cutting nature of the Internet and the synergies that it creates among key service sector infrastructures. Such a person can fashion pro-active alliances among government agencies and businesses that wish to promote liberalization, deregulation, and competition to achieve the benefits of Internet technologies. Such a Minister can help ensure that private sector competitors-both domestic and foreign-actively engage in creating the new environment in which both they and new firms can flourish.

Create "Internet E-Government Teams" to make government a leader in the network economy. Just as private firms are changing the way they do business, the Internet and electronic commerce will change how government performs its core functions, including raising tax revenues, procuring goods and services, and providing for the needs of the public. To both lead the way and pave the way for economic benefits to accrue, governments must proactively embrace the new environment. The Internet e-government team will help put government activities on-line.

The Internet team is composed of global consultants, local private sector firms, and people from within the specific agency of government. The team is a "systems integrator" with the agencies of the government as clients. After putting the agency "on-line" (with equipment, software, and training) the team moves to the next agency.

A key advantage is that the team leaves systems in each agency that will work together. So, for example, the tax authority will be integrated into the customs authority with clear benefits to the fiscal balance overall. A second key advantage is that technology transfer-hardware, software, and human capital-is part of what is delivered. The global private sector has a very important role to play as both support structure and key member of the team.

Without transformation of activities, the benefits of the e-commerce will not be evident. Moreover, without transformation, trade competitiveness is risk. Structural policy reforms are key to shape the environment where transformation can take place. These reforms, because they are comprehensive are more difficulty than a "technology policy". These reforms go to the heart of the relationship between the policy and economic environment. Therefore, they require domestic commitment and leadership at the top. By the same token, since the transformation takes places at the individual firm or community, local vision is needed too.

## Technology transfer

Technology transfer is meant to provide the technical knowledge lacking in a particular production environment. It is the transfer of the stock of production knowledge in both the private and public domains and it takes place through direct and indirect mechanisms.

Direct mechanisms include the purchase of capital goods and equipment, the training of nationals of recipient countries in specific technologies, and the hiring of foreign experts and consulting firms. Indirect mechanisms may include turnkey construction of plants and facilities, joint venture partnerships between foreign companies and local companies in the recipient countries, and the establishment of wholly owned subsidiaries of multinational companies.

While the different mechanisms provide different opportunities for the transfer of technologies, the outcome is not always assured. Transfer depends on a number of factors, which include, among others, the level of the existing stock of knowledge within the recipient country, the absorptive capacity of the recipient country's firms and individuals, and the policy, legal and institutional framework of the recipient country.

Technology transfer does not take place in a vacuum: it is only effective if transferred to an environment with adequate scientific and technological capability and infrastructure as well as the proper institutional and legal framework. Technology transfer is also determined by the existence and enforcement of national and international property rights regimes, and the bargaining power and negotiating capacities of the parties, as well as the balance of market and other factors on which the outcomes of such negotiations are dependent.

In today's networked knowledge-based global economy, knowledge and technological development are critical determinants of economic growth and sustainable development. The need for technology transfer arises from the fact that there is considerable concentration of knowledge, and the technologies deriving from it, in a limited number of countries and, furthermore, in a few large firms.

The multinational corporations are now responsible for most of the technology transfer through foreign direct investment (FDI) and international trade. This reality - the concentration of technological know-how in a few firms from a few countries -exposes many countries of the developing world to technological dependence, to monopolistic pricing of technology and knowledge products and services and, in some cases, to the imposition of inappropriate technological solutions to their unique set of problems.

Furthermore, the patterns of FDIs and international trade - only about 10 of the largest developing countries receive over 90 per cent of FDIs and enjoy a broader participation in international trade that extends beyond selling commodities - suggest that only a few developing countries are recipients of technology transfer through the predominant channels of FDIs and international trade undertaken by multinational corporations.

Moreover, there is a large body of knowledge in the public domain that is not accessible to developing countries and their firms and individuals owing to various factors related to the lack of human and institutional capacity, as well as costs. That body of knowledge is potentially useful to developing countries, and a deliberate effort needs to be pursued in order to harness this knowledge and transfer it to developing countries.

All these factors necessitate a concerted effort, on the part of the international community, at technology transfer to developing countries, especially the least developed countries. Urgency should be the hallmark of efforts at technology transfer because technology is advancing at a very rapid pace.

New advances in the fields of ICT, biotechnologies, and material sciences, to mention a few, are every day further enhancing the already huge potential for dramatically boosting development through "leapfrogging" stages of technological development, providing developing countries with access to markets, information and knowledge that has hitherto been inaccessible to them. However, the fact that this immense potential is not currently being adequately harnessed threatens to further marginalize the economies and peoples of developing countries. It is this potential and the urgent necessity to put it firmly at the service of development for all that should inform the work of the United Nations system in the area of transfer of technology and knowledge, especially ICT.

Another major factor that defines the work of the United Nations system in this area is the appreciation of the capabilities and, at the same time, the limits of both the national and international public sectors in assuring optimal outcomes to development efforts undertaken on their own. The private sector is the primary source of technological innovation, the engine of economic growth, employment and wealth creation.

The civil society, especially non-governmental organizations, provide networks of community organization and a framework within which wider consultations on the development process and its intended outcomes can be carried out.

The many initiatives of the United Nations system in the area of technology and knowledge transfer have therefore been increasingly characterized not only by cooperation among different agencies of the system, but also by partnerships with civil society, in particular the private sector.

The initiatives have been concentrated in a number of areas, such as developing knowledge and technology transfer networks through the utilization of the new technologies, especially the Internet, providing technical assistance to developing countries, building the capacity of developing countries, and assisting them in the creation of a conducive policy environment for the absorption, adaptation and utilization of knowledge and technology.

## Developing Networks

Poor countries - and poor people - differ from rich ones not only because they have less capital but also because they have less knowledge. Knowledge is often complex and costly to create and disseminate, and that is why much of it is created in industrialized countries. Developing countries can acquire knowledge from external sources as well as create their own. The success of the development experience in Asia relative to Africa and Latin America is due in part to the ability of East Asian countries to acquire and apply knowledge by attracting FDI and international trade.

There are two kinds of knowledge: technical knowledge or "know-how" and knowledge about attributes. The latter is knowledge that illuminates every economic transaction, revealing preferences, giving clarity to exchanges etc. The lack of such knowledge results in imperfect markets, the collapse of markets or, worse still, the absence of markets, all of which are detrimental to development and hurt the poor.

The lack of technical knowledge or know-how has dire consequences; for example, knowledge about how to treat a simple ailment such as diarrhoea has existed for centuries but millions of children continue to die from this ailment because their parents do not know how to treat them.

Further, greater amounts of knowledge and information are incorporated into goods and services. Knowledge and information are sources of wealth creation and value added in their own right. As their amount and value increase, there is a proportionate decrease in the amount and value of other inputs such as labour, capital, materials etc.

The concentration of knowledge and information-intensive industries in the industrialized countries contributes significantly to the development and technology gap between industrialized and developing countries. However, knowledge is now more readily accessible than ever before in the history of the human race.

The changing economics of information will make knowledge even more accessible in future, as the unit costs of computing, communications and transactions continue to decline. Despite this potentially easy accessibility, there are constraints on accessing knowledge, particularly by citizens and institutions of developing countries, and a deliberate effort is needed to generate and share knowledge, hence to establish knowledge networks.

Currently, there are four major networks that are pertinent to the issue of knowledge and technology transfer, especially ICT: the Global Development Network, the Knowledge and Technology for Development Network, WIPONET and the Sustainable Technologies Alternatives Network.

The Global Development Network (GDN), led by the World Bank in partnership with the United Nations Development Programme (UNDP) and a number of bilateral aid agencies, is an emerging network of institutes around the world that generates and shares knowledge about development.

It aims to enhance the quality and availability of policy-oriented research and strengthen the institutions, especially in developing countries, that undertake this work.

GDN offers tools, services and networking opportunities to help these institutions and their members join together in the fight against poverty.

GDN aims at supporting the generation and sharing of knowledge for development and helping to bridge the gap between the development of ideas and their practical implementation. It operates along two tracks: generating knowledge and sharing knowledge. Generating knowledge will be effected through:

— *A research grant competition*, which is funded by the World Bank and is administered through a competitive process by regional networks that are partners with the Bank in GDN;
— *A global research project*, which was launched in coordination with all the regional networks focusing on the broad topic of explaining economic growth or lack of it across regions, using a comprehensive and comparative approach that looks at the following four areas: macro -growth, political economy, private agents, and markets as institutions in the growth process;
— *A data initiative*, which will sponsor and provide information about training and other activities to support the broader and better use of microdata in macro- and socio-economic research.

Sharing knowledge has the following aspects:

- *Networking and knowledge management*: helping research and policy institutions by fostering vibrant global, regional and electronic networking activities designed to ensure sharing among the development community of the latest research, best practices and new ideas;
- *Support activities* that emphasize the organizational side of think-tank activity, such as fund-raising, evaluation, and effective dissemination of research products;
- *Training*: GDN will provide researchers and staff from policy institutions with a range of training and skills -building activities.

The use and assimilation of new technologies depend on the existence of basic technological capabilities in developing countries to choose, acquire, generate and apply technologies that are suited to their development objectives.

Developing countries need not reinvent the wheel in terms of basic scientific and technological research. This would be a waste of their already limited resources. They need useful technological information on sources and conditions of technology transfer. However, researchers and policy makers from developing countries tend to lack the resources to link into the scientific and technological research debate. In order to address this situation, the United Nations Conference on Trade and Development (UNCTAD) established the Knowledge and Technology for Development Network (KTD.Net).

KTD.Net is an electronic network and information exchange system for science and technology for development. The aim of this network is to improve:

— Information-sharing by providing access to the latest and relevant information on science and technology for development as well as links to information on science and technology activities of United Nations bodies;

— Knowledge diffusion, by providing information and identifying best practices with respect to mechanisms, strategies and channels needed to promote technology transfer, diffusion, adaptation and development of technological capabilities in developing countries. News and reports containing information and case studies on science and technology will also be posted online;

— Awareness-building of scientific and technological developments that are of particular importance with respect to fostering socio -economic development in member States.

KTD.Net seeks to be an important reference web site on science and technology for development. It therefore has, in addition to hyperlinks to science and technology activities in the United Nations system and other international organizations, links to partnerships and networking programmes in the United Nations system and the public and private sector. These links cover categories such as research partner locator, technology marketplace, technology partnership practices, regulations and policies facilitating international science and technology partnerships, promotion and technical assistance for networks in developing countries, and register of other international science and technology networks.

Technical knowledge and science and technology developments involve intellectual property rights (IPR) considerations. While there is a lot of knowledge and information available in the public domain, increasingly most of the knowledge and information embedded in technological advances is subject to IPR protection. This is especially the case in the areas of new technologies that are having a significant impact on the competitiveness of firms and economies and the well-being of peoples within the context of globalization - biotechnology, ICT and new synthetic materials.

An effective understanding of the IPR regime is crucial for developing countries in their search for technology transfer and for institutions that assist them in this endeavour. Given that international trade is, besides FDI, the main channel for technology transfer, an important IPR instrument is the Agreement on Trade-related Aspects of Intellectual Property Rights (TRIPS), which entered into force on 1 January 1995.

The agreement maintains that the protection and enforcement of IPR should contribute to the promotion of technological innovation and to the transfer and dissemination of technology, to the mutual advantage of producers and users of technological knowledge and in a manner conducive to socio-economic welfare, and to a balance of rights and obligations. The agreement also provides for specific requirements, such as the disclosure requirement of a patent application, in order to provide incentives for and to facilitate the transfer of technology to developing countries.

In 1996, the World Intellectual Property Organization (WIPO) and the World Trade Organization entered into an agreement that provides for WIPO to continue with its legal-technical assistance and technical cooperation activities for developing countries. It also extends such assistance in relation to the TRIPS agreement to those developing countries that are not members of WIPO but are members of the World Trade Organization.

One critical element in WIPO's strategy in relation to this specific mandate as well as to its broader mandate is to network the IPR community and to build an IPR resource base at both the global and national levels, hence WIPONET. WIPONET is a global digital information network enabling the integration of intellectual property (IP) information resources, processes and systems of the worldwide intellectual property communities, particularly the intellectual property offices (IPO) of the member States. It is intended to interconnect 332 intellectual property offices in 171 countries, and will be largely based on existing worldwide communication infrastructures and will also provide a portal for other WIPO-provided systems, such as the Intellectual Property Digital Libraries.

WIPONET seeks to ensure equitable access for all member States by establishing connectivity for those IPOs that have no Internet access, as well as through the training and development of the necessary human resources.

The 1992 United Nations Conference on Environment and Development highlighted the need for access to environmentally sound technologies developed elsewhere and the development of solutions for environmental problems specific to developing countries, which were deemed as being among the major strategic options to meet the challenge of environmentally sustainable development in developing countries.

The transfer of technology to developing countries, especially those technologies that reduce waste, cut energy consumption and minimize pollution, combined with the application of local knowledge and the preservation of biodiversity, sustainable use of renewable resources and the prevention of soil erosion, is an important measure in the preservation of the global common.

With this in mind, the United Nations Environment Programme (UNEP) in partnership with the Global Environment Facility (GEF) initiated the Sustainable Technologies Alternatives Network in order to enhance improved knowledge management and information-sharing for environmentally sound decision-making and implementation of multilateral environmental agreements, especially in relation to the transfer of environmentally sound technologies to developing countries.

The regional commissions have also been active in developing regional networks. For example, the Economic and Social Commission for Asia and the Pacific (ESCAP) has a number of information networks such as the Trade and Investment Information Service Network (TISNET), the International Network for Transfer of Environmentally Sound Technology (INTET) for Asia, and the regional Maritime Information Network (MARINET), among others.

International trade is one of the main channels of knowledge and technology transfer to developing countries. A new and emerging dimension to international trade is e-commerce.

Along with its potential to enhance developing-country access to markets, there is the obvious danger of e-commerce's emerging as a new barrier to trade by many developing countries because of the lack of the necessary infrastructure development to ensure connectivity as well as the lack of the necessary human and institutional capacity for effective participation in e-commerce transactions.

However e-commerce itself offers possibilities for firms in developing countries, which tend to be small, to access markets for goods and services to their advantage. E-commerce will make it easier for artisans and small and medium-sized enterprises (SMEs) to access business-to-consumer (B-2-C) markets as well as to tap into business-to-business (B-2-B) and business-to-government (B-2-G) supply chains; it will also facilitate activity, including market information acquisition, on the global market for agricultural and tropical products.

E-commerce will also allow individuals and enterprises in developing countries to operate more efficiently and to provide services anywhere in the world irrespective of location and physical distance.

In order for the possibilities of e-commerce to be realized by developing countries, there is an urgent need for action to overcome infrastructural bottlenecks in telecommunications, transport, logistics and customs operations. There is also a need to actively promote and nurture the development of e-commerce in developing countries. A number of United Nations bodies, notably UNCTAD and the International Telecommunication Union (ITU), have been very active in this area.

UNCTAD has been providing technical assistance, through seminars, workshops, advisory services and training, in the application and diffusion of ICT in the areas of trade promotion, transport and other trade-related services. It has also created programmes such as the Trade Analysis and Information System (TRAINS), the Automated System for Customs Data (ASYCUDA), the Advance Cargo Information System (ACIS), and the Trade Point Programme.

TRAINS is a computerized information system available to external users to increase transparency in trading conditions. It is intended for use by policy makers and economic operators engaged in exporting.

ASYCUDA is applied in over 80 developing countries and countries with economies in transition as an instrument to reform and modernize the management of their customs administrations. The objective is to speed up customs clearance through the introduction of computerization and simplification of procedures, thus minimizing administrative costs to the business community and the economy as a whole.

The introduction of ASYCUDA also allows an increase in customs revenue by ensuring that all goods are declared, that duty/tax calculations are correct and that duty/exemptions, preference regimes etc. are correctly applied and managed.

Furthermore, it helps producing reliable and timely trade and fiscal data to assist in the economic planning process. In order to be responsive to the needs of trade operators, in the development and implementation of ASYCUDA, UNCTAD consulted and continues to consult with all the stakeholders, especially the private sector.

ACIS is a logistics information system that uses ICT and microcomputing technology to improve transport efficiency in developing countries by tracking equipment and cargo on the different transport modes and at interfaces, and providing information in advance of cargo arrival.

ACIS provides both public and private sector operators and ancillaries with reliable, useful and timely information on transport operations. ACIS also produces regular performance indicators that enable management to remedy deficiencies and to make full use of the existing infrastructure and equipment capacity. It also provides data for economic planning and fosters optimal modal distribution patterns.

An important area of assistance has been the transfer of knowledge with regard to the use of the Internet for the promotion of local enterprises and the dissemination of information about developing countries. The Trade Point Programme -implemented in partnership with the Economic Commission for Europe (ECE), which contributes its expertise in standards for electronic data, and the International Trade Centre (ITC), which provides the trade information - uses ICT, especially the Internet, as a tool to increase the participation of developing and especially least developed countries in international trade and to enhance their competitiveness by reducing their costs.

Trade Points have been serving as centres of Internet access for SMEs in developing countries that could not afford their own Internet connections. In order to overcome the problems of inadequate telecommunications lines in a number of developing countries, the Trade Point Programme also set up an Internet incubator service for interested government agencies and enterprises from developing countries.

In order to attract private sector participation, the Trade and Development Board of UNCTAD recently took a decision to transfer the Electronic Trading Opportunities (ETO) system - a key part of the Trade Point Programme - to a suitable non-profit entity. This led to the creation, in November 2000, of the World Trade Point Federation, a non-profit organization representing all the trade points. Its main aim is to conclude strategic partnerships with private sector players capable of contributing to a further development of the programme.

ITU launched the Electronic Commerce for Developing Countries (EC-DC) initiative to enable developing countries, in particular the least developed countries, to be active participants in the networked economy. The EC-DC Initiative has the following four objectives:

(a) to coordinate the establishment of e-business infrastructure;

(b) to enable the transfer of e-business technologies;

(c) to address e-business policy and strategy issues; and

(d) to forge neutral and nonexclusive partnerships with industry.

This initiative is being carried out in partnership with the World Trade Centre (WTC), Geneva, and a private sector entity and is now being expanded to 110 countries from all regions.

One of the main activities is aimed at working with industry partners and local governments to deploy multipurpose community telecentres (MCTs). ITU, working with the United Nations Educational, Scientific and Cultural Organization (UNESCO), the International Development Research Centre (IDRC) and a number of other partners, has already deployed MCTs in Bhutan, India, the United Republic of Tanzania, Mali and Uganda and more are planned for other developing countries.

The ability of a developing country to participate actively in e-commerce and also to successfully acquire, adapt and utilize a range of other technologies depends not only on its having the right infrastructure, but also on its human and institutional capability. A country will need individuals embodying skills, training and experience as well as inclination. It will also need institutions that facilitate the sharing and management as well as the legitimization of knowledge.

Finally, it will also need a common strategic framework for technology acquisition and utilization. The following are examples of the work of agencies of the United Nations system in the area of human and institutional capacity-building.

UNDP established a Sustainable Development Networking Programme (SDNP) which is part of its effort to address the increasing "information gap" between industrialized countries and developing countries. SDNP operates at the country level, launching and supporting local Internet sites, and building national capacities and knowledge resources.

The programme focuses on connectivity, capacity-building and content creation and dissemination based on a participatory and multisectoral approach.

In 1996, the programme launched the Small Island Developing States Information Network (SIDSNET) as a community of 42 developing-country islands connected through the Internet for sharing information and coordinating action on key issues, as identified at the 1994 Global Conference on the Sustainable Development of Small Island Developing States. SIDSNET is implemented in close cooperation with the Alliance of Small Island States (AOSIS) and provides dedicated networking and training to SIDSNET partners at the national and regional levels.

Other agencies of the United Nations system are also making use of the possibilities provided by Internet technologies in their development capacity-building work. FAO, for example, has launched an initiative, the Farmer Information Network (FarmNet), which links organized groups of farmers in developing countries to service agencies and thus cuts costs and empowers the farmers in their market transactions as well as strengthens their productive capacities. This builds on FAO's experience in Chile and Mexico where electronic networks provided farmers with essential information and data on crops, inputs, prices, markets, credit services, weather conditions etc.

The International Civil Aviation Organization (ICAO) has begun efforts to extend the use of its ICAO-Net worldwide to all its member States; it is now being extended to include other aviation-related online information. ICAO has a long-established partnership with a private sector entity, the Société Internationale de Télécommunications Aéronautiques (SITA), which will be expanded to include the provision of internet access to those States that currently lack connectivity. Also in cooperation with SITA, ICAO will promote the use of the top-level domain name ".aero" by legitimate aviation-related entities.

The United Nations Centre for Human Settlements (Habitat), working in close cooperation with civil society partners, especially the foundations and the private sector, has established various extranets, databases and graphical information systems to improve the information flow and knowledge-sharing on human settlement issues. One such extranet is the Best Practice Extranet, which serves as a communication and knowledge-sharing platform for an expanding global network of training, capacity-building and policy advocacy institutions. The platforms content is dedicated to the documentation, dissemination, exchange and discussion of successful solutions for sustainable human settlements.

WIPO Worldwide Academy uses Web-based and other methods enabled by technology such as videoconferencing to bring teachers specializing in IPR issues closer to students and other interested parties in all corners of the world. Enhanced connectivity will further facilitate the availability and scalability of this approach to learning and training, especially in developing countries, and WIPO is therefore working at providing connectivity through its WIPONET initiative.

The United Nations Relief and Works Agency for Palestine Refugees in the Near East (UNRWA) has a Vocational and Educational Training

Programme for Palestinian refugees in Jordan, Lebanon, the Syrian Arab Republic and the Palestinian territories.

In 1998, it launched a Computer and Information Technology Initiative (CITI) with the assistance of a donor grant. This initiative is providing computer training facilities and is introducing a series of instructor and management training programmes to raise both the instructional and administrative standards at the various vocational training centres as well as to provide relevant skills to its trainees as necessitated in response to demands by the market. This programme is being carried out in cooperation with UNESCO and the European Union (EU).

The human resource development activities at ITU include a number of courses delivere d through the ITU Centres of Excellence, the Global Telecommunication University and the ITU Virtual Training Centre. ITU has also delivered a host of distance learning seminars on topics ranging from telecommunications regulation to national frequency management.

The International Labour Organization (ILO) is increasingly taking the opportunity afforded by new technologies to deliver its technical assistance, for example by making use of interactive distance learning modalities in its training programmes in Bosnia and Herzegovina, which are aimed at ensuring the speedy reintegration into the labour market of the displaced population.

At its International Training Centre in Turin, ILO is also making use of the Internet to supplement its residential programmes by providing Web-based learning assistance services and training modules for clients. The Centre is also developing a new computer programme, called the Internet Course Reader, which allows learners to quickly retrieve their messages from the tutor on the Internet and then cut off the connection and work offline. This is quite important for many developing countries with poor telephone connections, expensive Internet service providers and unreliable electricity sources.

The transfer and diffusion of knowledge and technology, including ICT, are dependent on a conducive policy environment. For example, for e-commerce to take hold and develop in a country, issues of governance, including consumer protection, security of transactions, privacy of records, taxation and intellectual property issues, will need to have been resolved.

Likewise, the trade policy stance of a country and its attitude to FDI will, in addition to natural factors such as resource endowments, determine the extent and nature of the technology transfers it receives. A country's education and training policies, inter alia, in relation to the education of girls and the training of women, will determine its capability to acquire, adapt and utilize technology, in cluding ICT. In short, policies do matter in the generation, acquisition, adaptation and utilization of technologies, including ICT.

Proceeding from the realization that policies do matter in ensuring optimal transfer of knowledge and technology to developing countries that would strengthen economic growth, employment creation and sustainable human development, agencies of the United Nations system have been engaged in a range of activities for facilitating policy development.

These vary from generating data and statistics that inform policy advice to arranging meetings for experts and policy makers at the national, regional and international levels. The following are examples of the work of some of the United Nations system agencies in this area.

In 2000, UNESCO launched the Information for All programme which provides a platform for international and regional policy discussions and partnerships as well as guidelines for action on preservation of information and universal access to information; participation of all in the emerging global information society; and ethical, legal and societal consequences of ICT developments.

It supports the development of common strategies, methods and tools for building a just and free information society and for narrowing the gap between the information-rich and the information-poor. The Programme is a key element in the fulfilment of UNESCO's mandate to contribute to "education for all", to the "free exchange of ideas and knowledge" and to "increase the means of communications between peoples".

The UNCTAD secretariat in conjunction with the Commission on Science and Technology for Development has addressed several important aspects of the diffusion and application of information technology for development and published them recently in the tenth issue of the Advanced Technology Assessment System (ATAS): Information Technology for Development.

UNCTAD, again in conjunction with the Commission, has also contributed to the preparation of the publication Knowledge Societies: Information Technology for Sustainable Development which contains a synthesis of a wealth of information and commentary on the social and economic benefits of ICT for developing countries. This publication was intended as a resource document for policy makers and ICT producers and users, especially in developing countries. It brings together the views of government policy makers, industrialists, researchers and other stakeholders in developing and industrialized countries and draws on the results of research in the field of science and technology policy studies.

ITU does considerable work in the area of policy development, research and dissemination. It has taken the lead in measuring the communication gaps among and within countries through its compilation of telecommunications indicators, and conducting of extensive country case-studies to measure the degree of Internet diffusion and the factors affecting its take -up. It also operates an Information Clearinghouse to disseminate the wealth of information it acquires. ITU is also the lead agency in the organization of the World Summit on the Information Society, scheduled for 2003, which is expected to adopt an action plan on bridging the digital divide.

ILO has been carrying out significant policy development work in the area of ICT and employment. It devoted its major publication this year - World Employment Report 2001: Life at Work in the Information Economy 4 - to an in -depth analysis of the implications of ICT for the world of work. Also, within its Sectoral Activities Programme, a global tripartite forum for discussions on issues of technology and labour at the industry level, ILO has recently examined issues such as the employment consequences of multimedia convergence and the effects of e-business on labour issues in the transport equipment industry. Conclusions from these global tripartite meetings are intended to influence the national policy debates.

The regional commissions have been actively engaged in the area of policy development. For example, the Economic Commission for Africa (ECA) has elaborated and adopted the Africa Information Society Initiative (AISI), an action framework to build Africa's information and communications infrastructure. AISI is also the principal activity on harnessing information technology for development within the United Nations System-wide Special Initiative for the Implementation of the United Nations New Agenda for the Development of Africa in the 1990s.

In another example, the Economic and Social Commission for Western Asia (ESCWA) launched a regional initiative aimed at assisting member countries in the design, implementation and management of novel institutional forms, namely, technology incubators, technology parks and high-technology industrial clusters, to facilitate the diffusion of new technologies, especially ICT in specific user sectors. This initiative was launched as a result of an extensive study of such institutions, which was presented at a regional meeting attended by experts and decision makers from Governments and enterprises in the member countries.

Experience gained in the design, implementation and management of new institutional forms is expected to lead to the formulation of more relevant policy frameworks and to the promotion of partnerships between the private and public sectors as well as new civil society institutions aimed at technology and knowledge acquisition and dissemination.

The United Nations system contains an unparalleled wealth of specialized agencies and entities that can mobilize the expertise needed to address all major policy issues. These agencies and entities have already demonstrated their capacity to facilitate broad multilateral negotiations that have set the global policy agenda. The challenge they face is implementing that policy agenda in order to realize the goals of poverty eradication and sustainable human development.

It is becoming increasingly clear that the further elaboration and implementation of the global policy agenda necessitate the forging of partnerships with other development actors, especially the private sector and non-governmental organizations. Non-governmental organizations have the capacity to galvanize the voices of many different sectors of society and to provide a framework for local consultation and action. Networks of non-governmental organizations are part of the social capital that is now emerging as a crucial input in ensuring beneficial outcomes to development efforts.

The private sector, on the other hand, has at its disposal the financial and technological resources that, if utilized appropriately within the context of a genuine partnership, can make a positive contribution to the development process. Also, the private sector, especially the multinational corporations, is the driving force of the process of globalization - the increasing integration and interdependence of national economies and societies. The private sector therefore has a role, if not an obligation, as well as an interest in ensuring that globalization is equitable to everyone.

## References

Frank Webster (2002) *Theories of the Information Society.* London: Routledge.

Jan Van Dijk (2006) *The Network Society*. London: Sage. Second Edition.

Nico Stehr (2002) *Knowledge & Economic Conduct.* Toronto: University of Toronto Press.

Seely Brown, John; Duguid, Paul (2000). *The Social Life of Information.* Harvard Business School Press.

Yannis Veneris (1984) *The Informational Revolution, Cybernetics and Urban Modelling,* PhD Thesis, University of Newcastle upon Tyne, UK.

# 4

# Cyber Crimes

Cyber crimes are defined as "offences that are committed against individuals or groups of individuals with a criminal motive to intentionally harm the reputation of the victim or cause physical or mental harm to the victim directly or indirectly, using modern telecommunication networks such as Internet (Chat rooms, emails, notice boards and groups) and mobile phones (SMS/MMS). Such crimes may threaten a nation's security and financial health. Issues surrounding this type of crime have become high-profile, particularly those surrounding cracking, copyright infringement, child pornography, and child grooming. There are also problems of privacy when confidential information is lost or intercepted, lawfully or otherwise.

Internationally, both governmental and non-state actors engage in cybercrimes, including espionage, financial theft, and other cross-border crimes. Activity crossing international borders and involving the interests of at least one nation state is sometimes referred to as cyber warfare. The international legal system is attempting to hold actors accountable for their actions through the International Criminal Court.

## Types of Cyber Crimes

Computer crime encompasses a broad range of activities. Generally, however, it may be divided into two categories: (1) crimes that target computers directly; (2) crimes facilitated by computer networks or devices, the primary target of which is independent of the cats network or device.

Crimes that primarily target computer networks or devices include:

- Computer viruses
- Denial-of-service attacks
- Malware (malicious code)

Crimes that use computer networks or devices to advance other ends include:

- Cyberstalking
- Fraud and identity theft
- Information warfare
- Phishing scams

### Spam

Spam, or the unsolicited sending of bulk email for commercial purposes, is unlawful in some jurisdictions. While anti-spam laws are relatively new, limits on unsolicited electronic communications have existed for some time.

### Fraud

Computer fraud is any dishonest misrepresentation of fact intended to let another to do or refrain from doing something which causes loss. In this context, the fraud will result in obtaining a benefit by:

- Altering computer input in an unauthorized way. This requires little technical expertise and is not an uncommon form of theft by employees altering the data before entry or entering false data, or by entering unauthorized instructions or using unauthorized processes;
- Altering, destroying, suppressing, or stealing output, usually to conceal unauthorized transactions: this is difficult to detect;
- Altering or deleting stored data;
- Altering or misusing existing system tools or software packages, or altering or writing code for fraudulent purposes.

Other forms of fraud may be facilitated using computer systems, including bank fraud, identity theft, extortion, and theft of classified information.

### Obscene or Offensive Content

The content of websites and other electronic communications may be distasteful, obscene or offensive for a variety of reasons. In some instances these communications may be illegal.

Over 25 jurisdictions place limits on certain speech and ban racist, blasphemous, politically subversive, libelous or slanderous, seditious, or inflammatory material that tends to incite hate crimes.

The extent to which these communications are unlawful varies greatly between countries, and even within nations. It is a sensitive area in which the courts can become involved in arbitrating between groups with strong beliefs.

One area of Internet pornography that has been the target of the strongest efforts at curtailment is child pornography.

### Harassment

Whereas content may be offensive in a non-specific way, harassment directs obscenities and derogatory comments at specific individuals focusing for example on gender, race, religion, nationality, sexual orientation. This often occurs in chat rooms, through newsgroups, and by sending hate e-mail to interested parties. Any comment that may be found derogatory or offensive is considered harassment.

There are instances where committing a crime, which involves the use of a computer, can lead to an enhanced sentence. For example, in the case of United States v. Neil Scott Kramer, Kramer was served an enhanced sentence according to the U.S. Sentencing Guidelines Manual §2G1.3(b)(3) for his use of a cell phone to "persuade, induce, entice, coerce, or facilitate the travel of, the minor to engage in prohibited sexual conduct."

Connecticut was the first state to pass a statute making it a criminal offense to harass someone by computer. Michigan, Arizona, and Virginia have also passed laws banning harassment by electronic means.

Harassment by computer statutes are typically distinct from cyberbullying laws, in that the former usually relates to a person's "use a computer or computer network to communicate obscene, vulgar, profane, lewd, lascivious, or indecent language, or make any suggestion or proposal of an obscene nature, or threaten any illegal or immoral act," while the latter need not involve anything of a sexual nature.

### Threats

Although freedom of speech is protected by law in most democratic societies (in US this is done by First Amendment) that does not include all types of speech. In fact spoken or written "true threat" speech/text is criminalized because of "intent to harm or intimidate", that also applies for online or any type of network related threats in written text or speech. The US Supreme Court definition of "true threat" is "statements where the speaker means to communicate a serious expression of an intent to commit an act of unlawful violence to a particular individual or group".

### Drug Trafficking

Drug traffickers are increasingly taking advantage of the Internet to sell their illegal substances through encrypted e-mail and other Internet Technology. Some drug traffickers arrange deals at internet cafes, use courier Web sites to track illegal packages of pills, and swap recipes for amphetamines in restricted-access chat rooms.

The rise in Internet drug trades could also be attributed to the lack of face-to-face communication. These virtual exchanges allow more intimidated individuals to more comfortably purchase illegal drugs. The sketchy effects that are often associated with drug trades are severely minimized and the filtering process that comes with physical interaction fades away.

### Cyber Terrorism

Government officials and Information Technology security specialists have documented a significant increase in Internet problems and server scans since early 2001. But there is a growing concern among federal officials that such intrusions are part of an organized effort by cyberterrorists, foreign intelligence services, or other groups to map potential security holes in critical systems. A cyberterrorist is someone who intimidates or coerces a government or organization to advance his or her political or social objectives by launching computer-based attack against computers, network, and the information stored on them.

Cyber terrorism in general, can be defined as an act of terrorism committed through the use of cyberspace or computer resources. As such, a simple propaganda in the Internet, that there will be bomb attacks during the holidays can be considered cyberterrorism. As well there are also hacking activities directed towards individuals, families, organized by groups within networks, tending to cause fear among people, demonstrate power, collecting information relevant for ruining peoples' lives, robberies, blackmailing etc.

Cyberextortion is a form of cyberterrorism in which a website, e-mail server, or computer system is subjected to repeated denial of service or other attacks by malicious hackers, who demand money in return for promising to stop the attacks. According to the Federal Bureau of Investigation, cyberextortionists are increasingly attacking corporate websites and networks, crippling their ability to operate and demanding payments to restore their service. More than 20 cases are reported each month to the FBI and many go unreported in order to keep the victim's name out of the public domain. Perpetrators typically use a distributed denial-of-service attack.

### Cyber Warfare

The U.S. Department of Defense (DoD) notes that cyberspace has emerged as a national-level concern through several recent events of geo-strategic significance. Among those are included the attack on Estonia's infrastructure in 2007, allegedly by Russian hackers. "In August 2008, Russia again allegedly conducted cyber attacks, this time in a coordinated and synchronized kinetic and non-kinetic campaign against the country of Georgia. Fearing that such attacks may become the norm in future warfare among nation-states, the concept of cyberspace operations impacts and will be adapted by warfighting military commanders in the future.

## Roots of Cyber Crime

It is difficult to determine when the first crime involving a computer actually occurred. The computer has been around in some form since the abacus, which is known to have existed in 3500 B.C. in Japan, China and India. In 1801 profit motives encouraged Joseph Jacquard, a textile manufacturer in France, to design the forerunner of the computer card. This device allowed the repetition of a series of steps in the weaving of special fabrics. So concerned were Jacquard's employees with the threat to their traditional employment and livelihood that acts of sabotage were committed to discourage Mr. Jacquard from further use of the new technology. A computer crime had been committed.

There has been a great deal of debate among experts on just what constitutes a computer crime or a computer-related crime. Even after several years, there is no internationally recognised definition of those terms. There is no doubt among the authors and experts who have attempted to arrive at definitions of computer crime that the phenomenon exists. However, the definitions that have been produced tend to relate to the study for which they were written. The intent of authors to be precise about the scope and use of particular definitions means, however, that using these definitions out of their intended context often creates inaccuracies. A global definition of computer crime has not been achieved; rather, functional definitions have been the norm.

Computer crime can involve criminal activities that are traditional in nature, such as theft, fraud, forgery and mischief, all of which are generally subject everywhere to criminal sanctions. The computer has also created a host of potentially new misuses or abuses that may, or should, be criminal as well. In 1989, expanding on work that had been undertaken by OECD, the European Committee on Crime Problems of the Council of Europe produced a set of guidelines for national legislators that enumerated activities that should be subject to criminal sanction. By discussing the functional characteristics of target activities, the Committee did not attempt a formal definition of computer crime but left individual countries to adapt the functional classification to their particular legal systems and historical traditions.

The terms "computer misuse" and "computer abuse" are also used frequently, but they have significantly different implications. Criminal law recognises the concepts of unlawful or fraudulent intent and of claim of right; thus, any criminal laws that relate to computer crime would need to distinguish between accidental misuse of a computer system, negligent misuse of a computer system and intended, unauthorised access to or misuse of a computer system, amounting to computer abuse. Annoying behaviour must be distinguished from criminal behaviour in law.

In relation to the issue of intent, the principle of claim of right also informs the determination of criminal behaviour. For example, an employee who has received a password from an employer, without direction as to whether a particular database can be accessed, is unlikely to be considered guilty of a crime if he or she accesses that database. However, the principle of claim of right would not apply to the same employee who steals a password from a colleague to access that same database, knowing his or her access is unauthorised; this employee would be behaving in a criminal manner. A distinction must be made between what is unethical and what is illegal; the legal response to the problem must be proportional to the activity that is alleged. It is only when the behaviour is determined to be truly criminal that criminal prohibition and prosecution should be sought. The criminal law, therefore, should be employed and implemented with restraint.

Recent and anticipated changes in technology arising from the convergence of communications and computing are truly breathtaking, and have already had a significant impact on many aspects of life. Banking, stock exchanges, air traffic control, telephones, electric power, and a wide range of institutions of health, welfare, and education are largely dependent on information technology and telecommunications for their operation. We are moving rapidly to the point where it is possible to assert that "everything depends on software". The exponential growth of this technology, the increase in its capacity and accessibility, and the decrease in its cost, has brought about revolutionary changes in commerce, communications, entertainment, and also crime. Along with this greater capacity, however, comes greater vulnerability. Information technology has begun to provide criminal opportunities of which Willie Sutton would never have dreamed.

Statistics on computer use and connectivity are notoriously evanescent. They are out of date before they appear in print. Suffice it to say that the number of people with internet connections will continue to increase dramatically, as will the volume of electronic commerce in Australia, and around the world. Not only does the increasing connectivity increase the number of prospective victims of computer related crime, it also increases the number of prospective offenders.

## Cyber Criminals

History has shown that computer crime is committed by a broad range of persons: students, amateurs, terrorists and members of organised crime groups. What distinguishes them is the nature of the crime committed. The individual who accesses a computer system without further criminal intent is much different from the employee of a financial institution who skims funds from customer accounts.

The cyber criminals constitute of various groups/category. This division may be justified on the basis of the object that they have in their mind. The following are the category of cyber criminals:

1. *Children and adolescents between the age group of 6 - 18 years*: The simple reason for this type of delinquent behaviour pattern in children is seen mostly due to the inquisitiveness to know and explore the things. Other cognate reason may be to prove themselves to be outstanding amongst other children in their group. Further the reasons may be psychological even. E.g. the Bal Bharati (Delhi) case was the outcome of harassment of the delinquent by his friends.

2. *Organised hackers*: These kinds of hackers are mostly organised together to fulfil certain objective. The reason may be to fulfil their political bias, fundamentalism, etc. The Pakistanis are said to be one of the best quality hackers in the world. They mainly target the Indian government sites with the purpose to fulfil their political objectives.
3. *Professional hackers/crackers*: Their work is motivated by the colour of money. These kinds of hackers are mostly employed to hack the site of the rivals and get credible, reliable and valuable information. Further they are ven employed to crack the system of the employer basically as a measure to make it safer by detecting the loopholes.
4. *Discontented employees:* This group include those people who have been either sacked by their employer or are dissatisfied with their employer. To avenge they normally hack the system of their employee.

The typical skill level of the computer criminal is a topic of controversy. Some claim that skill level is not an indicator of a computer criminal, while others claim that potential computer criminals are bright, eager, highly motivated subjects willing to accept a technological challenge, characteristics that are also highly desirable in an employee in the data-processing field.

It is true that computer criminal behaviour cuts across a wide spectrum of society, with the age of offenders ranging from 10 to 60 years and their skill level ranging from novice to professional. Computer criminals, therefore, are often otherwise average persons rather than super criminals possessing unique abilities and talents. Any person of any age with a modicum of skill, motivated by the technical challenge, by the potential for gain, notoriety or revenge, or by the promotion of ideological beliefs, is a potential computer criminal.

According to a number of studies, however, employees represent the largest threat, and indeed computer crime has often been referred to as an insider crime. One study estimated that 90 per cent of economic computer crimes were committed by employees of the victimised companies. A recent survey in North America and Europe indicated that 73 per cent of the risk to computer security was attributable to internal sources and only 23 per cent to external criminal activity. As advances continue to be made in remote data processing, the threat from external sources will probably increase. With the increasing connectedness of systems and the adoption of more user-friendly software, the sociological profile of the computer offender may change. Owing to the greater complexity of certain computer routines and augmented security measures, it is becoming increasingly unlikely that any one person will possess all the information needed to use a computer system for criminal purposes.

Organised computer criminal groups, composed of members from all over the world, are beginning to emerge. Corresponding with this increasing cooperation in criminal activity, the escalating underground use of electronic bulletin boards for clandestine criminal communication has been detected around the world. Rapidly improving telecommunication technology has added to the threat from external sources. Computer-based voice mailbox systems, for example, are being used by the computer criminal community to exchange stolen access numbers, passwords and software.

The advent of viruses and similar mechanisms whereby computer software can be made to act almost on its own initiative poses a new and significant threat. Sophisticated viruses and devices such as "logic bombs" and "trojan horses", discussed below, can be targeted for specific objectives at specific industries to commit a variety of traditional criminal offences, from mere mischief of extortion. These crimes, furthermore, can be committed immediately or can be planted to spring at a future date. Computer criminals have gained notoriety in the media and appear to have gained more social acceptability than traditional criminals. The suggestion that the computer criminal is a less harmful individual, however, ignores the obvious. The current threat is real. The future threat will be directly proportional to the advances made in computer technology.

The motivations of those who would commit computer related crime are diverse, but hardly new. Computer criminals are driven by time-honoured motivations, the most obvious of which are greed, lust, power, revenge, adventure, and the desire to taste 'forbidden fruit'. The ability to make an impact on large systems may, as an act of power, be gratifying in and of itself. The desire to inflict loss or damage on another may also spring from revenge, as when a disgruntled employee shuts down an employer's computer system, or to ideology, as when one defaces the web page of an institution that one regards as abhorrent. Much activity on the electronic frontier entails an element of adventure, the exploration of the unknown. The very fact that some activities in cyberspace are likely to elicit official condemnation is sufficient to attract the defiant, the rebellious, or the irresistibly curious. Given the degree of technical competence required to commit many computer-related crimes, there is one other motivational dimension worth noting here. This, of course, is the intellectual challenge of mastering complex systems. None of the above motivations is new. The element of novelty resides in the unprecedented capacity of technology to facilitate acting on these motivations.

## Vulnerability of Computer Systems

There are three kinds of offences which involve the use of communications technology, including the internet:

1. *Computers as means to an offence:* The first kind is an offence which is committed using the technology; effectively it is a conventional crime such as fraud which is committed by technological means.
2. *Computers as targets*: The second kind involves offences which target the computers themselves, and seek to destroy or alter information or data held in them, sometimes with a view to interfering in the processes which that data governs. An example would be an attempt to disrupt a city's water supply by interfering with the computers which control it. The interference can be exercised by a number of means including by hackers, worms, viruses and Trojans.
3. *Computers as storage:* This category includes offences in which the computer is used as storage for information about an offence, for example a drug offence in which supply records are kept on computer.

Computer systems are particularly vulnerable to threats because of a number of interacting factors. The more significant of these are analysed briefly below.

### Density of Information and Processes

Storage technology has allowed the development of filing systems that can accommodate billions of characters of data on-line. Providing different access privileges for different users of such systems is often difficult. A further problem lies in the fact that, owing to the methods for accessing stored information, a single error can have widespread impact. This fact can be used to great advantage by a party who wants to corrupt data or disrupt service.

At the same time, memory management techniques allow many independent processes to be supported concurrently within a single operating system. Independent data files can be combined to produce new and unforeseen relationships. Data items may be linked to produce a new item with a higher level of sensitivity than the original discrete data components. The centralisation of information and processing functions provides an attractive target for the infiltrator or saboteur intent on attacking the functions or information assets of an organisation. The density of data stored on such media as tapes, diskettes, cassettes and microfilms means that the loss or theft of such items can be very significant.

**System Accessibility**

Before security became a significant design criterion, the goal was often to provide the maximum computing capability to the largest possible user community. Access concerns once confined to the restricted computer room area must now be extended to remote terminal locations and interconnecting communications links. However, remote terminal stations and transmission circuits are often not subject to the same controls as those in the main centre. Two forms of attack that exploit remote access are the use of fraudulent identification and access codes to obtain the use of system resources and the unauthorised use of an unattended terminal, logged on by an authorised person.

Because of the desire to give system users maximum capability, unrestricted access privileges are often granted rather than allowing only the privileges necessary to perform an intended function. A transaction-oriented system permitting read-only or inquiry-only access offers a greater degree of protection than a system offering full programming capability.

Many systems in current use offer very limited ability to control user capabilities related to passive data and programmes on a read-only, read-write or execute basis. This situation frequently necessitates operating on the assumption that every user has the capability to use the full computing potential of the operating system. A known penetration technique that utilises this weakness involves disguising user instructions intended for clandestine purposes as a common utility, such as a file-copying routine, or inserting them into an existing routine. When the illicit code is activated, it performs functions more privileged than were intended for that user.

Finally, computer control functions are normally made accessible to numerous support and maintenance personnel. Tampering with software or hardware logic to obtain extended privilege or to disable protection features has been known to occur. The exposure provided through increasingly easy access to electronic data processing (EDP) resources is an important contributor to the vulnerability of modern computer systems.

**Complexity**

The typical operating environment of medium- and large-scale systems is characterised by support for local batch, remote batch, interactive and, occasionally, real-time user modes. Typical operating systems contain from 200,000 to 25 million individual instructions. The number of logic states that are possible during execution in a multiprogramming or multiprocessing environment approaches infinity. It is not surprising that such systems are not fully understood by anyone, including the designers, or that they are often unreliable.

It is only possible to prove the presence of errors, not their absence, and any system error can result in down time or a potential security fault. Even when systems have been carefully designed, errors in implementation, maintenance and operation can still occur. The prospective infiltrator can be expected to take full advantage of the uncertainties created by system complexity. Incidents have been noted where deliberate attempts to confuse operators, or to interrupt systems by attacking little-known weaknesses, have been instrumental in producing security violations.

**Electronic Vulnerability**

The reliance of computer systems on electronic technology means that they are subject to problems of reliability, fragility, environmental dependency and vulnerability to interference and interception. On systems using telecommunications, these vulnerabilities extend to the whole communications network in use.

Traditional forms of electronic eavesdropping can be readily adapted to exploit data-processing systems. They include wire-tapping and bugging, the analysis of electromagnetic radiations from equipment and monitoring of the cross-talk induced in adjacent electrical circuits. Interconnecting data communications circuits also suffer the same vulnerabilities, and communications on them can be subject to misrouting. A variation on wire-tapping involves the illegal use of a minicomputer to intercept data communications and to generate false commands or responses to other system components.

In the commission of a fraud, electronic technology has an advantage over manual data manipulation, which generally leaves behind an audit trail. Computer data, however, can be instantly changed or erased with minimal chance of detection, by, for example, a virus or logic bomb. The computer criminal can easily modify systems to perpetrate the fraud and then cover the evidence of the offence. It is suggested, moreover, that data processing is protected by only one tenth of the controls afforded to the same process in the manual environment, an insufficiency that facilitates the opportunity to commit crime without detection.

The performance of EDP systems may also be adversely affected by electromagnetic interference. Conducted or radiated electrical disturbances can interfere with the operation of electronic equipment. The system may suffer only very temporary and intermittent impairment, measurable in microseconds and from which recovery is possible, or it may suffer complete equipment failure, resulting in an inability to process. All hardware is susceptible to failure through ageing, physical damage and environmental change. To ensure that error propagation is confined to non-sensitive functions, i.e., that the system fails safely, malfunctions must be detected immediately. Progress is being made towards this goal, but few designs in current use offer the desired level of reliability.

**Vulnerability of Electronic Data-processing Media**

It is sometimes inferred that a degree of security is provided by the inability of humans to translate machine-readable data in the form of punched holes in cards or tape, magnetic states on tapes, drums and disks, and electrical states in processing or transmission circuits. In practice, not only can such computerised information codes be readily interpreted by most technical personnel, but the data obscurity created has the additional negative effect of creating identification and accounting problems.

Because the contents of most EDP media are not visually evident, data-processing personnel are often required to handle sensitive files without being aware they are doing so. As a result, the control of data items becomes a problem. Scratched tapes, discarded core memories can all contain residual data that may demand special attention. Because identity and accountability have been lost, safeguards are frequently relaxed for these items even though the same information is protected elsewhere in the system. The ease with which such sources of information can be utilised has resulted in several well-publicised system penetrations.

## Human Factors

Employees represent the greatest threat in terms of computer crime. It is not uncommon, operators, media librarians, hardware technicians and other staff members to find themselves in positions of extraordinary privilege in relation to the key functions and assets of their organisation. A consequence of this situation is the probability that such individuals are frequently exposed to temptation.

A further complication is the tendency on the part of management to tolerate less stringent supervisory controls over EDP personnel. The premise is that the work is not only highly technical and specialised but difficult to understand and control. As an example systems software support is often entrusted to a single programmer who generates the version of the operating system in use, establishes password or other control lists and determines the logging and accounting features to be used.

In addition, such personnel are often permitted, and sometimes encouraged, to perform these duties during non-prime shift periods, when demands on computer time are light. As a result, many of the most critical software development and maintenance functions are performed in an unsupervised environment. It is also clear that operators, librarians and technicians often enjoy a degree of freedom quite different from that which would be considered normal in a more traditional employment area.

There is another factor at play in the commission of computer crime. Criminological research has identified a variation of the Robin Hood syndrome: criminals tend to differentiate between doing harm to individual people, which they regard as highly immoral, and doing harm to a corporation, which they can more easily rationalise. Computer systems facilitate these kinds of crimes, as a computer does not show emotion when it is attached. Situations in which personnel at junior levels are trusted implicitly and given a great deal of responsibility, without commensurate management control and accountability, occur frequently in the EDP environment. Whether the threat is from malicious or subversive activities or from honest errors on the part of staff members, the human aspect is perhaps the most vulnerable aspect of EDP systems.

## Internet's Vulnerability to Crime

The most common internet access is through a personal computer and a phone line. However, emerging technologies will provide the capacity to access the internet and other online services using a range of devices, including mobile devices. The internet has features which favour criminal activity. They include:

— unregulated establishment of, and access to internet and email sites;
— anonymity; and
— lack of security and public awareness.

***Unregulated establishment and access***

Internet Service Providers are not required to be licensed, and are not regulated except by voluntary codes of conduct. Free email providers such as AOL, Yahoo and Hotmail require minimal information from the user, making the detection of offenders difficult. It is also possible to falsify email software to make an email appear to come from a particular source, but in reality be sent by a third party. One of the most familiar effects of unregulated email is SPAM; these are unwanted emails which may be used to harass, to acquire funds fraudulently or to distribute pornography.

***Anonymity***

Internet and computer criminal activity is supported by the anonymity of the environment. In email, free email services allow the creation of as many different email identities as the user wishes, without any useful information about the identity of that person. A short-term fix which would make life a lot easier would be to do away with free internet accounts such as AOL and Hotmail because if internet accounts are not free, people have to pay by credit card, and the vast majority of people who use credit cards have provided appropriate information when obtaining the credit cards and that gives law enforcement some starting point.

Chat rooms on the internet were described during the Inquiry as being similar to a conference call on a telephone. Chat rooms use internet technology to allow a group of people with similar interests to communicate using the one internet location. Access is readily available although in some cases a password might be required. In chat rooms, the participants may also assume identities which are untraceable, or false, which is why these are an ideal environment for paedophiles.

Chat rooms are an instant form of communication—unlike email which is relayed, and then read. The danger inherent in a chat room is its immediacy and somewhat clandestine nature. Children in particular, can be using chat rooms without their parents being any the wiser — the activity would simply appear in the same way as any typing or entering of text. Although some witnesses indicated it has been possible for police to enter chat rooms to monitor proceedings, gathering evidence in the environment is difficult, time consuming, and may not be cost effective.

The technological barriers to monitoring chat rooms are not insurmountable: If you look at the whole instant messaging or chat room space, there are a lot of third party solutions out there which you can bolt on to existing instant messaging and chat room technologies to record the conversations. It is just a matter of going out and finding the right bits that fit together and knowing how they work. We do not see that there are any real technology barriers there. It is just an extension of email, which we are all used to and is logged and recorded. There are also devices which can mask the source of information, making it appear that the content is actually from another source.

***Security and public awareness***

The evidence showed there are two areas of vulnerability for users of the internet. One is the potential for access by children to unsuitable content and to features such as chat rooms, and the other is a lack of general awareness of the need to secure a computer. This protects the user not only from nuisance email but also from malicious content (including viruses) and from hacking to obtain details such as internet banking and on-line shopping transactions. These are of varying degrees of usefulness, as the filter tends to eliminate material which appears to be objectionable but which is not. Filters can also do the opposite, and fail to filter very much content at all. There is nothing available at present which will restrict access to sites such as chat rooms.

Many consumers install virus protection, but do not update it. 'Firewall' programs are available (and are often supplied with computer packages) to assist with blocking malicious content, but consumers either don't install or don't update them, or are unaware that this kind of protection is available. The consequences of not having such protection can be serious, as they can be easily attacked by computer hackers, worms and viruses. The virus protection packages are a small expense compared to the havoc which can be caused to personal records, as well as major networks. Even keeping virus and firewall protection up to date does not guarantee full immunity, but most anti virus software companies are able to advise consumers of the latest potential dangers, and the appropriate action to take to minimise damage.

## Extent of Crime and Losses

Only a small portion of crimes come to the attention of the law enforcement authorities. In his book Computer Security, J. Carroll states that "computer crime may be the subject of the biggest cover-up since Watergate". While it is possible to give an accurate description of the various types of computer offences committed, it has proved difficult to give an accurate, reliable overview of the extent of losses and the actual number of criminal offences. At its Colloquium on Computer Crimes and Other Crimes against Information Technology, held at Wurzburg, Germany, from 5 to 8 October 1992, AIDP released a report on computer crime based on reports of its member countries that estimated that only 5 per cent of computer crime was reported to law enforcement authorities.

The number of verifiable computer crimes is not, therefore, very high. This fact notwithstanding, authorities point out that the evidence of computer crime discernible from official statistical sources, studies and surveys indicates the phenomenon should be taken seriously. The American Bar Association conducted a survey in 1987: of 300 corporations and government agencies, 72 claimed to have been the victim of computer-related crime in the 12-month period prior to the survey, sustaining losses estimated to range from $ 145 million to $ 730 million.

In 1991, a survey of security incidents involving computer-related crime was conducted at 3,000 Virtual Address Extension (VAX) sites in Canada, Europe and the United States of America. Seventy-two per cent of the respondents said that a security incident had occurred within the previous 12-month period; 43 per cent indicated that the security incident they had sustained had been a criminal offence. A further 8 per cent were uncertain whether they had sustained a security incident. Similar surveys conducted around the world report significant and widespread abuse and loss.

Law enforcement officials indicate from their experience that recorded computer crime statistics do not represent the actual number of offences; the term "dark figure", used by criminologists to refer to unreported crime, has been applied to undiscovered computer crimes. The invisibility of computer crimes is based on several factors. First, sophisticated technology, that is, the immense, compact storage capacity of the computer and the speed with which computers function, ensures that computer crime is very difficult to detect. In contrast to most traditional areas of crime, unknowing victims are often informed after the fact by law enforcement officials that they have sustained a computer crime. Secondly, investigating officials often do not have sufficient training to deal with problems in the complex environment of data processing. Thirdly, many victims do not have a contingency plan for responding to incidents of computer crime, and they may even fail to acknowledge that a security problem exists.

An additional cause of the dark figure is the reluctance of victims to report computer offences once they have been discovered. In the business sector, this reluctance is related to two concerns. Some victims may be unwilling to divulge information about their operations for fear of adverse publicity, public embarrassment or loss of goodwill. Other victims fear the loss of investor or public confidence and the resulting economic consequences. Some experts have suggested that these factors have a significant impact on the detection of computer crime.

Historically, economic value has been placed on visible and tangible assets. With the increasing appreciation that intangible data can possess economic value, they have become an economic asset that can be targeted for crime. Tangible assets in the computer environment, therefore, often have a double value. The replacement cost of a piece of computer equipment may represent only a small portion of the economic loss caused by the theft of, or damage to, that equipment. Of much greater significance is the value of the information lost or made inaccessible by the misappropriation or damage.

## Computer-related Frauds

Intangible assets represented in data format, such as money on deposit or hours of work, are the most common targets of computer-related fraud. Modern business is quickly replacing cash with deposits transacted on computer systems, creating an enormous potential for computer abuse. Credit card information, as well as personal and financial information on credit-card clients, have been frequently targeted by the organised criminal community. The sale of this information to counterfeiters of credit cards and travel documents has proven to be extremely lucrative. Assets represented in data format often have a considerably higher value than traditionally targeted economic assets, resulting in potentially greater economic loss. In addition, improved remote access to databases allows the criminal the opportunity to commit various types of fraud without ever physically entering the premises of the victim.

Computer fraud by input manipulation is the most common computer crime, as it is easily perpetrated and difficult to detect. Often referred to as "data diddling", it does not require any sophisticated computer knowledge and can be committed by anyone having access to normal data-processing functions at the input stage.

Programme manipulation, which is very difficult to discover and is frequently not recognised, requires the perpetrator to have computer-specific knowledge. It involves changing existing programmes in the computer system or inserting new programmes or routines. A common method used by persons with specialised knowledge of computer programming is the trojan horse, whereby computer instructions are covertly placed in a computer program so that it will perform an unauthorised function concurrent with its normal function. A trojan horse can be programmed to self-destruct, leaving no evidence of its existence except the damage that it caused. Remote access capabilities today also allow the criminal to easily run modified routines concurrently with legitimate programs.

Output manipulation is effected by targeting the output of the computer system. The obvious example is cash dispenser fraud, achieved by falsifying instructions to the computer in the input stage. Traditionally, such fraud involved the use of stolen bank cards. However, specialised computer hardware and software is now being widely used to encode falsified electronic information on the magnetic strips of bank cards and credit cards. There is a particular species of fraud conducted by computer manipulation that takes advantage of the automatic repetitions of computer processes. Such manipulation is characteristic of the specialised "salami technique", whereby nearly unnoticeable, "thin slices" of financial transactions are repeatedly removed and transferred to another account.

## Computer Forgery

Where data are altered in respect of documents stored in computerised form, the crime is forgery. In this and the above examples, computer systems are the target of criminal activity. Computers, however, can also be used as instruments with which to commit forgery. The created a new library of tools with which to forge the documents used in commerce. A new generation of fraudulent alteration or counterfeiting emerged when computerised colour laser copiers became available. These copiers are capable of high-resolution copying, the modification of documents and even the creation of false documents without benefit of an original, and they produce documents whose quality is indistinguishable from that of authentic documents except by an expert.

**Modifications of Computer Programs**

This category of criminal activity involves either direct or covert unauthorised access to a computer system by the introduction of new programmes known as viruses, "worms" or logic bombs. The unauthorised modification, suppression or erasure of computer data or functions with the internet to hinder normal functioning of the system is clearly criminal activity and is commonly referred to as computer sabotage.

Computer sabotage can be the vehicle for gaining economic advantage over a competitor, for promoting the illegal activities of ideologically motivated terrorists or for stealing data or programmes for extortion purposes. In one reported incident at London, Ontario, in 1987, a former employee of a company sought unsuccessfully to sabotage the computer system of the company by inserting a programme into the system that would have wiped it out completely.

A virus is a series of programme codes that has the ability to attach itself to legitimate programmes and propagate itself to other computer programs. A virus can be introduced to a system by a legitimate piece of software that has been infected. The potential purposes of viruses are many, ranging from the display of harmless messages on several computer terminals to the irreversible destruction of all data on a computer system. In 1990, Europe first experienced a computer virus, used to commit extortion in the medical research community. The virus threatened to destroy increasing amounts of data if no ransom was paid for the "cure". A significant amount of valuable medical research data was lost as a result.

A worm is similarly constructed to infiltrate legitimate data-processing programmes and to alter or destroy the data, but it differs from a virus in that it does not have the ability to replicate itself. In a medical analogy, the worm can be compared to a benign tumor, the virus to a malignant one. However, the consequences of a worm attack can be just as serious as those of a virus attack: for example, a bank computer can be instructed, by a worm programme that subsequently destroys itself, to continually transfer money to an illicit account.

A logic bomb, also known as a "time bomb", is another technique by which computer sabotage can be perpetrated. The creation of logic bombs requires some specialised knowledge, as it involves programming the destruction or modification of data at a specific time in the future. Unlike viruses or worms, however, logic bombs are very difficult to detect before they blow up; thus, of all these computer crime schemes, they have the greatest potential for damage. Detonation can be timed to cause maximum damage and to take place long after the departure of the perpetrator. The logic bomb may also be used as a tool of extortion, with a ransom being demanded in exchange for disclosure of the location of the bomb. Irrespective of motive, the fact remains that the use of viruses, worms and logic bombs constitutes unauthorised modification of legitimate computer data or programmes and thus fall under the rubric computer sabotage, although the motive of the sabotage may be circumstantial to the alteration of the data.

## Unauthorised Access to Computer Services

The desire to gain unauthorised access to computer systems can be prompted by several motives, from simple curiosity, as exemplified by many hackers, to computer sabotage or espionage. Intentional and unjustified access by a person not authorised by the owners or operators of a system may often constitute criminal behaviour. Unauthorised access creates the opportunity to cause additional unintended damage to data, system crashes or impediments to legitimate system users by negligence. Access is often accomplished from a remote location along a telecommunication network, by one of several means. The perpetrator may be able to take advantage of lax security measures to gain access or may find loopholes in existing security measures or system procedures. Frequently, hackers impersonate legitimate system users; this is especially common in systems where users can employ common passwords or maintenance passwords found in the system itself.

Password protection is often mischaracterised as a protective device against unauthorised access. However, the modern hacker can easily circumvent this protection using one of three common methods. If a hacker is able to discover a password allowing access, then a trojan horse programme can be placed to capture the other passwords of legitimate users. This type of programme can operate concurrently with the normal security function and is difficult to detect. The hacker can later retrieve the programme containing the stolen passwords by remote access.

Password protection can also be bypassed successfully by utilising password cracking routines. Most modern software effects password security by a process that converts a user's selected password into a mathematical series, a process known as encryption. Encryption disguises the actual password, which is then almost impossible to decrypt. Furthermore, legitimate security software has been developed that allows access to data only after it checks encrypted passwords against a dictionary of common passwords so as to alert system administrators of potential weakness in security.

However, this same security process can be imitated for illegitimate purposes. Known as a "cracker" programme when used for illegitimate purposes, these tools encrypt some or all of the data of the system. This creates a dictionary of data to compare with cracker software, for the purpose of identifying common passwords and gaining access to the system. A variety of these system-specific encryption routines can be obtained from hacker bulletin boards around the world and are regularly updated by the criminal community as security technology develops.

The third method commonly used to access a system is the "trapdoor" method, whereby unauthorised access is achieved through access points, or trapdoors, created for legitimate purposes, such as maintenance of the system. The international criminal hacker community uses electronic bulletin boards to communicate system infiltration incidents and methods. In one case, details of a Canadian attempt to access a system were found on suspects in an unrelated matter in England; they had removed the material from a bulletin board in Germany. This sharing of information can facilitate multiple unauthorised infiltrations of a system from around the globe, resulting in staggering telecommunication charges to the victim.

With the development of modern telecommunications system, a new field for unauthorised infiltration was created. Personal telecommunications have been expanded with the advent of portable, cellular telecommunication devices. The criminal community has responded to these advances by duplicating the microchip technology. Modern telecommunications systems are equally vulnerable to criminal activity. Office automation systems such as voice mail boxes and private business exchanges are, in effect, computer systems, designed for the convenience of users. However, convenience features such as remote access and maintenance capabilities, call-forwarding and voice-messaging are easily infiltrated by computer criminals.

Modern telecommunications systems, like other computer systems, are also susceptible to abuse by remote access. The integration of telecommunications systems means that once one system is accessed, a computer operator with sufficient skill could infiltrate the entire telecommunications network of a city. The usual motive for telecommunications crime is to obtain free telecommunications services. However, more innovative telecommunications fraud has also been uncovered, and telecommunications systems have been used to disguise other forms of criminal activity.

### Unauthorised Reproduction of Protected Computer Programs

The unauthorised reproduction of computer programmes can mean a substantial economic loss to the legitimate owners. Several jurisdictions have dictated that this type of activity should be the subject of criminal sanction. The problem has reached transnational dimensions with the trafficking of these unauthorised reproductions over modern telecommunication networks.

## Modus Operandi of Cyber Criminals

### Hacking

Hacking is the unauthorised access to computer systems or networks. Hackers are people with sufficient technical ability to gain access to another person's computer or to a network through the use of stolen passwords, or interference technology which provides access to networks and individual computers. It is a recognised and for some, an accepted form of computer activity.

There are three different hacking groups:

The first group are young kids, 15 to 21 years old, who download the latest hacking tools straight off a web site. If you go into any search engine, type in 'hacking tools' and hit return, a plethora of sites come up that will give you the ability to generate your own malicious codes, worms, viruses, hack attacks. Most of that is filtered out as noise by the technology They are known vulnerabilities and they are known attacks, so they are fairly easy to block.

The second group would be politically motivated organisations that are attempting to hack into specific countries, for example, organisations that are anti global trade and that sort of thing. You see attacks on high-profile commercial organisations launched by special interest groups of that nature on occasions.

The final group is those that are a little more talented in what they do. They are specifically after personal gain. They tend to launch the attacks that are not as high profile because you tend not to hear about them. They are trying to steal credit card information or deploy keystroke loggers without people knowing about it. These things are not designed to bring down infrastructure or hack into web sites they are trying to specifically pick up their own information without people knowing. They are predominantly male, predominantly 15 to 35 years of age.

Hacking is the deliberate gaining unauthorised access to an information system and, in extreme cases, it may amount to industrial espionage or a national security crime when the defendant accesses commercially or nationally sensitive materials. Hackers may identify and exploit security flaws. Although this may represent a threat to commercially or militarily sensitive sites, this form of activity is not necessarily against the public interest and should be distinguished from both nuisance attacks and the more serious, malicious assaults, even though all "victims" may still incur financial "loss" whether through the unexpected cost of having to repair insecure systems, or downtime on a retail portal.

The more genuinely criminal can be external threats, i.e. those who wish to break into the systems from outside, or internal in that employees wish to steal from their employers or to place a logic bomb or similar presents when leaving their employment. The cost and inconvenience involved can be substantial. For example, the development of computer viruses such as the "love bug", worms, trojans, etc. represent major threats. Less obvious but no less costly is telephone hacking or "phreaking", i.e. unauthorised access into an organisation's telephone system to make free long-distance calls.

Hacking frequently involves people acting in different states. Criminal jurisdiction is usually invoked both when the defendant and/or the accessed computer is physically within the territory of the prosecuting state.

### Theft of Electronic Information

This includes information stored in computer hard disks, removable storage media etc. Theft may be either by appropriating the data physically or by tampering them through the virtual medium.

### Email Bombing

This kind of activity refers to sending large numbers of mail to the victim, which may be an individual or a company or even mail servers there by ultimately resulting into crashing.

### Data Diddling

This kind of an attack involves altering raw data just before a computer processes it and then changing it back after the processing is completed. The electricity board faced similar problem of data diddling while the department was being computerised.

### Salami Attacks

This kind of crime is normally prevalent in the financial institutions or for the purpose of committing financial crimes. An important feature of this type of offence is that the alteration is so small that it would normally go unnoticed. E.g. the Ziegler case wherein a logic bomb was introduced in the bank's system, which deducted 10 cents from every account and deposited it in a particular account.

### Denial of Service Attack

The computer of the victim is flooded with more requests than it can handle which cause it to crash. Distributed Denial of Service (DDoS) attack is also a type of denial of service attack, in which the offenders are wide in number and widespread. E.g. Amazon, Yahoo.

### Virus/Worm Attacks

Viruses are programs that attach themselves to a computer or a file and then circulate themselves to other files and to other computers on a network. They usually affect the data on a computer, either by altering or deleting it. Worms, unlike viruses do not need the host to attach themselves to. They merely make functional copies of themselves and do this repeatedly till they eat up all the available space on a computer's memory. E.g. love bug virus, which affected at least 5% of the computers of the globe. The losses were accounted to be $ 10 million. The world's most famous worm was the internet worm let loose on the internet by Robert Morris sometime in 1988. Almost brought development of internet to a complete halt.

### Logic Bombs

These are event dependent programs. This implies that these programs are created to do something only when a certain event (known as a trigger event) occurs. E.g. even some viruses may be termed logic bombs because they lie dormant all through the year and become active only on a particular date (like the Chernobyl virus).

### Trojan Attacks

This term has its origin in the word 'Trojan horse'. In software field this means an unauthorised programme, which passively gains control over another's system by representing itself as an authorised programme. The most common form of installing a Trojan is through e-mail. E.g. a Trojan was installed in the computer of a lady film director in the U.S. while chatting. The cyber criminal through the web cam installed in the computer obtained her nude photographs. He further harassed this lady.

### Internet Time Thefts

Normally in these kinds of thefts the internet surfing hours of the victim are used up by another person. This is done by gaining access to the login ID and the password. E.g. Colonel Bajwa's case—the internet hours were used up by any other person. This was perhaps one of the first reported cases related to cyber crime in India. However this case made the police infamous as to their lack of understanding of the nature of cyber crime.

### Web Jacking

This term is derived from the term hi jacking. In these kinds of offences the hacker gains access and control over the web site of another. He may even mutilate or change the information on the site. This may be done for fulfilling political objectives or for money. E.g. recently the site of MIT (Ministry of Information Technology) was hacked by the Pakistani hackers and some obscene matter was placed therein. Further the site of Bombay crime branch was also web jacked. Another case of web jacking is that of the 'gold fish' case. In this case the site was hacked and the information pertaining to gold fish was changed. Further a ransom of US $ 1 million was demanded as ransom. Thus web jacking is a process where by control over the site of another is made backed by some consideration for it.

## Legislation against Cyber Crime

Almost all developed and developing countries have established rules and regulations to control and cyber crime. In India, The Information Technology Act 2000 was undoubtedly a welcome step at a time when there was no legislation on this specialised field. The Act has however during its application has proved to be inadequate to a certain extent. The hurry in which the legislation was passed, without sufficient public debate, did not really serve the desired purpose. Experts are of the opinion that one of the reasons for the inadequacy of the legislation has been the hurry in which it was passed by the parliament and it is also a fact that sufficient time was not given for public debate.

Cyber laws, in their very preamble and aim, state that they are targeted at aiding e-commerce, and are not meant to regulate cyber crime. The main intention of the legislators has been to provide for a law to regulate the e-commerce and with that aim the I.T.Act 2000 was passed, which also is one of the reasons for its inadequacy to deal with cases of cyber crime.

The recent cases including Cyber stalking cyber harassment, cyber nuisance, and cyber defamation have shown that the I.T.Act 2000 has not dealt with those offences. Further it is also contended that in future new forms of cyber crime will emerge which even need to be taken care of. Therefore India should sign the cyber crime convention. However the I.T.Act 2000 read with the Penal Code is capable of dealing with these felonies.

Cyber crime in the Act is neither comprehensive nor exhaustive. We need dedicated legislation on cyber crime that can supplement the Indian Penal Code. The IT Act, 2000 is not comprehensive enough and doesn't even define the term 'cyber crime. India, as a nation, has to cope with an urgent need to regulate and punish those committing cyber crimes, but with no specific provisions to do so. Supporters of the Indian Penal Code School vehemently argue that IPC has stood the test of time and that it is not necessary to incorporate any special laws on cyber crime. This is because it is debated by them that the IPC alone is sufficient for all kinds of crime. However, in practical terms, the argument does not have appropriate backing. It has to be distinctly understood that cyber crime and cyber space are completely new whelms, where numerous new possibilities and opportunities emerge by the day in the form of new kinds of crimes.

A new legislation on cyber crime is totally unwarranted. The reason is that the new legislation not come alone but will bring with it the same confusion, the same dissatisfaction and the same desire to supplant it by further new legislation. Mr. Duggal has stated above the need to supplement IPC by a new legislation. If that is the issue then the present legislation along with the Penal Code when read harmoniously and co-jointly is sufficient to deal with the present problems of cyber crime. Further there are other legislations to deal with the intellectual property crimes on the cyber space such as the Patents Act, Copy Right Act, Trade Marks Act.

The need of the hour is a worldwide uniform cyber law to combat cyber crime. Cyber crime is a global phenomenon and therefore the initiative to fight it should come from the same level. One important reason that the Act of 2000 is not achieving complete success is the lack of awareness among the netizens about their rights. Further most of the cases are going unreported. If the people are vigilant about their rights the law definitely protects their right. E.g. the Delhi high court in October 2002 prevented a person from selling Microsoft pirated software over an auction site. Achievement was also made in the case before the court of metropolitan magistrate Delhi wherein a person was convicted for online cheating by buying Sony products using a stolen credit card.

Jurisdiction is also one of the debatable issues in the cases of cyber crime due to the very universal nature of cyber space. With the ever-growing arms of cyber space the territorial concept seems to vanish. New methods of dispute resolution should give way to the conventional methods. The Act of 2000 is very silent on these issues. The government has taken a leap in this direction by constituting cyber crime cells in all metropolitan and other important cities. Further the establishment of the Cyber Crime Investigation Cell (CCIC) of the Central Bureau of Investigation (CBI) 11) is definitely a welcome step in this direction. There are many cases in which the C.B.I has achieved success. Cyber savvy judges are also the need of the day.

## Prevention of Computer Crimes

Prevention is always better than cure. It is always better to take certain precaution while operating the net. A netizen should make them his part of cyber life. He should keep in mind the following things:

1. To prevent cyber stalking avoid disclosing any information pertaining to oneself. This is as good as disclosing your identity to strangers in public place.
2. Always avoid sending any photograph online particularly to strangers and chat friends as there have been incidents of misuse of the photographs.
3. always use latest and up date anti virus software to guard against virus attacks.
4. Always keep back up volumes so that one may not suffer data loss in case of virus contamination
5. Never send your credit card number to any site that is not secured, to guard against frauds.
6. Always keep a watch on the sites that your children are accessing to prevent any kind of harassment or depravation in children.
7. It is better to use a security programme that gives control over the cookies and send information back to the site as leaving the cookies unguarded might prove fatal.
8. Web site owners should watch traffic and check any irregularity on the site. Putting host-based intrusion detection devices on servers may do this.
9. Use of firewalls may be beneficial.
10. Web servers running public sites must be physically separate protected from internal corporate network.

## Challenge of Controlling Computer Crime

Crime can be explained in part by the supply of motivated offenders. Given the diversity of computer-related crime, it is not surprising that the various types of behaviour discussed above flow from a wide range of motives. Some of these are as old as human society, including greed, lust, revenge and curiosity. Revenge in the modern era can also entail an ideological dimension. Of considerable significance, if not unique to computer-related crime, is the intellectual challenge of defeating a complex system. Motivations, whether on the part of individuals or in the aggregate, are very difficult to change. For this reason, the most strategically advantageous approaches to computer-related crime will be concerned with the reduction of opportunities, and with the enhancement of guardianship.

While motives tend not to change, the variety and number of opportunities for cyber crime are proliferating. The exponential growth in connectivity of computing and communications creates parallel opportunities for prospective offenders, and parallel risks for prospective victims. As the internet becomes increasingly a medium of commerce, it will become increasingly a medium of fraud.

The most effective way of eliminating opportunities for on-line crime is simply to pull the plug. This is of course unrealistic; the affluent nations of the world are now highly dependent on information technology. For the poorer nations, information technology is probably a necessary, if not sufficient, path to economic development. Thus, the challenge lies in managing risk so as to achieve the maximum benefits which flow from new technologies, while minimising the downside. A merchant could scrutinise every credit card transaction so as to drastically reduce the risk of fraud, but in the process drive away legitimate customers. At a higher level, nations around the world are in the process of forging policies on where to draw the line on such fundamental questions as the balance between the citizen's privacy and the imperatives of law enforcement, and freedom of expression versus the protection of certain cultural values.

There are many technologies which reduce the opportunity to commit computer-related crime. Given that so much computer-related crime depends upon unauthorised access to information systems, access control and authentication technologies have become essential. Sophisticated advice and products for computer crime prevention are provided by one of the world's growth industries of today, namely computer security.

Denning offers a comprehensive inventory of technologies for reducing opportunities for computer crime. She describes technologies of encryption and anonymity, which permit concealment of the content of communications such as a consumer's credit card details, or of the identity of the communicator. Denning also outlines technologies of authentication, from basic passwords, to various biometric devices such as finger print or voice recognition technology, and retinal imaging, which greatly enhance the difficulty of obtaining unauthorised access to information systems. Virus detectors can identify and block malicious computer code; blocking and filtering programs can screen out unwanted content. A rich variety of commercial software now exists with which to block access to certain sites.

Another basic factor which explains computer related crime is the absence of a capable guardian. Capable guardianship has evolved over human history, from feudalism, to the rise of the state and the proliferation of public institutions of social control, to the post-modern era in which employees of private security services vastly outnumber sworn police officers in many industrial democracies. Here again, it may be instructive to compare computer related crime with more conventional types of crime.

Guardianship against conventional crime involves preventive efforts on the part of prospective victims, contributions by members of the general public or commercial third parties, as well as the activities of law enforcement agencies. Indeed, it is often only when private efforts at crime prevention fail that the criminal process is mobilised. So it is that owners of motor vehicles are encouraged to lock their vehicles at all times, that insurance contracts may offer premium discounts for crime prevention measures such as theft alarms, and that some car parks have video surveillance or private security guards in attendance. Often, it is only when these systems fail that the assistance of law enforcement is sought.

Technology can also enhance guardianship. Denning describes various technologies for detecting attempted intrusions of information systems. Alarms can indicate when repeated login attempts fail because of incorrect passwords, or when access is sought outside of normal working hours. Other anomaly detection devices will identify unusual patterns of system use, including atypical destination and duration of telephone calls, or unusual spending patterns using credit cards. Guardianship can also be enhanced by market forces. A market is currently emerging for internet service providers specialising in content suitable for family consumption, guaranteed to be free of sex, violence, and vilification.

Market forces may also generate second-order controlling influences. As large organisations begin to appreciate their vulnerability to electronic theft or vandalism, they may be expected to insure against potential losses. It is very much in the interests of insurance companies to require appropriate security precautions on the part of their policyholders. Indeed, decisions to set and to price insurance may well depend upon security practices of prospective policy holders. Subcontractors may also be required to have strict IT integrity programs in place as a condition of doing business.

Citizen concern about the availability of undesirable content has given rise to the private monitoring and surveillance of cyber space. Among the more prominent organisations involved in such surveillance is the Simon Wiesenthal Center, whose CyberWatch Hotline invites notification of anti-Semitic and racist material. Citizen co-production can complement activities undertaken by agencies of the state. An example of collaborative public-private effort in furtherance of controlling objectionable content is the Netherlands Hotline for Child Pornography on internet, an initiative of the Foundation for Dutch Internetproviders (NLIP), the Dutch National Criminal Intelligence Service (CRI), internet users, and the National Bureau against Racism (LBR). Users who encounter child pornography originating in the Netherlands, identifiable by a domain name address ending in "nl" are encouraged to report the site. The originator is warned about the posting, and asked to desist from further such activity. If the warning is ignored, then the hotline will forward any available information to the vice-squad of the local police.

The policing of terrestrial space is now very much a pluralistic endeavour, and so too is the policing of cyber space. Responsibilities for the control of computer crime will be similarly shared between agents of the state, information security specialists in the private sector, and the individual user. In cyber space today, as on terrestrial space two millennia ago, the first line of defence will be self defence — in other words, minding one's own store.

One of the more significant aspects of computer-related crime is its global reach. While international offending is by no means a uniquely modern phenomenon, the global nature of cyber space significantly enhances the ability of offenders to commit crimes in one country which will affect individuals in a variety of other countries. This poses great challenges for the detection, investigation and prosecution of offenders.

Two problems arise in relation to the prosecution of telecommunications offences which have an inter-jurisdictional aspect: first, the determination of where the offence occurred in order to decide which law to apply and, secondly, obtaining evidence and ensuring that the offender can be located and tried before a court. Both these questions raise complex legal problems of jurisdiction and extradition.

Even if one is able to decide which law is applicable, further difficulties may arise in applying that law. In a unitary jurisdiction, such as New Zealand, where there is one law and one law enforcement agency, determining and applying the applicable law is difficult enough. Criminal activities committed from across the globe, however, pose even greater problems. Sovereign governments are finding it difficult to exercise control over online behaviour at home, not to mention abroad. A resident of Chicago who falls victim to a telemarketing scam originating in Albania, for example, can expect little assistance from law enforcement agencies in either jurisdiction. As a result, regulation by territorially-based rules may prove to be inappropriate for these types of offences.

Extraterritorial law enforcement costs are also often prohibitive. The time, money and uncertainty required by international investigations, and if successful, extradition proceedings, can be so high as to preclude attention to all but the most serious offending. Moreover, the cooperation across international boundaries in furtherance of such enforcement usually requires a congruence of values and priorities which, despite prevailing trends towards globalisation, exists only infrequently.

Other issues which may complicate investigation entail the logistics of search and seizure during real time, the sheer volume of material within which incriminating evidence may be contained, and the encryption of information, which may render it entirely inaccessible, or accessible only after a massive application of decryption technology.

Traditionally, the jurisdiction of courts was local. That is, courts could only entertain prosecutions in respect of offences committed against local laws where there existed a sufficient link between the offence and the jurisdiction in question. There is, however, always the possibility that legislatures will confer extraterritorial jurisdiction for some crimes. Some common examples include offences committed on the high seas, counterfeiting offences and crimes committed by members of the defence forces. In rare circumstances, a nation's laws may apply to acts committed overseas by foreign nationals. Recent war crimes prosecutions in Australia involved defendants resident elsewhere at the times the alleged offences were committed. These circumstances are, to say the least, most unusual. But in a shrinking world where the financial burdens of extradition are unlikely to decline, they may become more common.

To the extent that international telecommunications-related crime is amenable to international enforcement, it will require concerted international cooperation. Past performance in the context of other forms of criminality would suggest that this cooperation is unlikely to be forthcoming except in the relatively infrequent types of illegality where there is widespread international consensus about the activity in question, and about the desirability of suppressing it. In many instances, extradition is likely to be more cumbersome, the greater the cultural and ideological distance between the two parties. Even so, this would assume a seamless world system of stable sovereign states; such a system does not exist today, nor is it likely to exist in our lifetime. Law enforcement and regulatory vacuums exist in some parts of the world, certainly in those settings where the state has effectively collapsed. Even where state power does exist in full force, the corruption of individual regimes can impede international cooperation.

Issues of transborder criminality aside, many law enforcement agencies as we know them, lack the capacity on their own to control computer-related crime which occurs entirely within their own jurisdiction. This arises from a number of factors, not the least of which is resource constraint. In most western industrial societies, police are being asked to do more with less. The broad sweep of the criminal law and the abundance of criminal activity means that police must often choose what matters to pursue and which to ignore. This is even more the case with transnational electronic crime than it is with domestic offending.

Another fundamental issue, at least at the present historical moment, is the difficulty faced by police services around the world in retaining expert computer crime investigators. Much like the priesthood, policing was formerly a lifetime vocation. In many police services today, trained computer crime investigators must battle for the equipment which they regard as necessary to do their job. The development of expertise in forensic computing, moreover, may require a concentration and specialisation that precludes the development of the more general expertise required for advancement through the ranks. With the traditional high status areas of policing such as homicide investigation now joined by those of general management as the most prestigious areas of policing, prospects for upward mobility on the part of the computer crime investigator are thus limited.

At the same time, very attractive opportunities exist in the private sector for persons with forensic computing skills. A competent police officer may well be able to double or triple his or her salary in the private sector, whether working for one of the big multinational accounting firms or a large financial institution. Whether this "brain drain" will continue indefinitely, or rather slow down as the supply of highly computer literate individuals in both public and private sectors catches up with demand, remains to be seen. For the time being, however, police will not be able to go it alone. They will remain dependent upon private and nonprofit institutions to combat crime in cyber space. In general, this division of labour will include elements of self protection by prospective victims of telecommunications-related illegality; market-based commercial solutions; self regulatory initiatives by the targets of regulation; traditional law enforcement or regulatory intervention by the state; and third party "co-production" of surveillance by private individuals and citizens' groups.

## References

McQuade, S. (ed) (2009) *The Encyclopedia of Cybercrime,* Westport, CT: Greenwood Press.

Parker D (1983) *Fighting Computer Crime,* U.S.: Charles Scribner's Sons.

Pattavina, A. (ed) *Information Technology and the Criminal Justice System,* Thousand Oaks, CA: Sage.

Walden, I. (2007) *Computer Crimes and Digital Investigations,* Oxford: Oxford University Press.

Wall, D.S. (2007) *Cybercrimes: The transformation of crime in the information age,* Cambridge: Polity.

# 5

# Principles of Information Security

Information security means protecting information and information systems from unauthorized access, use, disclosure, disruption, modification, perusal, inspection, recording or destruction.

The terms information security, computer security and information assurance are frequently used interchangeably. These fields are interrelated often and share the common goals of protecting the confidentiality, integrity and availability of information; however, there are some subtle differences between them.

These differences lie primarily in the approach to the subject, the methodologies used, and the areas of concentration. Information security is concerned with the confidentiality, integrity and availability of data regardless of the form the data may take: electronic, print, or other forms. Computer security can focus on ensuring the availability and correct operation of a computer system without concern for the information stored or processed by the computer. Information assurance focuses on the reasons for assurance that information is protected, and is thus reasoning about information security.

Governments, military, corporations, financial institutions, hospitals, and private businesses amass a great deal of confidential information about their employees, customers, products, research, and financial status. Most of this information is now collected, processed and stored on electronic computers and transmitted across networks to other computers.

Should confidential information about a business' customers or finances or new product line fall into the hands of a competitor, such a breach of security could lead to negative consequences. Protecting confidential information is a business requirement, and in many cases also an ethical and legal requirement.

For the individual, information security has a significant effect on privacy, which is viewed very differently in different cultures.

The field of information security has grown and evolved significantly in recent years. There are many ways of gaining entry into the field as a career. It offers many areas for specialization including: securing network(s) and allied infrastructure, securing applications and databases, security testing, information systems auditing, business continuity planning and digital forensics science, etc.

## Origin and Development

Since the early days of writing, politicians, diplomats and military commanders understood that it was necessary to provide some mechanism to protect the confidentiality of correspondence and to have some means of detecting tampering. Julius Caesar is credited with the invention of the Caesar cipher ca. 50 B.C., which was created in order to prevent his secret messages from being read should a message fall into the wrong hands, but for the most part protection was achieved through the application of procedural handling controls. Sensitive information was marked up to indicate that it should be protected and transported by trusted persons, guarded and stored in a secure environment or strong box. As postal services expanded governments created official organisations to intercept, decipher, read and reseal letters.

In the mid 19th century more complex classification systems were developed to allow governments to manage their information according to the degree of sensitivity. The British Government codified this, to some extent, with the publication of the Official Secrets Act in 1889 and by the time of the First World War multi-tier classification systems were used to communicate information to and from various fronts. The war and wider use of electronic communications systems encouraged greater use of code making and breaking sections in diplomatic and military headquarters. In the United Kingdom this led to the creation of the Government Codes and Cypher School in 1919. Encoding became more sophisticated between the wars as machines were employed to scramble and unscramble information. The volume of information shared by the Allied countries during the Second World War necessitated formal alignment of classification systems and procedural controls. An arcane range of markings evolved to indicate who could handle documents (usually officers rather than men) and where they should be stored as increasingly complex safes and storage facilities were developed. Procedures evolved to ensure documents were destroyed properly and it was the failure to follow these procedures which led to some of the greatest intelligence coups of the war.

The end of the 20th century and early years of the 21st century saw rapid advancements in telecommunications, computing hardware and software, and data encryption. The availability of smaller, more powerful and less expensive computing equipment made electronic data processing within the reach of small business and the home user. These computers quickly became interconnected through a network generically called the Internet.

The rapid growth and widespread use of electronic data processing and electronic business conducted through the Internet, along with numerous occurrences of international terrorism, fueled the need for better methods of protecting the computers and the information they store, process and transmit. The academic disciplines of computer security and information assurance emerged along with numerous professional organizations – all sharing the common goals of ensuring the security and reliability of information systems.

## Basic Principles

The CIA triad (confidentiality, integrity and availability) is one of the core principles of information security.

There is continuous debate about extending this classic trio Other principles such as Accountability have sometimes been proposed for addition – it has been pointed out that issues such as Non-Repudiation do not fit well within the three core concepts, and as regulation of computer systems has increased (particularly amongst the Western nations) Legality is becoming a key consideration for practical security installations.

In 1992 and revised in 2002 the OECD's Guidelines for the Security of Information Systems and Networks proposed the nine generally accepted principles: Awareness, Responsibility, Response, Ethics, Democracy, Risk Assessment, Security Design and Implementation, Security Management, and Reassessment. Building upon those, in 2004 the NIST's Engineering Principles for Information Technology Security proposed 33 principles. From each of these derived guidelines and practices.

In 2002, Donn Parker proposed an alternative model for the classic CIA triad that he called the six atomic elements of information. The elements are confidentiality, possession, integrity, authenticity, availability, and utility. The merits of the Parkerian hexad are a subject of debate amongst security professionals.

### Confidentiality

Confidentiality is the term used to prevent the disclosure of information to unauthorized individuals or systems. For example, a credit card transaction on the Internet requires the credit card number to be transmitted from the buyer to the merchant and from the merchant to a transaction processing network. The system attempts to enforce confidentiality by encrypting the card number during transmission, by limiting the places where it might appear (in databases, log files, backups, printed receipts, and so on), and by restricting access to the places where it is stored. If an unauthorized party obtains the card number in any way, a breach of confidentiality has occurred.

Confidentiality is necessary (but not sufficient) for maintaining the privacy of the people whose personal information a system holds.

### Integrity

In information security, integrity means that data cannot be modified undetectably. This is not the same thing as referential integrity in databases, although it can be viewed as a special case of Consistency as understood in the classic ACID model of transaction processing. Integrity is violated when a message is actively modified in transit. Information security systems typically provide message integrity in addition to data confidentiality.

### Availability

For any information system to serve its purpose, the information must be available when it is needed. This means that the computing systems used to store and process the information, the security controls used to protect it, and the communication channels used to access it must be functioning correctly. High availability systems aim to remain available at all times, preventing service disruptions due to power outages, hardware failures, and system upgrades. Ensuring availability also involves preventing denial-of-service attacks.

### Authenticity

In computing, e-Business, and information security, it is necessary to ensure that the data, transactions, communications or documents (electronic or physical) are genuine. It is also important for authenticity to validate that both parties involved are who they claim to be.

### Non-repudiation

In law, non-repudiation implies one's intention to fulfill their obligations to a contract. It also implies that one party of a transaction cannot deny having received a transaction nor can the other party deny having sent a transaction.

Electronic commerce uses technology such as digital signatures and public key encryption to establish authenticity and non-repudiation.

## Risk Management

The Certified Information Systems Auditor (CISA) Review Manual 2006 provides the following definition of risk management: "Risk management is the process of identifying vulnerabilities and threats to the information resources used by an organization in achieving business objectives, and deciding what countermeasures, if any, to take in reducing risk to an acceptable level, based on the value of the information resource to the organization."

There are two things in this definition that may need some clarification. First, the process of risk management is an ongoing, iterative process. It must be repeated indefinitely. The business environment is constantly changing and new threats and vulnerability emerge every day. Second, the choice of countermeasures (controls) used to manage risks must strike a balance between productivity, cost, effectiveness of the countermeasure, and the value of the informational asset being protected.

Risk analysis and risk evaluation processes have their limitations since, when security incidents occur, they emerge in a context, and their rarity and even their uniqueness give rise to unpredictable threats. The analysis of these phenomena which are characterized by breakdowns, surprises and side-effects, requires a theoretical approach which is able to examine and interpret subjectively the detail of each incident.

Risk is the likelihood that something bad will happen that causes harm to an informational asset (or the loss of the asset). A vulnerability is a weakness that could be used to endanger or cause harm to an informational asset. A threat is anything (manmade or act of nature) that has the potential to cause harm.

The likelihood that a threat will use a vulnerability to cause harm creates a risk. When a threat does use a vulnerability to inflict harm, it has an impact. In the context of information security, the impact is a loss of availability, integrity, and confidentiality, and possibly other losses (lost income, loss of life, loss of real property). It should be pointed out that it is not possible to identify all risks, nor is it possible to eliminate all risk. The remaining risk is called "residual risk".

A risk assessment is carried out by a team of people who have knowledge of specific areas of the business. Membership of the team may vary over time as different parts of the business are assessed. The assessment may use a subjective qualitative analysis based on informed opinion, or where reliable dollar figures and historical information is available, the analysis may use quantitative analysis.

The research has shown that the most vulnerable point in most information systems is the human user, operator, designer, or other human The ISO/IEC 27002:2005 Code of practice for information security management recommends the following be examined during a risk assessment:

- security policy,
- organization of information security,
- asset management,
- human resources security,
- physical and environmental security,
- communications and operations management,
- access control,
- information systems acquisition, development and maintenance,

- information security incident management,
- business continuity management, and
- regulatory compliance.

In broad terms, the risk management process consists of:

- Identification of assets and estimating their value. Include: people, buildings, hardware, software, data (electronic, print, other), supplies.
- Conduct a threat assessment. Include: Acts of nature, acts of war, accidents, malicious acts originating from inside or outside the organization.
- Conduct a vulnerability assessment, and for each vulnerability, calculate the probability that it will be exploited. Evaluate policies, procedures, standards, training, physical security, quality control, technical security.
- Calculate the impact that each threat would have on each asset. Use qualitative analysis or quantitative analysis.
- Identify, select and implement appropriate controls. Provide a proportional response. Consider productivity, cost effectiveness, and value of the asset.
- Evaluate the effectiveness of the control measures. Ensure the controls provide the required cost effective protection without discernible loss of productivity.

For any given risk, management can choose to accept the risk based upon the relative low value of the asset, the relative low frequency of occurrence, and the relative low impact on the business. Or, leadership may choose to mitigate the risk by selecting and implementing appropriate control measures to reduce the risk. In some cases, the risk can be transferred to another business by buying insurance or outsourcing to another business. The reality of some risks may be disputed. In such cases leadership may choose to deny the risk.

## Security Controls

When management chooses to mitigate a risk, they will do so by implementing one or more of three different types of controls.

### Administrative

Administrative controls (also called procedural controls) consist of approved written policies, procedures, standards and guidelines. Administrative controls form the framework for running the business and managing people. They inform people on how the business is to be run and how day to day operations are to be conducted. Laws and regulations created by government bodies are also a type of administrative control because they inform the business. Some industry sectors have policies, procedures, standards and guidelines that must be followed – the Payment Card Industry (PCI) Data Security Standard required by Visa and MasterCard is such an example. Other examples of administrative controls include the corporate security policy, password policy, hiring policies, and disciplinary policies.

Administrative controls form the basis for the selection and implementation of logical and physical controls. Logical and physical controls are manifestations of administrative controls. Administrative controls are of paramount importance.

### Logical

Logical controls (also called technical controls) use software and data to monitor and control access to information and computing systems. For example: passwords, network and host based firewalls, network intrusion detection systems, access control lists, and data encryption are logical controls.

An important logical control that is frequently overlooked is the principle of least privilege. The principle of least privilege requires that an individual, program or system process is not granted any more access privileges than are necessary to perform the task. A blatant example of the failure to adhere to the principle of least privilege is logging into Windows as user Administrator to read Email and surf the Web. Violations of this principle can also occur when an individual collects additional access privileges over time. This happens when employees' job duties change, or they are promoted to a new position, or they transfer to another department. The access privileges required by their new duties are frequently added onto their already existing access privileges which may no longer be necessary or appropriate.

### Physical

Physical controls monitor and control the environment of the work place and computing facilities. They also monitor and control access to and from such facilities. For example: doors, locks, heating and air conditioning, smoke and fire alarms, fire suppression systems, cameras, barricades, fencing, security guards, cable locks, etc. Separating the network and workplace into functional areas are also physical controls.

An important physical control that is frequently overlooked is the separation of duties. Separation of duties ensures that an individual can not complete a critical task by himself. For example: an employee who submits a request for reimbursement should not also be able to authorize payment or print the check. An applications programmer should not also be the server administrator or the database administrator – these roles and responsibilities must be separated from one another.

## Defence in Depth

Information security must protect information throughout the life span of the information, from the initial creation of the information on through to the final disposal of the information. The information must be protected while in motion and while at rest. During its lifetime, information may pass through many different information processing systems and through many different parts of information processing systems. There are many different ways the information and information systems can be threatened. To fully protect the information during its lifetime, each component of the information processing system must have its own protection mechanisms. The building up, layering on and overlapping of security measures is called defense in depth. The strength of any system is no greater than its weakest link. Using a defense in depth strategy, should one defensive measure fail there are other defensive measures in place that continue to provide protection.

Recall the earlier discussion about administrative controls, logical controls, and physical controls. The three types of controls can be used to form the basis upon which to build a defense-in-depth strategy. With this approach, defense-in-depth can be conceptualized as three distinct layers or planes laid one on top of the other. Additional insight into defense-in- depth can be gained by thinking of it as forming the layers of an onion, with data at the core of the onion, people the next outer layer of the onion, and network security, host-based security and application security forming the outermost layers of the onion. Both perspectives are equally valid and each provides valuable insight into the implementation of a good defense-in-depth strategy.

## Security Classification for Information

An important aspect of information security and risk management is recognizing the value of information and defining appropriate procedures and protection requirements for the information. Not all information is equal and so not all information requires the same degree of protection. This requires information to be assigned a security classification.

The first step in information classification is to identify a member of senior management as the owner of the particular information to be classified. Next, develop a classification policy. The policy should describe the different classification labels, define the criteria for information to be assigned a particular label, and list the required security controls for each classification.

Some factors that influence which classification information should be assigned include how much value that information has to the organization, how old the information is and whether or not the information has become obsolete. Laws and other regulatory requirements are also important considerations when classifying information.

The type of information security classification labels selected and used will depend on the nature of the organisation, with examples being:

- In the business sector, labels such as: Public, Sensitive, Private, Confidential.
- In the government sector, labels such as: Unclassified, Sensitive But Unclassified, Restricted, Confidential, Secret, Top Secret and their non-English equivalents.
- In cross-sectoral formations, the Traffic Light Protocol, which consists of: White, Green, Amber, and Red.

All employees in the organization, as well as business partners, must be trained on the classification schema and understand the required security controls and handling procedures for each classification. The classification of a particular information asset has been assigned should be reviewed periodically to ensure the classification is still appropriate for the information and to ensure the security controls required by the classification are in place.

## Access Control

Access to protected information must be restricted to people who are authorized to access the information. The computer programs, and in many cases the computers that process the information, must also be authorized. This requires that mechanisms be in place to control the access to protected information. The sophistication of the access control mechanisms should be in parity with the value of the information being protected – the more sensitive or valuable the information the stronger the control mechanisms need to be. The foundation on which access control mechanisms are built start with identification and authentication.

Identification is an assertion of who someone is or what something is. If a person makes the statement "Hello, my name is John Doe" they are making a claim of who they are. However, their claim may or may not be true. Before John Doe can be granted access to protected information it will be necessary to verify that the person claiming to be John Doe really is John Doe.

Authentication is the act of verifying a claim of identity. When John Doe goes into a bank to make a withdrawal, he tells the bank teller he is John Doe—a claim of identity. The bank teller asks to see a photo ID, so he hands the teller his driver's license. The bank teller checks the license to make sure it has John Doe printed on it and compares the photograph on the license against the person claiming to be John Doe. If the photo and name match the person, then the teller has authenticated that John Doe is who he claimed to be.

There are three different types of information that can be used for authentication: something you know, something you have, or something you are. Examples of "something you know" include such things as a PIN, a password, or your mother's maiden name. Examples of "something you have" include a driver's license or a magnetic swipe card. "'Something you are" refers to biometrics, including palm prints, fingerprints, voice prints and retina (eye) scans. Strong authentication requires providing more than one type of authentication information (two-factor authentication). The username is the most common form of identification on computer systems today and the password is the most common form of authentication. Usernames and passwords have served their purpose but in our modern world they are no longer adequate. Usernames and passwords are slowly being replaced with more sophisticated authentication mechanisms.

After a person, program or computer has successfully been identified and authenticated then it must be determined what informational resources they are permitted to access and what actions they will be allowed to perform (run, view, create, delete, or change). This is called authorization. Authorization to access information and other computing services begins with administrative policies and procedures. The policies prescribe what information and computing services can be accessed, by whom, and under what conditions. The access control mechanisms are then configured to enforce these policies. Different computing systems are equipped with different kinds of access control mechanisms—some may even offer a choice of different access control mechanisms. The access control mechanism a system offers will be based upon one of three approaches to access control or it may be derived from a combination of the three approaches.

The non-discretionary approach consolidates all access control under a centralized administration. The access to information and other resources is usually based on the individuals function (role) in the organization or the tasks the individual must perform. The discretionary approach gives the creator or owner of the information resource the ability to control access to those resources. In the Mandatory access control approach, access is granted or denied basing upon the security classification assigned to the information resource.

Examples of common access control mechanisms in use today include role-based access control available in many advanced database management systems—simple file permissions provided in the UNIX and Windows operating systems, Group Policy Objects provided in Windows network systems, Kerberos, RADIUS, TACACS, and the simple access lists used in many firewalls and routers.

To be effective, policies and other security controls must be enforceable and upheld. Effective policies ensure that people are held accountable for their actions. All failed and successful authentication attempts must be logged, and all access to information must leave some type of audit trail.

Also, need-to-know principle needs to be in affect when talking about access control. Need-to-know principle gives access rights to a person to perform their job functions. This principle is used in the government, when dealing with difference clearances. Even though two employees in different departments have a top-secret clearance, they must have a need-to-know in order for information to be exchanged. Within the need-to-know principle, network administrators grant the employee least amount privileges to prevent employees access and doing more than what they are supposed too. Need-to-know helps to enforce the confidential-integrity-availability (C-I-A) triad. Need-to-know directly impacts the confidential area of the triad.

## Cryptography

Information security uses cryptography to transform usable information into a form that renders it unusable by anyone other than an authorized user; this process is called encryption. Information that has been encrypted (rendered unusable) can be transformed back into its original usable form by an authorized user, who possesses the cryptographic key, through the process of decryption. Cryptography is used in information security to protect information from unauthorized or accidental disclosure while the information is in transit (either electronically or physically) and while information is in storage.

Cryptography provides information security with other useful applications as well including improved authentication methods, message digests, digital signatures, non-repudiation, and encrypted network communications.

Older less secure applications such as telnet and ftp are slowly being replaced with more secure applications such as ssh that use encrypted network communications. Wireless communications can be encrypted using protocols such as WPA/WPA2 or the older (and less secure) WEP. Wired communications (such as ITU-T G.hn) are secured using AES for encryption and X.1035 for authentication and key exchange. Software applications such as GnuPG or PGP can be used to encrypt data files and Email.

Cryptography can introduce security problems when it is not implemented correctly. Cryptographic solutions need to be implemented using industry accepted solutions that have undergone rigorous peer review by independent experts in cryptography. The length and strength of the encryption key is also an important consideration.

A key that is weak or too short will produce weak encryption. The keys used for encryption and decryption must be protected with the same degree of rigor as any other confidential information. They must be protected from unauthorized disclosure and destruction and they must be available when needed. Public key infrastructure (PKI) solutions address many of the problems that surround key management.

## Process

The terms reasonable and prudent person, due care and due diligence have been used in the fields of Finance, Securities, and Law for many years. In recent years these terms have found their way into the fields of computing and information security. U.S.A. Federal Sentencing Guidelines now make it possible to hold corporate officers liable for failing to exercise due care and due diligence in the management of their information systems.

In the business world, stockholders, customers, business partners and governments have the expectation that corporate officers will run the business in accordance with accepted business practices and in compliance with laws and other regulatory requirements. This is often described as the "reasonable and prudent person" rule. A prudent person takes due care to ensure that everything necessary is done to operate the business by sound business principles and in a legal ethical manner. A prudent person is also diligent (mindful, attentive, and ongoing) in their due care of the business.

In the field of Information Security, Harris offers the following definitions of due care and due diligence:

"Due care are steps that are taken to show that a company has taken responsibility for the activities that take place within the corporation and has taken the necessary steps to help protect the company, its resources, and employees." And, [Due diligence are the] "continual activities that make sure the protection mechanisms are continually maintained and operational."

Attention should be made to two important points in these definitions. First, in due care, steps are taken to show - this means that the steps can be verified, measured, or even produce tangible artifacts. Second, in due diligence, there are continual activities - this means that people are actually doing things to monitor and maintain the protection mechanisms, and these activities are ongoing.

## Change Management

Change management is a formal process for directing and controlling alterations to the information processing environment. This includes alterations to desktop computers, the network, servers and software. The objectives of change management are to reduce the risks posed by changes to the information processing environment and improve the stability and reliability of the processing environment as changes are made. It is not the objective of change management to prevent or hinder necessary changes from being implemented.

Any change to the information processing environment introduces an element of risk. Even apparently simple changes can have unexpected effects. One of Management's many responsibilities is the management of risk. Change management is a tool for managing the risks introduced by changes to the information processing environment. Part of the change management process ensures that changes are not implemented at inopportune times when they may disrupt critical business processes or interfere with other changes being implemented.

Not every change needs to be managed. Some kinds of changes are a part of the everyday routine of information processing and adhere to a predefined procedure, which reduces the overall level of risk to the processing environment. Creating a new user account or deploying a new desktop computer are examples of changes that do not generally require change management. However, relocating user file shares, or upgrading the Email server pose a much higher level of risk to the processing environment and are not a normal everyday activity. The critical first steps in change management are (a) defining change (and communicating that definition) and (b) defining the scope of the change system.

Change management is usually overseen by a Change Review Board composed of representatives from key business areas, security, networking, systems administrators, Database administration, applications development, desktop support and the help desk. The tasks of the Change Review Board can be facilitated with the use of automated work flow application. The responsibility of the Change Review Board is to ensure the organizations documented change management procedures are followed. The change management process is as follows:

- *Requested:* Anyone can request a change. The person making the change request may or may not be the same person that performs the analysis or implements the change. When a request for change is received, it may undergo a preliminary review to determine if the requested change is compatible with the organizations business model and practices, and to determine the amount of resources needed to implement the change.

- *Approved:* Management runs the business and controls the allocation of resources therefore, Management must approve requests for changes and assign a priority for every change. Management might choose to reject a change request if the change is not compatible with the business model, industry standards or best practices. Management might also choose to reject a change request if the change requires more resources than can be allocated for the change.
- *Planned:* Planning a change involves discovering the scope and impact of the proposed change; analyzing the complexity of the change; allocation of resources and, developing, testing and documenting both implementation and backout plans. Need to define the criteria on which a decision to back out will be made.
- *Tested*: Every change must be tested in a safe test environment, which closely reflects the actual production environment, before the change is applied to the production environment. The backout plan must also be tested.
- *Scheduled:* Part of the change review board's responsibility is to assist in the scheduling of changes by reviewing the proposed implementation date for potential conflicts with other scheduled changes or critical business activities.
- *Communicated*: Once a change has been scheduled it must be communicated. The communication is to give others the opportunity to remind the change review board about other changes or critical business activities that might have been overlooked when scheduling the change. The communication also serves to make the Help Desk and users aware that a change is about to occur. Another responsibility of the change review board is to ensure that scheduled changes have been properly communicated to those who will be affected by the change or otherwise have an interest in the change.
- *Implemented*: At the appointed date and time, the changes must be implemented. Part of the planning process was to develop an implementation plan, testing plan and, a back out plan. If the implementation of the change should fail or, the post implementation testing fails or, other "drop dead" criteria have been met, the back out plan should be implemented.

- *Documented*: All changes must be documented. The documentation includes the initial request for change, its approval, the priority assigned to it, the implementation, testing and back out plans, the results of the change review board critique, the date/time the change was implemented, who implemented it, and whether the change was implemented successfully, failed or postponed.
- *Post change review:* The change review board should hold a post implementation review of changes. It is particularly important to review failed and backed out changes. The review board should try to understand the problems that were encountered, and look for areas for improvement.

Change management procedures that are simple to follow and easy to use can greatly reduce the overall risks created when changes are made to the information processing environment. Good change management procedures improve the over all quality and success of changes as they are implemented. This is accomplished through planning, peer review, documentation and communication.

ISO/IEC 20000, The Visible OPS Handbook: Implementing ITIL in 4 Practical and Auditable Steps (Full book summary), and Information Technology Infrastructure Library all provide valuable guidance on implementing an efficient and effective change management program information security.

## Business Continuity

Business continuity is the mechanism by which an organization continues to operate its critical business units, during planned or unplanned disruptions that affect normal business operations, by invoking planned and managed procedures.

Unlike what most people think business continuity is not necessarily an IT system or process, simply because it is about the business. Today disasters or disruptions to business are a reality. Whether the disaster is natural or man-made, it affects normal life and so business. So why is planning so important? Let us face reality that "all businesses recover", whether they planned for recovery or not, simply because business is about earning money for survival.

The planning is merely getting better prepared to face it, knowing fully well that the best plans may fail. Planning helps to reduce cost of recovery, operational overheads and most importantly sail through some smaller ones effortlessly.

For businesses to create effective plans they need to focus upon the following key questions. Most of these are common knowledge, and anyone can do a BCP.

Should a disaster strike, what are the first few things that I should do? Should I call people to find if they are OK or call up the bank to figure out my money is safe? This is Emergency Response. Emergency Response services help take the first hit when the disaster strikes and if the disaster is serious enough the Emergency Response teams need to quickly get a Crisis Management team in place.

What parts of my business should I recover first? The one that brings me most money or the one where I spend the most, or the one that will ensure I shall be able to get sustained future growth? The identified sections are the critical business units. There is no magic bullet here, no one answer satisfies all. Businesses need to find answers that meet business requirements.

How soon should I target to recover my critical business units? In BCP technical jargon this is called Recovery Time Objective, or RTO. This objective will define what costs the business will need to spend to recover from a disruption. For example, it is cheaper to recover a business in 1 day than in 1 hour.

What all do I need to recover the business? IT, machinery, records...food, water, people...So many aspects to dwell upon. The cost factor becomes clearer now...Business leaders need to drive business continuity. Hold on. My IT manager spent $200000 last month and created a DRP (Disaster Recovery Plan), whatever happened to that? a DRP is about continuing an IT system, and is one of the sections of a comprehensive Business Continuity Plan. Look below for more on this.

And where do I recover my business from... Will the business center give me space to work, or would it be flooded by many people queuing up for the same reasons that I am.

But once I do recover from the disaster and work in reduced production capacity, since my main operational sites are unavailable, how long can this go on. How long can I do without my original sites, systems, people? this defines the amount of business resilience a business may have.

Now that I know how to recover my business. How do I make sure my plan works? Most BCP pundits would recommend testing the plan at least once a year, reviewing it for adequacy and rewriting or updating the plans either annually or when businesses change.

## Disaster Recovery Planning

While a business continuity plan (BCP) takes a broad approach to dealing with organizational-wide effects of a disaster, a disaster recovery plan (DRP), which is a subset of the business continuity plan, is instead focused on taking the necessary steps to resume normal business operations as quickly as possible. A disaster recovery plan is executed immediately after the disaster occurs and details what steps are to be taken in order to recover critical information technology infrastructure. Disaster recovery planning includes establishing a planning group, performing risk assessment, establishing priorities, developing recovery strategies, preparing inventories and documentation of the plan, developing verification criteria and procedure, and lastly implementing the plan.

## Laws and Regulations

Below is a partial listing of European, United Kingdom, Canadian and USA governmental laws and regulations that have, or will have, a significant effect on data processing and information security. Important industry sector regulations have also been included when they have a significant impact on information security.

- UK Data Protection Act 1998 makes new provisions for the regulation of the processing of information relating to individuals, including the obtaining, holding, use or disclosure of such information. The European Union Data Protection Directive (EUDPD) requires that all EU member must adopt national regulations to standardize the protection of data privacy for citizens throughout the EU.
- The Computer Misuse Act 1990 is an Act of the UK Parliament making computer crime (e.g. hacking) a criminal offence. The Act has become a model upon which several other countries including Canada and the Republic of Ireland have drawn inspiration when subsequently drafting their own information security laws.

- EU Data Retention laws requires Internet service providers and phone companies to keep data on every electronic message sent and phone call made for between six months and two years.
- The Family Educational Rights and Privacy Act (FERPA) (20 U.S.C. § 1232 g; 34 CFR Part 99) is a USA Federal law that protects the privacy of student education records. The law applies to all schools that receive funds under an applicable program of the U.S. Department of Education. Generally, schools must have written permission from the parent or eligible student in order to release any information from a student's education record.
- Health Insurance Portability and Accountability Act (HIPAA) of 1996 requires the adoption of national standards for electronic health care transactions and national identifiers for providers, health insurance plans, and employers. And, it requires health care providers, insurance providers and employers to safeguard the security and privacy of health data.
- Gramm-Leach-Bliley Act of 1999 (GLBA), also known as the Financial Services Modernization Act of 1999, protects the privacy and security of private financial information that financial institutions collect, hold, and process.
- Sarbanes–Oxley Act of 2002 (SOX). Section 404 of the act requires publicly traded companies to assess the effectiveness of their internal controls for financial reporting in annual reports they submit at the end of each fiscal year. Chief information officers are responsible for the security, accuracy and the reliability of the systems that manage and report the financial data. The act also requires publicly traded companies to engage independent auditors who must attest to, and report on, the validity of their assessments.
- Payment Card Industry Data Security Standard (PCI DSS) establishes comprehensive requirements for enhancing payment account data security. It was developed by the founding payment brands of the PCI Security Standards Council, including American Express, Discover Financial Services, JCB, MasterCard Worldwide and Visa International, to help facilitate the broad adoption of consistent data security measures on a global basis. The PCI DSS is a multifaceted security standard that includes requirements for security management, policies, procedures,

network architecture, software design and other critical protective measures.

- State Security Breach Notification Laws (California and many others) require businesses, nonprofits, and state institutions to notify consumers when unencrypted "personal information" may have been compromised, lost, or stolen.
- Personal Information Protection and Electronics Document Act (PIPEDA) – An Act to support and promote electronic commerce by protecting personal information that is collected, used or disclosed in certain circumstances, by providing for the use of electronic means to communicate or record information or transactions and by amending the Canada Evidence Act, the Statutory Instruments Act and the Statute Revision Act.

## Sources of Standards

International Organization for Standardization (ISO) is a consortium of national standards institutes from 157 countries, coordinated through a secretariat in Geneva, Switzerland. ISO is the world's largest developer of standards. ISO 15443: "Information technology - Security techniques - A framework for IT security assurance", ISO/IEC 27002: "Information technology - Security techniques - Code of practice for information security management", ISO-20000: "Information technology - Service management", and ISO/IEC27001: "Information technology - Security techniques - Information security management systems - Requirements" are of particular interest to information security professionals.

The USA National Institute of Standards and Technology (NIST) is a non-regulatory federal agency within the U.S. Department of Commerce. The NIST Computer Security Division develops standards, metrics, tests and validation programs as well as publishes standards and guidelines to increase secure IT planning, implementation, management and operation. NIST is also the custodian of the USA Federal Information Processing Standard publications (FIPS).

The Internet Society is a professional membership society with more than 100 organization and over 20,000 individual members in over 180 countries. It provides leadership in addressing issues that confront the future of the Internet, and is the organization home for the groups responsible for

Internet infrastructure standards, including the Internet Engineering Task Force (IETF) and the Internet Architecture Board (IAB). The ISOC hosts the Requests for Comments (RFCs) which includes the Official Internet Protocol Standards and the RFC-2196 Site Security Handbook.

The Information Security Forum is a global nonprofit organization of several hundred leading organizations in financial services, manufacturing, telecommunications, consumer goods, government, and other areas. It undertakes research into information security practices and offers advice in its biannual Standard of Good Practice and more detailed advisories for members.

The IT Baseline Protection Catalogs, or IT-Grundschutz Catalogs, ("IT Baseline Protection Manual" before 2005) are a collection of documents from the German Federal Office for Security in Information Technology (FSI), useful for detecting and combating security-relevant weak points in the IT environment (IT cluster). The collection encompasses over 3000 pages with the introduction and catalogs.

## References

Allen, Julia H. (2001). *The CERT Guide to System and Network Security Practices.* Boston, MA: Addison-Wesley.

Dhillon, Gurpreet (2007). *Principles of Information Systems Security: text and cases.* NY: John Wiley & Sons.

Layton, Timothy P. (2007). *Information Security: Design, Implementation, Measurement, and Compliance.* Boca Raton, FL: Auerbach publications.

Krutz, Ronald L.; Russell Dean Vines (2003). *The CISSP Prep Guide* (Gold Edition ed.). Indianapolis, IN: Wiley.

Peltier, Thomas R. (2002). *Information Security Policies, Procedures, and Standards: guidelines for effective information security management.* Boca Raton, FL: Auerbach publications.

# 6

# Internet Protocol Security

Internet Protocol Security (IPsec) is a protocol suite for securing Internet Protocol (IP) communications by authenticating and encrypting each IP packet of a communication session. IPsec also includes protocols for establishing mutual authentication between agents at the beginning of the session and negotiation of cryptographic keys to be used during the session.

IPsec is an end-to-end security scheme operating in the Internet Layer of the Internet Protocol Suite. It can be used in protecting data flows between a pair of hosts (host-to-host), between a pair of security gateways (network-to-network), or between a security gateway and a host (network-to-host).

Some other Internet security systems in widespread use, such as Secure Sockets Layer (SSL), Transport Layer Security (TLS) and Secure Shell (SSH), operate in the upper layers of the TCP/IP model. In the past, the use of TLS/SSL had to be designed into an application to protect the application protocols. In contrast, since day one, applications did not need to be specifically designed to use IPsec. Hence, IPsec protects any application traffic across an IP network.

## History of IPsec

In December 1993, the experimental of IP Security swIPe (protocol) was researched at Columbia University and AT&T Bell Labs. In July 1994, Wei Xu at Trusted Information Systems continued this research. After several months, the research was completed successfully on BSDI system. By hacking the binary kernels, Wei had quickly extended his development on to Sun OS, HP UX, and other UNIX system. One of the challenges was slow performance of DES and 3DES. The software encryption can't even support a T1 speed under the Intel 80386 architecture. By exploring the Crypto cards from Germany, Wei Xu further developed an automated device driver, known as plug-and-play today. By achieving the throughput for more than a T1s, this work made the commercial product practically feasible, that was released as a part of the well-known Gauntlet firewall. In December 1994, it was the first time in production for securing some of remote sites between east and west coastal states of the United States.

Another IP Security Protocol was developed in 1995 at the Naval Research Laboratory as part of a DARPA-sponsored research project. ESP was originally derived from the SP3D protocol, rather than being derived from the ISO Network-Layer Security Protocol (NLSP). The SP3D protocol specification was published by NIST, but designed by the Secure Data Network System project of the National Security Agency (NSA), AH is derived in part from previous IETF standards work for authentication of the Simple Network Management Protocol (SNMP).

Since 1996, the IP Security workshops were organized for standardizing the protocols. IPsec is officially specified by the Internet Engineering Task Force (IETF) in a series of Request for Comments documents addressing various components and extensions. It specifies the spelling of the protocol name to be IPsec.

## Technologies in Internet Security

The base of Internet protocol (IP) is the large networks. It underlies networks from medium-sized corporate LANs through to the Internet itself. More so than any other protocol at any level of network architecture, IP is the universal medium of communications—the lingua franca—of computers all around the world. IP deserves its popularity. It is flexible, powerful, and well-suited to negotiate communications between platforms with divergent capabilities.

However, IP-based networks have a weakness related to the structure of IP itself. IP's original architects had no reason to provide security features at the IP level, and IP's flexibility allows for some creative uses of the protocol that defeat traffic auditing, access control and many other security measures. IP-based network data is, therefore, wide open to tampering and eavesdropping.

Mass media reports of the Internet's fundamental unsuitability for sending sensitive communications, while sometimes sensationalised, have their basis in fact. The public and business know about the Internet's weakness, and they should.

Technologies now exist to secure communications over the Internet, but mostly for specific software applications. These technologies generally use powerful new encryption techniques to get the job done. PGP/Web-of-Trust technology encrypts e-mail. Browser-based authentication and encryption between the browser and the web server (SSL) protect commercial web traffic. While these technologies have their respective strengths and niches, they are limited to specific uses. This doesn't address the challenges faced by the large enterprise and the average Internet service provider (ISP) that may never know precisely what applications may be running tomorrow over the networks they're building today.

**Network Layer**

There is a solution to the security problem, however, and it isn't restricted to a single application. The key is in understanding the nature of the network layer in IP networks. To isolate the various problems in building networks and making them work, we picture them in layers. Each layer solves specific problems unique to that layer. Broadly speaking, you can imagine an IP network as having three layers—the physical layer, the IP network layer and the application layer. Each layer provides services to the level above.

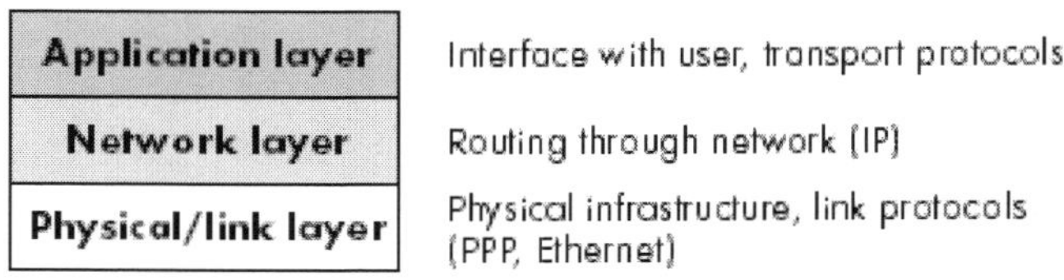


**Figure 1. Network layers (simplified)**

The physical/link layer (the lowest layer) consists of the electrical cables, network cards, and/or radio links on which information travels, as well as the simple data carrying protocols that provide an interface for the higher level protocols. In an IP network, different parts of the network use different types of physical media - Ethernet in some places, point-to-point lines in others.

Above the physical layer, the network layer (the IP layer in IP networks) deals with getting information from network node to network node across the entire network. It uses the lower level protocols to move the data, and its own routing logic to work out the most sensible subnets through which to send the data.

Above the network layer are a few higher level protocols that set up the links between nodes for different types of communications, and the application layer in which the applications run. Applications use the services of the network layer to determine how to move data from network node to network node, and the network layer, in turn, uses the physical layer to get the data from one computer's network card to the next.

The significant feature of IP networks is that the network layer in IP networks is entirely homogeneous, and it's the only layer that is. This means that any communication passing through an IP network, including the Internet, has to use the IP protocol. In other network layers, different protocols hold sway in different areas for different reasons (depending on the network architecture and the type of communication). But sooner or later everything has to go through the network layer, and there is only one protocol used in that layer—IP. So if you secure the IP layer, you secure the network.

An international working group organised under the IETF has developed a method of doing exactly that. They call it the IP security (IPSec) protocol suite. The IPSec protocol suite is based in powerful new encryption technologies, and adds security services to the IP layer in a fashion that is compatible with the existing IP standard (IPv.4), and which is mandatory in the upcoming one (IPv.61). This means that if you use the IPSec suite where you would normally use IP, you secure all communications in your network for all applications and for all users more transparently than you would using any other approach.

With IPSec, you can build something called a secure virtual private network (VPN) - a secure, private network that is as safe or safer than an isolated office LAN, but that is built on an unsecured, public network. With IPSec, you can create a secure VPN on the fly, on demand, and with anyone else using the standard. But because IPSec works with the existing and future IP standards, you can still use regular IP networks in between to carry data. You have to be IPSec-compliant, and the recipient of the information has to be IPSec-compliant, but the rest of the network in between can work just as it works now.

The fundamental strength of the IPSec group's approach is that their security works at a low network level. So just as IP is transparent to the average user, so are IPSec-based security services—unseen servants functioning in the background, ensuring that your communications are secure. Just as IP's power and flexibility make it universal, IPSec promises to become the new international standard, answering to a diverse range of security needs, allowing vastly different networks around the world to interconnect and communicate securely.

And just as IP provides services in networks of any size -from LANs with hundreds of nodes to global networks with millions—IPSec promises painless scalability. IPSec promises quiet and reliable service, however complex your security needs.

### Security in the Network Environment

To know you have security in the network environment, you want to be confident of three things:

— that the person with whom you're communicating really is that person

— that no one can eavesdrop on your communication

— that the communication you've received has not been altered in any way during transmission

These three security needs, in industry terms, are:

— authentication

— confidentiality

— integrity

The architecture of the modern, large, IP-based network, unfortunately, makes all of this difficult to ensure.

### IP Spoofing

The first difficulty IP networks pose is that it is difficult to know where information really comes from. A technique called IP spoofing takes advantage of this weakness. To understand spoofing, you need to understand how information travels across the network. At the IP level, information is broken into small, manageable chunks of data called packets. Each of these packets contains three things:

— the data

— the IP address of the data source

— the IP address of the data destination

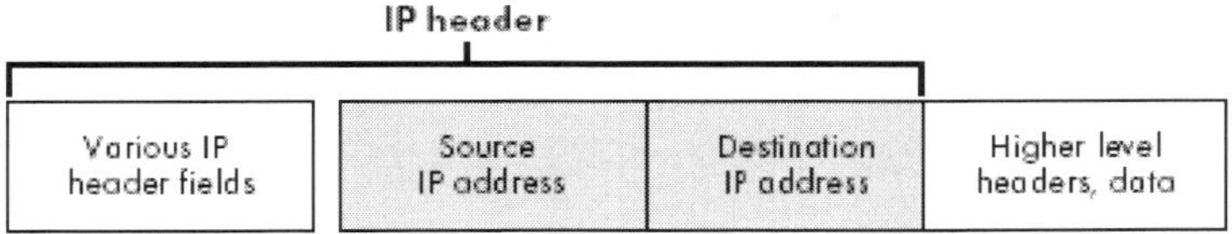


**Figure 2. The basic IP packet**

The structure of the IP packet, together with the logic of IP subnetting, gives IP much of its adaptability in terms of routing and traffic management, and much of its scalability. When two nodes on an IP network are communicating, the data stream between them is broken up into these packets, and released into the network. The route each packet takes to get to its destination isn't controlled by any particular network element—neither the sending node, nor any single device in between. Nor does any single device on the network have to know all the details of the network architecture to direct the packet to its destination.

Most of the devices in between need only know the relative directions of the sending and receiving nodes, and need only be responsible for pointing the packet the right way, subject to traffic levels and bandwidth availability. So the packet wends its way through whatever nets and subnets are available to get where it's going. Two adjacent parts of an e-mail message need not even travel the same route.

The net can direct them however it wishes, according to how busy the various network segments are. At the other end, the receiving node takes the packets, reads the sending address, and puts it all back together. The difficulty with this from a security perspective, however, is that source IP addresses in IP packet headers are easily changed. The attack—called spoofing—makes a packet coming from one machine appear to come from somewhere else altogether.

### Session Hijacking

Spoofing is one level of attack. It makes possible another. If your TCP/IP-based e-mail client program trusts an IP source address to know that it's really communicating with the mail server, nothing prevents someone with sufficiently advanced tools from taking over the connection, sending the mail server a message to cut the link, and thereafter communicating through the same TCP link with your client. The fact that you've identified the person with whom you're communicating once, doesn't mean you can depend on IP to ensure it will be the same person through the rest of the session. You need a scheme that authenticates the data's source throughout the transmission.

### Sniffing in Ethernet Networks

Sniffing is another attack that's possible in Ethernet-based IP networks. Ethernet LANs make up a large part of most networks. Ethernet technology has the advantages of being cheap, universally available, well-understood and easy to expand. It has the disadvantage of making sniffing easy. In most Ethernet LANs, packets are available to every Ethernet node on the network. Conventionally, each node's network interface card (NIC) only listens and responds to packets specifically addressed to it.

It's relatively easy, however, to put many Ethernet NICs in what's called "promiscuous mode"—meaning they can collect every packet that passes on the wire. There's no way to detect such a NIC from elsewhere on the network, because the NIC doesn't do anything to the packets when it picks them up.

A type of software colloquially called a "sniffer" can take advantage of this feature of Ethernet technology. Such tools can record all the network traffic going past them. As such they are a necessary part of the tool kit of any network diagnostician working with Ethernets—allowing them to determine quickly what's going through any segment of the network. However, in the hands of someone who wants to listen in on sensitive communications, a sniffer is a powerful eavesdropping tool.

### Use of Encryption Technologies

The most obvious solution to the problems of IP security threats is the use of encryption technologies that conceal and authenticate the data passed in IP packets. But there are complications in doing this. To use encryption, you first have to exchange encryption keys. Encryption keys are bits of information—a little like passwords - that are used with encryption algorithms to scramble and unscramble data. The purpose of the key is that once you've encrypted data with that key you need the same key to decrypt it.

But exchanging unprotected keys through the network might easily defeat the whole purpose, since those keys could easily be intercepted and open up yet another type of attack—a threat academic cryptographers refer to as a man-in-themiddle attack. A sophisticated attacker employing spoofing, hijacking and sniffing could actually work his way into such a key exchange, in a system that left the way open. He could plant his own key early in the process so that, while you believed you were communicating with one party's key, you would actually be using a key known to the man-in-the-middle. IPSec presupposes that such an attacker may exist somewhere in the public network - and provides mechanisms to defeat him.

**Interlocking Technologies**

IPSec offers three interlocking technologies, that combine to defeat all the traditional threats to IP-based networks:

— Authentication header (AH)—ties data in each packet to a verifiable signature (similar to PGP e-mail signatures) that allows you to verify both the identity of the person sending the data and that the data has not been altered.

— Encapsulating security payload (ESP)—scrambles the data (and even certain sensitive IP addresses) in each packet using hard core encryption - so a sniffer somewhere on the network doesn't get anything usable.

— Internet key exchange (IKE)—a powerful, flexible negotiation protocol that allows users to agree on authentication methods, encryption methods, the keys to use, how long to use the keys before changing them, and that allows smart, secure key exchange.

The IPSec protocol suite provides everything you need for secure communications—authentication, integrity and confidentiality—and makes key exchange practical even in larger networks. The end result is that with IPSec-compliant products you can build a secure VPN in any existing IP-based network. The basic building blocks of IPSec, the encapsulating security payload (ESP) and the authentication header (AH), use cryptographic techniques for ensuring data confidentiality and digital signatures for authenticating the data's source.

***Encapsulating Security Payload (ESP)***

The IP datagram, or IP packet, is the fundamental unit of communications in IP networks. IPSec handles the encryption at the packet level. The protocol it uses is called ESP. ESP supports pretty much any kind of symmetric encryption. The default standard built into ESP that assures basic interoperability is 56-bit DES. ESP also supports some authentication (as can the AH—the two have been designed with some overlap).

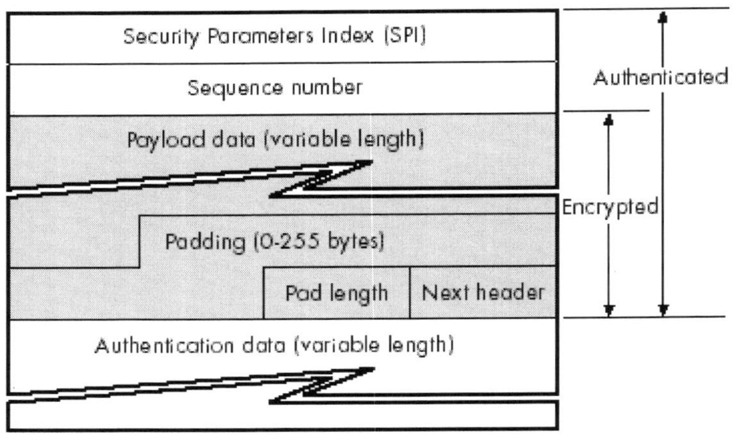


**Figure 3. The encapsulating security payload**

The ESP (Figure 3) follows the standard IP header in an IP datagram, and contains both the data and all higher level protocol headers relying on IP for routing. To explain more fully, from a chronological perspective, the ESP is inserted after the higher level header. Normally, headers are assembled and added to the front of the packet with higher level protocols first, so lower level protocols are earliest in the packet—at the outside, and deciphered first, since the system needs them first. For example, in an IP packet carrying TCP data across an Ethernet LAN, it would go like this (Figure 4):

1. First, the TCP packet header is assembled and appended to the data.
2. Then the IP header is assembled and appended to the TCP header (in front of it).

| Ethernet header | IP header | TCP header | Data | Ethernet checksum |
|---|---|---|---|---|

**Figure 4. A typical TCP/IP packet on an Ethernet LAN**

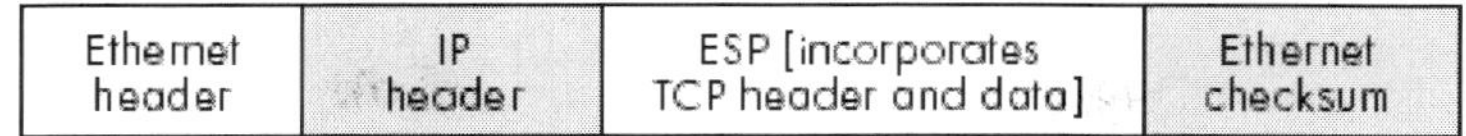


**Figure 5. A TCP/IP packet using ESP on an Ethernet LAN**

3. Then the Ethernet header is assembled and appended to the IP header (in front of it—though there's also a checksum on the end with Ethernet).

With the ESP (Figure 5), this chain becomes:

1. First, the TCP packet header is assembled and appended to the data.
2. Second, the ESP packet is assembled. With encryption, it encapsulates the TCP packet in totality, including the header.
3. Third, the IP header is assembled and added to the front of this.
4. Finally, the Ethernet header and checksum are assembled and tacked onto the front and the end.

The ESP contains six parts. The first two parts are not encrypted but are authenticated:

— The security parameter index (SPI) is an arbitrary 32-bit number that specifies to the device receiving the packet what group of security protocols the sender is using for communication—which algorithms, which keys, and how long those keys are valid.

— The sequence number is a counter that increases each time a packet is sent to the same address using the same SPI. It indicates which packet is which and how many packets have been sent with the same group of parameters. The sequence number provides protection against replay attacks—in which an attacker copies a packet and sends it out of sequence, to confuse communicating nodes. The remaining parts (with the exception of the authentication data) are all encrypted during transmission across the network. When unencrypted, they look like this:

— The payload data is the actual data being carried by the packet.

— The padding—from 0 to 255 bytes of data—allows for the fact that certain types of encryption algorithms require the data to be a multiple of a certain number of bytes—to confuse sniffers trying to estimate how much data is being transmitted.

— The pad length field specifies how much of the payload is padding as opposed to data.

— The next header field, like a normal IP next header field, identifies the type of data carried and the protocol above. The final field is an authentication field.

The ESP can support any number of encryption protocols; it's up to the user to decide which ones to use. You can even use different protocols for each party with whom you're communicating. But IPSec specifies a basic DES-CBC (cipher block chaining mode) as its default, to guarantee minimal interoperability among IPSec networks.

The ESP's encryption support is designed for use by symmetric encryption algorithms. IPSec mostly uses asymmetric algorithms for such specialised purposes as negotiating which keys to use for the symmetric encryption. The ESP also provides for a secure VPN service called tunneling. Tunneling takes the original IP packet header and encapsulates it within the ESP. Then it adds to the packet a new IP header containing the address of a gateway.

Tunneling allows you to pass illegal IP addresses through a public network (like the Internet) that otherwise wouldn't accept them. Tunneling with the ESP also has the advantage of hiding the original source and destination addresses from users on the public network—defeating or at least reducing the power of traffic analysis attacks. A traffic analysis attack uses network monitoring to determine who's saying how much to whom. An attacker doing traffic analysis doesn't know what is being said, but does know how much is being said, and that can be valuable information too.

The ESP authentication field, an optional field in the ESP, contains something called an integrity check value (ICV)—essentially a digital signature computed over the remaining part of the ESP (minus the authentication field itself). It varies in length depending on the authentication algorithm used. It may also be omitted entirely, if authentication services are not selected for the ESP. The authentication is calculated on the ESP packet once encryption is complete. The ICV supports symmetric (classical) authentication schemes. The source encrypts a hash of the data payload (or just composes a keyed hash of the payload), and attaches this as the authentication field.

The recipient confirms that there has been no tampering and that the payload did come from the expected source by checking the authentication field. The current IPSec standard specifies HMAC (a symmetric signature scheme) with hashes SHA-1 and MD5 as mandatory algorithms for doing authentication.

***Authentication Header (AH)***

The IPSec suite's second protocol, the authentication header, provides authentication services but does not address confidentiality. The AH may be applied alone, in concert with the ESP, or in a nested fashion when using tunnel mode. Authentication provided by the AH differs from that provided in the ESP in that the ESP's authentication services do not protect the IP header that precedes the ESP. The AH services protect this external IP header, along with the entire contents of the packet.

The AH does not protect all of the fields in the external IP header because some of them change in transit, and the sender cannot predict how they might change. The standard is designed so AH works around these fields. In the packet, the AH goes after the IP header but before the ESP (if present) or other higher level protocol (like TCP, in the absence of ESP). Figure 6, below, shows the AH format.

| Pad length | Next header | Reserved |
|---|---|---|
| Security Parameters Index (SPI) | | |
| Sequence number | | |
| Authentication data (variable length) | | |

**Figure 6. The authentication header**

The parts are as follows:

— The next header field indicates what the higher level protocol following the AH is (ESP or TCP, for example).

— The payload length field is an 8-bit field specifying the size of the AH, in 32-bit words (groups of 4 bytes), minus two.

— The reserved field is reserved for future use and is currently always set to zero.

— The SPI, as in the ESP packet, identifies a set of security parameters (algorithms and keys) to use for this connection.

— The sequence number, also as in the ESP packet, is a number that increases for each packet sent with a given SPI, for the purposes of keeping track of the order in which the packets go, and to make sure that the same set of parameters is not used for too many packets.

— Finally, the authentication data is the actual ICV, or digital signature, for the packet. It's much the same as the ICV used in the ESP authentication field. It may include padding to bring the length of the header to an integral multiple of 32 bits (in IPv.4) or 64 bits (IPv.6). Like the ESP, the AH can be used to implement tunneling mode. Also as in the ESP, IPSec requires specific algorithms to be available for implementing the AH. These are the minimum any IPSec implementation must support to guarantee minimal interoperability. All IPSec implementations, under the standard, must support at least HMAC-MD5 and HMACSHA-1 (the HMAC symmetric authentication scheme supported by MD5 or SHA-1 hashes) for the AH.

**AH in IPv.4 vs. IPv.6**

IPv.6 is the next IP standard coming down the road. The IPv.6 header is quite different from the existing IPv.4 header. Among the more dramatic changes, IPv.6 headers carry 128-bit addresses instead of 32-bit addresses. Among other things, IPv.6 is expected to solve the problems of coming up with new IP addresses in an expanding Internet. It is also expected to make a more flexible network architecture.

One of the difficulties with IPv.6 headers, and the host of optional headers that IPv.6 specifies, is that there is more in them that can change in transit through the network. This makes wrapping the AH's authentication around an IPv.6 packet a little more complicated. However, the IPSec group is developing the AH in concert with IPv.6 standards, and has developed protocols for flexible ranges of authentication and intelligent placing of the AH header in the IP packet so that it can work under either IPv.4 or IPv.6.

You can view the AH and ESP protocols as the building blocks of IPSec. The two protocols provide the pieces you need to build a secure VPN.

They provide the fundamental services you need—confidentiality, authentication and integrity. What you need next is the mortar that holds them together. The encryption services provided by the AH and ESP represent a powerful technology for keeping your data secret, for verifying its origin, and for protecting it from undetected tampering. But they mean little without a wisely designed infrastructure to support them, to distribute keys, and to negotiate protocols between communicating parties. Proposed secure VPN systems will succeed or fail based on the strength of this infrastructure and its scalability. And that's where IPSec's IKE protocol suite comes in.

## Management of Protocol Negotiation

The password and its numerical analogue, the PIN, are among the simplest ways available of guaranteeing security. Easy to implement and generally suitable to a range of security needs, they're everywhere now. The concept is simple: a password or PIN is something you know that no one else does, that therefore identifies you. But they're a pain to remember. Probably everyone has at least one embarrassing incident to recount—the day they drew a blank at the bank machine and couldn't remember their PIN. Or the time building security almost called the police.

The same basic difficulty faces anyone trying to implement security measures based on keyed encryption techniques. Keys are like passwords, and you've got to keep track of them. And the more keys you have, the harder it is to keep track. Factor in that keys often change regularly, and you've got the makings of a real nightmare on your hands.

For example, 20 stock traders have interests that are sometimes compatible and sometimes competing. They want to talk to each other privately and safely, through a public network. If they use a symmetric encryption scheme to do this, they will need a total of 190 keys among them. Each of them has to keep track of 19 keys—one to communicate with each of the other group members.

Add to this that they want to keep changing those keys, at least monthly, and that they have to do it in person (which is safest). So each trader has to meet with each of the 19 other traders monthly, for a total of 190 two-person meetings each month. The first thing you can do to improve this situation is to use asymmetric encryption instead of symmetric. With asymmetric encryption, each trader issues a public key that all the other traders use. Each trader also has his own private key. So each trader actually has to remember 20 keys (the 19 public keys of the other traders, plus his own private key). But exchanging them is far simpler. They could all meet at one big meeting, and each publicly announce his public key.

This artificial example illustrates two important points:

— Key exchange is fundamentally a complicated business.

— Key exchange gets more complicated as the group of communicating players expands.

So just because a system says it does encryption, that alone doesn't mean it's going to be appropriate for your needs, even if the system does that encryption well. Any proposed secure VPN solution is only as good as its method of key exchange, especially if it serves large enterprise needs. IPSec does support large enterprise needs, and its industrial strength key exchange and protocol negotiation scheme sets it apart from all other security systems.

To communicate with someone using authentication and encryption services (like those provided by IPSec's ESP and AH), you need to do three things:

— Negotiate with other people the protocols, encryption algorithms, and keys, to use.

— Exchange keys easily (this might include changing them often).

— Keep track of all these agreements.

IPSec provides mechanisms to do all three.

**Security Association**

The first problem IPSec's designers solved was actually number three, how to keep track of all the details, and which keys and algorithms to use. They did it by bundling everything together in something called the Security Association (SA). The SA groups together all the things you need to know about how you communicate securely with someone else. The SA, under IPSec, specifies:

— the mode of the authentication algorithm used in the AH and the keys to that authentication algorithm

— the ESP encryption algorithm mode and the keys to that encryption algorithm

— the presence and size of (or absence of) any cryptographic synchronisation to be used in that encryption algorithm

— how you authenticate your communications (using what protocol, what encrypting algorithm and what key)
— how you make your communications private (again, what algorithm and what key)
— how often those keys are to be changed
— the authentication algorithm, mode and transform for use in ESP plus the keys to be used by that algorithm
— the key lifetimes
— the lifetime of the SA itself
— the SA source address
— a sensitivity level descriptor

You can think of the SA as your secure channel through the public network to a certain person, group of people, or network resource. It's like a contract with whomever is at the other end. The SA also has the advantage that it lets you construct classes of security channels. If you need to be a little more careful talking to one party than another, the rules of your SA with that party can reflect extra caution—specifying stronger encryption, for example.

***SA in business***

SAs are good for building multiple secure VPNs. Imagine your company has its own secure VPN. You develop a business relationship with another company that also has a secure VPN. You're perfectly happy to give them some access to your network by linking the two secure VPNs, as this facilitates business, but you don't want them to have full access. Some things do not belong outside the company, or even outside Human Resources' filing cabinets. So you have specific SAs between your secure VPN and theirs, controlling who has what access to which resources. And you have another set of specific SAs within your secure VPN. And another within Human Resources. And so on. You can layer your secure VPN like an onion using the SA concept. That's what the SA is for.

***SA in SPI***

The SA is a concept, whereas he SPI is more concrete. The SPI is a number that uniquely identifies an SA. The SPI, together with the SA concept, makes keeping track of keys and protocols easy and automatic. Specifically, the SPI is the 32-bit number we mentioned earlier when describing the ESP and

AH packet formats. The SPI is an arbitrary 32-bit number your system picks to represent that SA whenever someone negotiates an SA with you. It identifies the SA. The SPI can not be encrypted in the packet because you use it to keep track of how to decrypt the packet. It works like this. When you negotiate an SA, the recipient node assigns an SPI it isn't already using, and preferably, one it hasn't used in a while. It then communicates this SPI to the node with which it negotiated the SA. From then until that SA expires, whenever that node wishes to communicate with yours using that SA, it uses that SPI to specify it.

Your node, on receipt, would look at the SPI to determine which SA it needs to use. Then it authenticates and/or decrypts the packet according to the rules of that SA, using the agreed-upon keys and algorithms to verify (depending on the terms of the SA) that the data really did come from the node it claims, that the data has not been modified, and that no one between those nodes has read the data. The next thing we need is to work out how to negotiate those SAs in the first place.

## IKE

IKE (industrial strength key exchange), the IPSec group's answer to protocol negotiation and key exchange through the Internet, is actually a hybrid protocol. It integrates the Internet Security Association and Key Management Protocol (ISAKMP) with a subset of the Oakley key exchange scheme.

IKE provides a way to:

— agree on which protocols, algorithms, and keys to use (negotiation services)

— ensure from the beginning of the exchange that you're talking to whom you think you're talking to (primary authentication services)

— manage those keys after they've been agreed upon (key management)

— exchange material for generating those keys safely Key exchange is a closely related service to SA management.

When you need to create an SA, you need to exchange keys. So IKE wraps them both up together, and delivers them as an integrated package.

### *Manual key exchange*

There is one other way to exchange keys. IPSec specifies that compliant systems support manual keying as well. That means if you wish to use manual (face-to-face) key exchange for certain situations, you still can. But IPSec's designers also assume that in most situations, for most large enterprises, this would be impractical. So IKE, the safe way to negotiate SAs and exchange keys through public networks, will probably do most of the work for most of the world.

***Functions fo IKE***

IKE functions in two phases. In phase one, two IKE peers establish a secure channel for doing IKE (called the IKE SA). In phase two, those two peers negotiate general purpose SAs. An IKE peer is an IPSec-compliant node capable of establishing IKE channels and negotiating SAs. It might be the computer on your desktop, or something called a security gateway that negotiates security services for you.

There are three modes of exchanging keying information and setting up SAs—two for IKE phase one exchanges, and one for phase two exchanges.

- Main mode accomplishes a phase one IKE exchange by establishing a secure channel.
- Aggressive mode is another way of accomplishing a phase one exchange—it's a little simpler and a little faster than main mode, but does not provide identity protection for the negotiating nodes, as they must transmit their identities before having negotiated a secure channel through which to do so.
- Quick mode accomplishes a phase two exchange by negotiating an SA for general purpose communications.

**Security for Channel Negotiation**

To establish an IKE SA, the initiating node proposes six things:

- encryption algorithms (to protect data)
- hash algorithms (to reduce data for signing)
- an authentication method (for signing data)
- information about a group over which to do a Diffie-

***Hellman exchange***

- a pseudo-random function (PRF) used to hash certain values during the key exchange for verification purposes
- the type of protection to use (ESP or AH)

### *Perfect forward secrecy*

One of the most annoying things about passing encrypted data around a public network is the number of opportunities an attacker has to get hold of encrypted material. You can reduce the risk of their ever deciphering it by using larger and larger keys. But the larger the key, the slower and more complex the encryption—and this can impair network performance. A good compromise solution is to use reasonably large keys, and to keep changing them. But this presents difficulties too. You need ways to generate those new keys so that the person at the other end can agree on them as well. But, to generate your new key, you can't use either the key you're changing from, or material used to generate the key you're changing from. The point is that if you do, and then someone gets hold of the current key, that person can easily deduce your new key.

What you need is a method of generating a new key that is in no way dependent on the value of the current key. So if someone gets hold of your current key, it only gives them a small part of the overall picture, and they would have to break yet another entirely unrelated key to get the next part. Cryptographers call this concept "perfect forward secrecy".

### *Diffe-Hellman scheme*

A Diffie-Hellman exchange works like this: two people independently and randomly generate values much like a public/private key pair. Each sends its public value to the other (using authentication to close out the man-in-themiddle). Each then combines the public key just received with the private key just generated, using the Diffie-Hellman combination algorithm.

The resulting value is the same on both sides, and therefore can be used for fast symmetric encryption by both parties. But no one else in the world can come up with the same value from the two public keys passed through the net, since the final value also depends on the private values, which remain secret. You can use the derived Diffie-Hellman key either as a session key for subsequent exchanges, or to encrypt yet another randomly generated key, which you can then pass through the net quite safely.

Note that yes, you do need authentication to protect even Diffie-Hellman exchanges against the man-in-the-middle. Diffie-Hellman alone does not solve this problem. It would be complicated, but without authentication a man-in-themiddle could use an active attack to get in on the action and plant his own keys. But if the key exchange mechanism you're using is protected by an authentication scheme, Diffie-Hellman allows you to generate new shared keys to use for symmetric encryption which are independent of older keys—providing perfect forward secrecy. And since symmetric encryption techniques are a lot faster, this can be quite useful in network communications. You may wish to agree on a few things to do a Diffie-Hellman exchange in the first place. That's what the Diffie-Hellman parameter in the IKE SA is for. The parameter contains information on a group to perform the Diffie-Hellman exchange. The group consists of generation material used for coming up with keys.

***Pseudo-random function***

A PRF is really just another name for a hash function. In IKE, you can use the PRF both for authentication purposes and to generate additional key material (as a randomiser).

***Main mode***

Main mode provides a mechanism for establishing the first phase IKE SA, which is used to negotiate future communications. Remember, the object here is to agree on enough things to be able to communicate securely long enough to set up an SA for future communication.

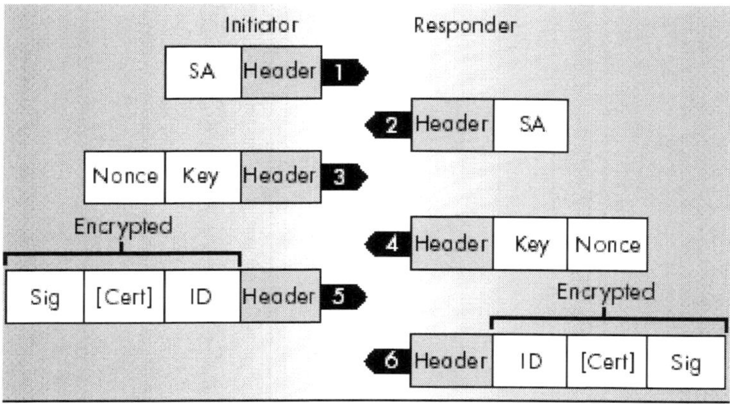


Cert: a certification payload
ID: an identification payload
Key: a key exchange payload
Nonce: a nonce payload
SA: a Security Association/proposal payload
Sig: a signature payload

**Figure 7. IKE main mode**

The steps in full will be:

1. Use main mode to bootstrap an IKE SA.
2. Use quick mode within that IKE SA to negotiate a general SA.
3. Use that SA to communicate from now until it expires.

The first step, securing an IKE SA using main mode, occurs in three two-way exchanges between the SA initiator and the recipient (Figure 7). In the first exchange (1 and 2 in the illustration below), the two agree on basic algorithms and hashes. In the second (3 and 4 in the illustration below), they exchange public keys for a Diffie-Hellman exchange, and pass each other nonces—random numbers the other party must sign and return to prove its identity. In the third (5 and 6 in the illustration below), they verify those identities. So the following is how IKE establishes its own IKE SA, step by step, using main mode and established digital signatures for authentication.

Each of the pieces is carried in its own payload, but you can pack any number of these payloads into a single IKE packet. The parties actually use the generated shared Diffie-Hellman value in three permutations, once they derive it. Both parties have to hash it three times—generating first a derivation key (to be used later for generating additional keys in quick mode), then an authentication key (for authentication), and then, finally, the encryption key to be used for the IKE SA.

***Aggressive mode***

Aggressive mode provides the same services as main mode. It establishes the original IKE SA. It looks much the same as main mode except that it is accomplished in two exchanges, rather than three, with only one round trip, and a total of three packets rather than six. In aggressive mode, the proposing party generates a Diffie-Hellman pair at the beginning of the exchange, and does as much as is practical with that first packet - proposing an SA, passing the Diffie-Hellman public value, sending a nonce for the other party to sign, and sending an ID packet that the responder can use to check its identity with a third party. The responder then sends back everything needed to complete the exchange—really an amalgamation of all three response steps in main mode, and all that's left for the initiator to do is to confirm the exchange (Figure 8).

The end result is that an aggressive mode exchange attains the same goal as a main mode exchange, except that aggressive mode does not provide identity protection for the communicating parties.

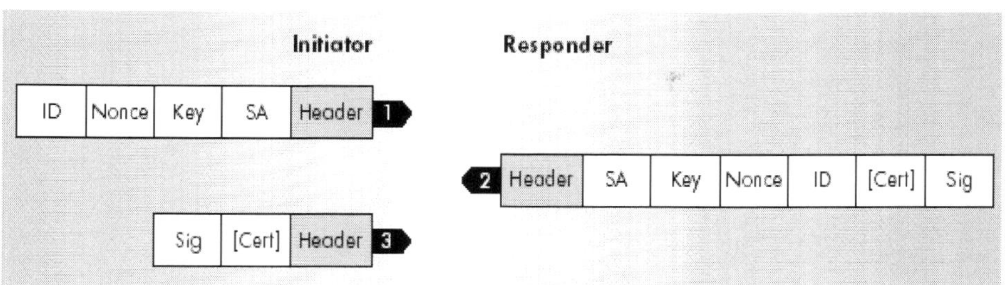


Cert: a certification payload
ID: an identification payload
Key: a key exchange payload
Nonce: a nonce payload
SA: a Security Association/proposal payload
Sig: a signature payload

**Figure 8. IKE aggressive mode**

That is to say, in aggressive mode, the parties exchange identification information prior to establishing a secure SA in which to encrypt it. So someone monitoring an aggressive exchange can actually identify who has just formed a new SA.

### *Quick mode*

Once two communicating parties have established an IKE SA using aggressive mode or main mode, they can use quick mode. Quick mode has two purposes—negotiating general IPSec security services and generating fresh keying material. Quick mode is less complex than either main or aggressive mode. Since it's already inside a secure tunnel (every packet is encrypted), it can also afford to be a little more flexible. Quick mode packets are always encrypted, and always start with a hash payload. The hash payload is composed using the agreed-upon PRF and the derived authentication key for the IKE SA. The hash payload is used to authenticate the rest of the packet. Quick mode defines which parts of the packet are included in the hash (Figure 9).

Key refreshing can be done one of two ways. If you don't want or need perfect forward secrecy, quick mode can just refresh the keying material already generated (in main or aggressive mode) with additional hashing. The two communicating parties can exchange nonces through the secure channel, and use these to hash the existing keys. If you do want perfect forward secrecy, you can still request an additional Diffie-Hellman exchange through the existing SA and change the keys that way.

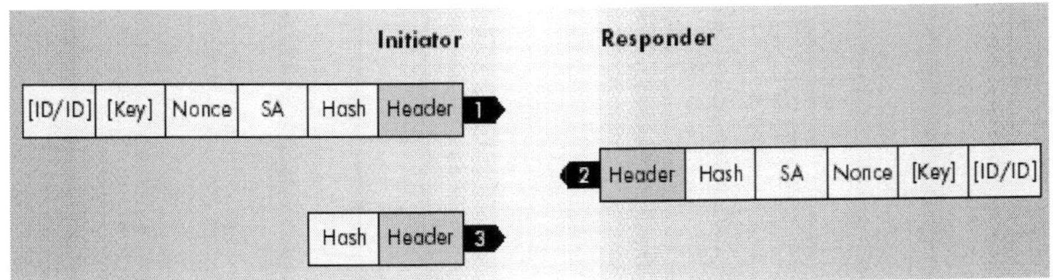


ID: an identification payload

Key: a key exchange payload

Nonce: a nonce payload

SA: a Security Association/proposal payload

**Figure 9. IKE quick mode**

Basic quick mode is a three packet exchange, like aggressive mode. If the parties do not require perfect forward secrecy, the initiator sends a packet with the quick mode hash, with proposals and a nonce. The respondent then replies with a similar packet, but generates its own nonce and includes the initiator's nonce in the quick mode hash for confirmation. The initiator then sends back a confirming quick mode hash of both nonces, completing the exchange. Finally, both parties perform a hash of a concatenation of the nonces, the SPI, and the protocol values from the ISAKMP header that initiated the exchange, using the derivation key as the key for the hash. The resulting hash becomes the new password for that SA.

If the parties do require perfect forward secrecy, the initiator first generates a public/private key pair, and sends the public key along with the initiation packet (along with the hash and nonce). The recipient then responds with its own public key and nonce, and both parties then generate the shared key using a Diffie-Hellman exchange - again fully protected by the quick mode hashes, and by full encryption within the IKE SA.

After all those exchanges to generate the IKE SA, actually establishing the general purpose SA is relatively simple. To generate a new SA, the initiator sends a quick mode message, protected by the IKE SA, requesting the new SA. A single SA negotiation actually results in two SAs—one inbound, to the initiator, and one outbound. Each IPSec SA is one way, and the node on the receiving end of that SA always chooses its own SPI to ensure it is the only SA using that reference.

So, using quick mode, the initiator tells the respondent which SPI to use in future communications with it, and the respondent follows up with its own selected SPI. Each SPI, in concert with the destination IP address and the protocol, uniquely identifies a single, IPSec SA. However, these SAs are always formed in pairs (inbound and outbound), and these pairs have identical parameters (keys, authentication and encryption algorithms, and hashes)—apart from the SPI itself.

### Certificate Authority (CA)

A CA is a trusted third party—someone whose identity you can already prove, and who can vouch for the identity of people with whom you're trying to communicate. The idea is easy enough to relate to the real world. The CA is like a public figure (for example, a notary public) who you know well enough to trust, and who vouches for other people. In the world of online verification, the CA software issues certificates tying three things together:

— someone's identity, anything that uniquely identifies them to you in a meaningful way so you can't confuse them with someone else (i.e., their name and place of residence)

— the public key that a person uses to sign their identity to online documents

— the CA's public key (used to sign and authenticate the entire package)

The CA is the defense against that man-in-the-middle working his way into key exchanges. Whenever you initiate an exchange with someone, he has to sign it with his digital signature. And then you in turn can check that signature against the one on record with the CA. They have to match. You then check that certificate's signature with the CA's signature. They have to match too.

What stops the man-in-the-middle from forging the CA's signature, and turning out his own certificates? Mostly smart distribution. Because it's a highly public entity, and a highly useful value, the CA's public key can be on record in a number of places—making it difficult for anyone to get away with forging it. You also usually design the CA's signature with strong encryption and an extremely large keyspace. This makes it long lived, so you can distribute it any number of ways, including on the disk on which the verification software is distributed. It makes it difficult indeed (provided the system is vigilant about checking) to introduce counterfeit signatures into the system.

IKE provides for third party verification using the established industry-standard X.509 format certificate. So when someone initiates an IKE exchange with you, or responds to one you have initiated, you first send the data they have to sign with their digital signature. They then send their certificate, signed by the CA, thereby proving the signature they used legitimately belongs to them. You first check the certificate signature against your copy of the CA's signature to make sure the CA really issued it. Provided it checks out, you then look up the signature attached to the certificate (the one belonging to the person you're trying to initiate an exchange with), and check the data they've just signed against it.

It's really a chain of trust—beginning with your trust in the CA's signature, which is then used to verify someone else's. All of this may look complicated, but it's part of the beauty of IPSec that this can all be done in the background -quickly, quietly and painlessly. It's far less trouble than checking the signature on the back of a credit card, in that your verification system checks for forgeries for you. You don't even have to think about it.

Altogether, IPSec's IKE system offers network users a great deal that other schemes have had difficulty delivering. But most critically, IPSec's designers have built the system's key exchange from the ground up to be genuinely scalable-so it works with any size of system. So to put all of it together, with an IPSec secure VPN:

— You can form SAs with a range of attributes, layering your network.

— You can build multiple domains of communication within the same secure VPN.

— You can update keys as frequently as you wish, and get the best of both worlds in doing so - perfect forward secrecy, and a silent, painless background mechanism that the user doesn't have to think about.

— You can do this in any IP network environment, of any size, for any size of enterprise.

— Finally, you can do this with anyone using IPSec technology, creating new SAs with whomever you wish to communicate.

## Security Policy

Essentially, all IPSec processing is the enforcement of a security policy to ensure IP communication between to end points is secure. The security policy defines the security services to be applied at the IPSec endpoint, and every IP packet processed has to be evaluated against the policy regardless of whether it is protected by IPSec or not. Security policies are maintained in a Security Policy Database (SPD). IPSec architecture specifies that a separate SPD be maintained for every IPSec enabled interface. Two tables are defined in the SPD for inbound and outbound policy.

RFC 2401 mandates that an administrative user interface be implemented to manage the SPD. Entries in the SPD are somewhat similar to a firewall rule set. Each entry has to indicate how the traffic that matches that entry is processed, and one of three actions need to be specified—bypass, reject or proceed with IPSec processing. Each policy entry also has a number of selectors that are used to identify and granulise the policy application process. These selectors include source address, destination address, user ID or system name, transport layer protocol and source and destination ports.

## IPSec Processing

IPSec uses two completely independent processes in outbound and inbound IPSec traffic processing. Regardless of whether the packet has to be processed by IPSec or not, every packet has to be compared against the security policy database (SPD). Based on the policy defined for that packet the packet is dropped, routed or passed on to the IPSec kernel for processing.

### *Outbound packet processing*

Once the routing decisions have been made, if the outbound packet has to be processed by IPSec, a number of selector fields in the packet are compared against the outbound policies in the SPD.

More than one selector fields are used for this matching because there could be more than one policy defined for that packet. Policies in the SPD are ordered, and the first matching policy is selected for enforcement. The policy usually includes information on the SA (or SA bundle) for that packet. If there is no SA defined, key management mechanisms are used to generate an SA for that packet. If key management mechanisms are not present, then the packet is dropped. If there is an SA, or an SA can be generated, then the packet is processed by IPSec, using the parameters defined by the SA.

### *Inbound packet processing*

As indicated above, inbound packets are processed differently to outbound packets. Firstly any fragmented packets need to be reassembled. Then the IP next protocol field is checked for the AH or ESP values that indicate IPSec has been applied to that packet. If the packet is authenticated or encrypted using IPSec, it will have a SPI included in the AH or ESP header. Using the SPI, and the destination IP address, the SAD is queried to identify the appropriate SA for that packet. If there is no SA that can be matched to packet the packet is dropped. If there is a match, the packet is processed.

The first step in processing the packet is to match the selectors of the packet to the selectors in the SA. This process is repeated until all IPSec headers are processed, and the next header is a transport or an IP header. Then the SPD is queried using the back pointers from the SAs or the packets selectors. Once match has been found, and the packet has been processed the packet is presented to the transport layer.

## Implementation of IPSec

RFC 2401 defines 3 ways in which IPSec could be implemented.

a) Integrating IPSec in to the native IP implementation of the host or security gateway.

b) Inserting an IPSec layer between the IP layer and the network drivers. This implementation is known as the "bump-in-the-stack" (BITS) implementation.

c) Using an external device such as an outboard crypto processor. This implementation is known as the "bump-in-the-wire" (BITW) implementation. IPSec is implemented at the IP layer, thus providing security services to the upper layer protocols.

IPSec can be implemented between, two hosts, two gateways or between a host and a gateway. Some examples of these of implementations are:

a) Two servers synchronising a database, either internally or across the Internet

b) Two gateways, providing secure communication between the two networks connected by the two gateways;

c) A gateway and host/s as in remote access solutions.

## Limitations of IPSec

Despite it being a standard and its wide acceptance, IPSec has a few limitations. IPSec secures the communication path, not the hosts/gateways that communicate. As per RFC 2401, IPSec "... can be used to protect one or more paths between a pair of hosts, between a pair of security gateways, or between a security gateway and a host". By implication then, there should be additional mechanisms in place to secure the communication endpoints. If the communication endpoint becomes compromised, then the data that traverses the IPSec communication channel can be tainted. Moreover the chances of detecting an intrusion made using such a compromised host is minimal as the end-to-end communication is encrypted and cannot be analysed by any detection mechanisms between the IPSec endpoints.

Since IPSec provides end-to-end encryption, intermediary routing devices cannot process any flags contained within the original IP headers. This affects special packet processing instructions such as Quality of Service (QoS). Therefore technologies such as IP Telephony that rely heavily on QoS cannot be secured using IPSec. In large deployments of IPSec, the administrative overhead of maintaining the numerous IPSec clients can be an issue. Installing and maintaining IPSec clients and managing the IPSec policies can be resource intensive, as IPSec does not provide a central administration mechanism for such environments.

IPSec does not interoperate with most firewall and gateway technologies that implement network address translation as part of their security/routing environment. This perhaps is the biggest drawback of IPSec. Although there is an IETF informational paper for NAT traversal using IPSec policy (RFC 2709), this has not been adopted as a standard. There has been an attempt to encapsulate IPSec packets within UDP packets for NAT traversal, but this too, has added more complexity to the already complex IPSec architecture. IPSec is too complex to implement, according to many critics of IPSec. There are too many options and too much flexibility. There are many options that IPSec offers to two IPSec endpoints, for example transport or tunnel mode with either AH or ESP. However, these multiple options do not afford more performance or functionality gains.

## References

Kent, S.; Atkinson, R. (November 1998). *IP Encapsulating Security Payload (ESP)*. IETF. RFC 2406.

Thayer, R.; Doraswamy, N.; Glenn, R. (November 1998). *IP Security Document Roadmap*. IETF. RFC 2411.

Kent, S.; Atkinson, R. (November 1998). *IP Authentication Header*. IETF. RFC 2402.

Harkins, D.; Carrel, D. (November 1998). *The Internet Key Exchange (IKE)*. IETF. RFC 2409.

Sakane, S.; Kamada, K.; Thomas, M.; Vilhuber, J. (November 1998). *Kerberized Internet Negotiation of Keys (KINK)*.IETF. RFC 4430.

Hoffman, P. (December 2005). *Cryptographic Suites for IPsec*. IETF. RFC 4308.

Kent, S. (December 2005). *IP Authentication Header*. IETF. RFC 4302.

# 7

# Cyber Security Management

Cybersecurity today is far worse than what known best practices can provide. Even without any new security technologies, much better security would be possible today if technology producers, operators of critical systems, and users took appropriate steps. But new technologies and new operating procedures—which would require additional investment for research and development—could make things even better. Because a secure system doesn't allow users to do any more than an insecure system, system and network operators in the private sector spend only as much on security as they can justify on business grounds—and this may be much less than the nation needs as a whole.

Because serious cyberattacks are rare, the payoff from security investments is uncertain (and in many cases, it is society rather than any individual firm that will capture the benefit of improved security). As a result, system and network operators tend to underinvest in security. Changing market incentives—for example, by adjusting the liability to which business users of technology might be subject or the insurance implications of good security—could have a dramatic impact on the market for security features.

For economic reasons, systems are generally built out of commercial off-the-shelf components. These are not very secure because there isn't much market demand: Customers buy features and performance rather than security. The failure of the U.S. government's Orange Book programme even within the federal marketplace is a striking example. The government demanded secure systems, industry produced them, and then government agencies refused to buy them because they were slower and less functional than other nonsecure systems available on the open market.

Because security measures are disaster-preventing rather than payoff-producing, a central aspect of security must be accountability. That is, users and operators must be held responsible by management for taking all appropriate security measures—one cannot count on financial and market incentives alone to drive appropriate action. Many security problems exist not because a fix is unknown but because some responsible party has not implemented a known fix. Of course, appropriate security measures are not free. Management must be willing to pay the costs and must demand from vendors the tools needed to minimise those costs. Management must resolve the conflict between holding people responsible and full reporting of problems, which tends to be easier in an environment in which individuals are not fearful of reporting problems.

## Operational Vulnerabilities

To promote accountability, frequent and unannounced penetration testing (so-called red-teaming) is essential to understand the actual operational vulnerabilities of deployed systems and networks. No other method is as effective at pointing to security problems that must be solved. Information about vulnerabilities thus gathered must be made available to those who are in a position to fix them—or to upper management, who can force them to be fixed. Note that effective red-teaming is undertaken independently of the system or network being tested—those being tested must not know when the test will occur or what aspects of security will be tested, while those doing the testing must be technically savvy and not constrained by operating orders that limit what they are permitted to do.

Many compromises of an information system or network result from improper configuration. For example, a given system on a network may have a modem attached to it that is not known to the network administrator, even if it was attached by a legitimate user for legitimate purposes. An installed operating system on a computer may lack critical "bug" fixes, because they were not applied or because the system was restored from a backup tape that did not include those fixes. A system firewall may be improperly configured in a way that allows Web access when, in fact, the system should only be able to transmit and receive e-mail. Or, a group of users may be given privileges that should, in fact, be restricted to one member of that group.

Because checking operational configurations is very labour-intensive if done manually, it is essential to have configuration management tools for both systems and networks that can automatically enforce a desired configuration or alert administrators when variances from the known configuration are detected. Such tools are miserably inadequate today. Building them does not require research, but it does require a considerable amount of careful engineering.

— Since perfect security is impossible, secure configurations need to be updated when new attacks are discovered. These updates need to be delivered automatically to millions of systems.

— Organisations must have concrete fallback action plans that instruct users and administrators about what they should do under conditions of cyberattack. Admonitions to "be more careful" are not actionable, especially since the effects of a cyberattack may not be obvious, nor will they be constant over time. Instead, the trade-offs between vulnerability and functionality must be understood, and appropriate responses to attacks must be defined. Usually these responses involve making the systems do less in order to make them less vulnerable: fewer authorised users, less software running, and less communication between systems. For example, software architects might design a system so that operators could close off certain routes of access to it when under attack, thereby losing the useful functionality associated with those routes but preserving critical functions that do not need those routes.

## Architectural Design

There are often tensions between security and other good things, such as features, ease of use, and interoperability. For example, if users have different passwords for different systems, it is harder for an unauthorised party to gain access to all of those systems, but users must bear the burden of remembering multiple passwords. Because the benefits of successful security can be seen only in events that usually do not happen, resources devoted to security are "wasted" in the same sense that resources devoted to insurance are "wasted." In both cases, the system user (or the insured party) does not gain additional functionality as the result of its expenditures. But that does not make investments in security worthless—rather, it changes the terms on which such investments should be evaluated, which include the value of being able to continue operation in the face of hostile attacks (and often natural or accidental disruptions as well).

Human error is usually not a useful explanation for security problems. Usually either operational or management practice is at fault: operational practice that requires people to get too many details right or that does too little red-team testing, and management practice that allows too little time for security procedures or fails to ensure that problems uncovered by testing are fixed.

While cryptography is not a magic bullet for security problems, it does play key roles in system and network security. Cryptography has three primary uses: authentication, integrity checks, and confidentiality. Cryptographic authentication is an important aspect of security techniques that deny access or system privileges to unauthorised users. Cryptographic integrity checks ensure that data cannot be modified without revealing the fact of modification. Cryptographic confidentiality can be used to keep unauthorised parties from reading data stored in systems and sent over networks. Of course, adversaries can also use cryptography, to the detriment of certain national security and law enforcement purposes, but its widespread use can promote and enhance crime prevention and national security efforts as well.

User authentication is essential for access control and for auditing. The most common method used today to authenticate users is passwords, which are known to be insecure compared with other authentication methods. A hardware token (e.g., smart card), supplemented by a personal identification number or biometrics (assuming good implementation), is much better. The user doesn't have to keep track of passwords, and a lost token is physically obvious and cannot be broadcast to a myriad of unauthorised parties.

A common approach to network security is to surround an insecure network with a defensive perimeter that controls access to the network. Once past the perimeter, a user is left unconstrained. A perimeter defence is good as part of a defence in depth, especially because the security burden is placed primarily on those who manage the perimeter rather than those who manage systems inside the perimeter. However, it is entirely vulnerable if a hostile party gains access to a system inside the perimeter or compromises a single authorised user. Another approach to network security is mutual suspicion:

Every system within a critical network regards every other system as a potential source of threat. Thus, a hostile party who gains access to one system does not automatically gain access to the whole network. Mutual suspicion can provide significantly higher levels of security, but it requires all system operators to pay attention to security rather than just those at the network perimeter. Perimeter defence and mutual suspicion can be used together to increase network security.

**Role of Individual Organisations**

Individual organisations should:

— Establish and provide adequate resources to an internal entity with responsibility for providing direct defensive operational support to system administrators throughout the organisation.

— Ensure that adequate information security tools are available, that everyone is properly trained in their use, and that enough time is available to use them properly. Then hold all personnel accountable for their information system security practices.

— Conduct frequent, unannounced red-team penetration testing of deployed systems and report the results to responsible management.

— Promptly fix problems and vulnerabilities that are known or that are discovered to exist.

— Mandate the organisation-wide use of currently available network/configuration management tools, and demand better tools from vendors.

— Mandate the use of strong authentication mechanisms to protect sensitive or critical information and systems.

— Use defence in depth. In particular, design systems under the assumption that they will be connected to a compromised network or a network that is under attack, and practice operating these systems under this assumption.

— Define a fallback plan for more secure operation when under attack and rehearse it regularly. Complement that plan with a disaster recovery programme.

**Vendors of Computer Systems**

Vendors of computer systems should:

— Drastically improve the user interface to security, which is totally incomprehensible in nearly all of today's systems. Users and administrators must be able to easily see the current security state of their systems; this means that the state must be expressible in simple terms.

— Develop tools to monitor systems automatically for consistency with defined secure configurations, and enforce these configurations. Extensive automation is essential to reduce the amount of human labor that goes into security. The tools must promptly and automatically respond to changes that result from new attacks.

— Provide well-engineered schemes for user authentication based on hardware tokens. These systems should be both more secure and more convenient for users than are current password systems.

— Develop a few simple and clear blueprints for secure operation that users can follow, since most organisations lack the expertise to do this properly on their own. For example, systems should be shipped with security features turned on, so that a conscious effort is needed to disable them, and with default identifications and passwords turned off, so that a conscious effort is needed to select them.

— Strengthen software development processes and conduct more rigorous testing of software and systems for security flaws, doing so before releasing products rather than use customers as implicit beta testers to shake out security flaws. Changing this mind-set is one necessary element of an improved cybersecurity posture.

**Policy Makers**

Policy makers should:

— Consider legislative responses to the failure of existing incentives to cause the market to respond adequately to the security challenge. Possible options include steps that would increase the exposure of software and system vendors and system operators to liability for system breaches and mandated reporting of security breaches that could threaten critical societal functions.

— Position the federal government as a leader in technology use and practice by requiring agencies to adhere to the practices recommended above and to report on their progress in implementing those measures.

Such a step would also help to grow the market for security technology, training, and other services.

— Provide adequate support for research and development on information systems security. Research and development on information systems security should be construed broadly to include R&D on defensive technology (including both underlying technologies and architectural issues), organisational and sociological dimensions of such security, forensic and recovery tools, and best policies and practices. Given the failure of the market to address security challenges adequately, government support for such research is especially important.

## Causes of Network Problems

It is useful to distinguish between accidental causes and deliberate causes. In general, accidental causes are natural (e.g., a lightning surge that destroys a power supply in a network that causes part of the network to fail) or human but nondeliberate (e.g., an accidental programming error that causes a computer to crash under certain circumstances, or the unintended cutting of a communications cable during excavation). Accidental causes figure prominently in many aspects of trustworthiness beside security, such as safety or reliability.

Deliberate problems are the result of conscious human choice. In the context of seeking to understand the laws of physics, Einstein once said that while nature may be subtle, it is not malicious. But in dealing with deliberate problems, one is faced with malicious intent. A malicious human may seek to hide his or her tracks, making it difficult to identify the nature of the problem caused (or even to identify that a problem has been caused). A malicious human can, in principle, tailor actions to produce a desired effect beyond the damage to the actual system attacked—unlike an accidental problem whose effects are randomly determined.

Security experts often refer to the efforts of these malicious people as "attacks." A central challenge in responding to an information system attack is identifying who the attacker is and distinguishing whether the motive is mischief, terrorism, or attack on the nation. A related challenge is determining whether events that are distant in time or space are related—parts of a given attack. Note also that an attacker—who seeks to cause damage deliberately—may be able to exploit a flaw accidentally introduced into a system. System design and/or implementation that is poor by accident can result in serious security problems that can be deliberately targeted in a penetration attempt by an attacker.

There are many ways to cause problems deliberately. One way—which receives a great deal of attention in the media—is through an attack that arrives "through the wires." The Internet makes it possible to mount such an attack remotely, anonymously, and on a large scale. One example of such "cyber-only" attacks are computer viruses that infect a user's computer, take some destructive action such as deleting files on the network or local hard drive, and propagate themselves further, such as by e-mailing copies of themselves.

The damage that a cyber-only attack causes may not be immediately (or ever) apparent. A successful attack may lay a foundation for later attacks, be set to cause damage well after the initial penetration, or enable the clandestine transmission of sensitive information stored on the attacked system. For example, a number of recent incidents have compromised the computers of unsuspecting home computer users by implanting unauthorised code; these computers were subsequently used as launch points in a coordinated and distributed denial-of-service attack.

Finally, the fact that the Internet connects many of the world's computers implies that a cyber-only attack can be launched from locations around the world, routed through other countries (perhaps clandestinely and unknown to anyone in those other countries), and directed against any U.S. computer on the Internet. The availability of a plethora of launch points and routes for cyberattack greatly complicates the ability to stop an attack before it reaches the security barriers of the U.S. computers in question, as well as to identify its source. The Internet's various intentional or inadvertent links to other communications networks make them potentially vulnerable to worldwide attacks as well.

A cyber-only attack is only one way to cause problems in a computer system or network. Other ways include the following:

— The compromise of a trusted insider who can provide system or network access to outsiders or use his or her access for improper purposes (e.g., providing passwords that permit outsiders to gain entry). This trusted insider may be recruited covertly by hostile parties, planted well in advance of any action associated with an actual attack (the so-called "sleeper" problem), or tricked into taking some action that breaches system security (e.g., tricked into disclosing a password or installing software that permits access by malicious outsiders).

— Physical destruction of some key element of the system or network, such as critical data centers or communications links. Examples of physical vulnerabilities are various backhoe incidents in which accidental cutting of fiber-optic cables (both primary and backup!) resulted in major network outages, and the severe damage to a Verizon central office in the World Trade Center attack on September 11, 2001.

It is useful to distinguish between three important concepts of cybersecurity. A vulnerability is an error or a weakness in the design, implementation, or operation of a system. A threat is an adversary that is motivated to exploit a system vulnerability and is capable of doing so. Risk refers to the likelihood that a vulnerability will be exploited, or that a threat may become harmful. In this lexicon, a system that allows computer viruses to replicate or unauthorised users to gain access exhibits vulnerabilities. The creator of the virus or the unauthorised user is the threat to the system. Operating a system with known vulnerabilities in the presence of possible threats entails some risk that harm or damage will result.

## Cybersecurity from Breashes

How do potential cyberdisasters compare with disasters in the physical world? As the catastrophic events of September 11, 2001, demonstrate, disasters in the physical world can involve massive loss of life and damage to physical infrastructure over a very short period of time. The damage from most cyberattacks is unlikely to be manifested in such a manner—although interference with medical information systems and devices could affect lives. If undertaken by themselves, cyberattacks could compromise systems and networks in ways that could render communications and electric power distribution difficult or impossible, disrupt transportation and shipping, disable financial transactions, and result in the theft of large amounts of money.

Economic and associated social harm is a likely consequence of a large-scale cyberattack that is successful. That harm would involve at least opportunity costs—interruption of business, forgoing of various activities and associated benefits, and so on. While such results would qualify on any scale as disastrous, additional harm can come from the interactions of cyber- and physical systems under attack that endanger human life directly and affect physical safety and well-being. In particular, a large-scale coordinated cyberattack could occur at the same time as an attack on the physical infrastructure.

For example, a successful cyberattack launched on the air traffic control system in coordination with airliner hijackings could result in a much more catastrophic disaster scenario than was seen on September 11, 2001. Or compromising communications channels during a physical attack of that magnitude could prevent government officials from responding to the attack, coordinating emergency response efforts, or even knowing whether the attack was still ongoing.

In the United States, information system vulnerabilities, from the standpoint of both operations and technology, are growing faster than the country's ability (and willingness) to respond. Security is expensive, not only in dollars but especially in interference with daily work. It has no value when there is no attack (or natural/accidental disruption in the system environment). Consequently, people tend to use as little of it as they think they can get away with. Exhortations to be more careful may work for a short time, but operational security can be maintained only by systematic and independently conducted "red team" attacks and correction of the defects that they reveal.

Moreover, there are no widely accepted metrics for characterising security, so it is difficult for a decision maker to know how much security a certain investment buys or whether that investment is enough. The overall security of a system is only as strong as its weakest link. System security is a holistic problem, in which technological, managerial, organisational, regulatory, economic, and social aspects interact. Weaknesses in any of these aspects can be very damaging, since competent attackers seek out weak points in the security of a network or system.

The best is the enemy of the good. Risk management is an essential element of any realistic strategy for dealing with security issues. Experience has demonstrated—sadly—that the quest for perfection is the enemy of concrete, actionable steps that can provide improved but not perfect security. It is true that given enough time and effort, almost any security system can be breached. But that does not diminish the value of steps that can increase the difficulty of breaching security.

Security is a game of action and reaction. When old vulnerabilities are corrected, attackers look for new paths of attack. On the other hand, it takes time to find those new paths, and during that time the system is more secure. Systems have many potential points of vulnerability, and an attacker is free to choose any one of them. For example, as antivirus software came to protect against conventional viruses, virus writers exploited a new channel—the macro capabilities of word processors—that was never intended to provide the capability for implementing viruses. Thus, security must be approached on a system level rather than on a piecemeal basis.

Because cyberattacks can be conducted without leaving publicly visible evidence (unlike, for example, a plane crash), it is easy to cover them up. Reporting of attempts, successful and unsuccessful, to breach security—the where, when, and how of attacks—is essential both for forensics (to determine who is responsible and whether incidents in different places are part of the same attack) and for prevention (to defend against future attacks). Researchers, developers, and operators need this information to redesign systems and procedures to avoid future incidents, and national security and law enforcement agencies need it to defend the nation as a whole.

Organisations that are attacked prefer to conceal attacks, because publicity may undermine public confidence, disclose adverse information, and make managers look bad. Weighing these costs and benefits should be a public policy issue, but so far the commercial and face-saving concerns of targets have dominated, and there is no effective reporting. The airline industry might be a good model to copy (in the sense that both accidents and near-misses are reported), and the information-sharing problem is being explored in the context of critical infrastructure protection, a perspective that emerged in the late 1990s.

## Safe Computing in the Information Age

Security refers to protection against unwanted disclosure, modification, or destruction of data in a system and also to the safeguarding of systems themselves. Security, safety, and reliability together are elements of system trustworthiness—which inspires the confidence that a system will do what it is expected to do. Organisations and people that use computers can describe their needs for information security and trust in systems in terms of three major requirements:

— *Confidentiality*: controlling who gets to read information;

— *Integrity*: assuring that information and programmes are changed only in a specified and authorised manner; and

— *Availability*: assuring that authorised users have continued access to information and resources.

These three requirements may be emphasised differently in various applications. For a national defence system, the chief concern may be ensuring the confidentiality of classified information, whereas a funds transfer system may require strong integrity controls. The requirements for applications that are connected to external systems will differ from those for applications without such interconnection. Thus the specific requirements and controls for information security can vary.

The framework within which an organisation strives to meet its needs for information security is codified as security policy. A security policy is a concise statement, by those responsible for a system (e.g., senior management), of information values, protection responsibilities, and organisational commitment. One can implement that policy by taking specific actions guided by management control principles and utilising specific security standards, procedures, and mechanisms. Conversely, the selection of standards, procedures, and mechanisms should be guided by policy to be most effective.

To be useful, a security policy must not only state the security need (e.g., for confidentiality—that data shall be disclosed only to authorised individuals), but also address the range of circumstances under which that need must be met and the associated operating standards. Without this second part, a security policy is so general as to be useless (although the second part may be realised through procedures and standards set to implement the policy). In any particular circumstance, some threats are more probable than others, and a prudent policy setter must assess the threats, assign a level of concern to each, and state a policy in terms of which threats are to be resisted.

For example, until recently most policies for security did not require that security needs be met in the face of a virus attack, because that form of attack was uncommon and not widely understood. As viruses have escalated from a hypothetical to a commonplace threat, it has become necessary to rethink such policies in regard to methods of distribution and acquisition of software. Implicit in this process is management's choice of a level of residual risk that it will live with, a level that varies among organisations.

## Vulnerability, Threat, and Countermeasures

The field of security has its own language and mode of thought, which focus on the processes of attack and on preventing, detecting, and recovering from attacks. In practice, similar thinking is accorded to the possibility of accidents that, like attacks, could result in disclosure, modification, or destruction of information or systems or a delay in system use. Security is traditionally discussed in terms of vulnerabilities, threats, and countermeasures. A vulnerability is an aspect of some system that leaves it open to attack. A threat is a hostile party with the potential to exploit that vulnerability and cause damage.

A countermeasure or safeguard is an added step or improved design that eliminates the vulnerability and renders the threat impotent. A safe containing valuables, for example, may have a noisy combination lock—a vulnerability—whose clicking can be recorded and analysed to recover the combination. It is surmised that safe-crackers can make contact with experts in illegal eavesdropping—a threat. A policy is therefore instituted that recordings of random clicking must be played at loud volume when the safe is opened—a countermeasure.

Threats and countermeasures interact in intricate and often counterintuitive ways: a threat leads to a countermeasure, and the countermeasure spawns a new threat. Few countermeasures are so effective that they actually eliminate a threat. New means of attack are devised (e.g., computerised signal processing to separate "live" clicks from recorded ones), and the result is a more sophisticated threat.

## Asymmetry Between Offence and Defence

The interaction of threat and countermeasure poses distinctive problems for security specialists: the attacker must find but one of possibly multiple vulnerabilities in order to succeed; the security specialist must develop countermeasures for all. The advantage is therefore heavily to the attacker until very late in the mutual evolution of threat and countermeasure. If one waits until a threat is manifest through a successful attack, then significant damage can be done before an effective countermeasure can be developed and deployed.

Therefore countermeasure engineering must be based on speculation. Effort may be expended in countering attacks that are never attempted. The need to speculate and to budget resources for countermeasures also implies a need to understand what it is that should be protected, and why; such understanding should drive the choice of a protection strategy and countermeasures. This thinking should be captured in security policies generated by management; poor security often reflects both weak policy and inadequate forethought.

Confidence in countermeasures is generally achieved by submitting them for evaluation by an independent team; this process increases the lead times and costs of producing secure systems. The existence of a successful attack can be demonstrated by an experiment, but the adequacy of a set of countermeasures cannot. Security specialists must resort to analysis, yet mathematical proofs in the face of constantly changing systems are impossible.

In practice, the effectiveness of a countermeasure often depends on how it is used; the best safe in the world is worthless if no one remembers to close the door. The possibility of legitimate users being hoodwinked into doing what an attacker cannot do for himself cautions against placing too much faith in purely technological countermeasures. The evolution of countermeasures is a dynamic process. Security requires ongoing attention and planning, because yesterday's safeguards may not be effective tomorrow, or even today.

**Network Vulnerabilities**

Interconnection gives an almost ecological flavour to security; it creates dependencies that can harm as well as benefit the community of those who are interconnected. An analogy can be made to pollution: the pollution generated as a by-product of legitimate activity causes damage external to the polluter. A recognised public interest in eliminating the damage may compel the installation of pollution control equipment for the benefit of the community, although the installation may not be justified by the narrow self-interest of the polluter. Just as average citizens have only a limited technical understanding of their vulnerability to pollution, so also individuals and organisations today have little understanding of the extent to which their computer systems are put at risk by those systems to which they are connected, or vice versa. The public interest in the safety of networks may require some assurances about the quality of security as a prerequisite for some kinds of network connection.

The threats to U.S. computer systems are international, and sometimes also political. The international nature of military and intelligence threats has always been recognised and addressed by the U.S. government. But a broader international threat to U.S. information resources is emerging with the proliferation of international computer networking—involving systems for researchers, companies, and other organisations and individuals—and a shift from conventional military conflict to economic competition. The concentration of information and economic activity in computer systems makes those systems an attractive target to hostile entities. This prospect raises questions about the intersection of economic and national security interests and the design of appropriate security strategies for the public and private sectors. Finally, politically motivated attacks may also target a new class of system that is neither commercial nor military: computerised voting systems.

**Influences of Market**

Even the best product will not be sold if the consumer does not see a need for it. Consumer awareness and willingness to pay are limited because people simply do not know enough about the likelihood or the consequences of attacks on computer systems or about more benign factors that can result in system failure or compromise. Consumer appreciation of system quality focuses on features that affect normal operations—speed, ease of use, functionality, and so on. This situation feeds a market for inappropriate or incomplete security solutions, such as antiviral software that is effective only against certain viruses but may be believed to provide broader protection, or password identification systems that are easily subverted in ordinary use.

Enhancing security requires changes in attitudes and behaviour that are difficult because most people consider computer security to be abstract and concerned more with hypothetical rather than likely events. Very few individuals not professionally concerned with security, from top management through the lowest-level employee, have ever been directly involved in or affected by a computer security incident. Such incidents are reported infrequently, and then often in specialised media, and they are comprehensible only in broadest outline. Further, most people have difficulty relating to the intricacies of malicious computer actions. Yet it is understood that installing computer security safeguards has negative aspects such as added cost, diminished performance (e.g., slower response times), inconvenience in use, and the awkwardness of monitoring and enforcement, not to mention objections from the work force to any of the above. The Internet worm experience showed that even individuals and organisations that understand the threats may not act to protect against them.

**Nontechnical Dimensions**

Computer security does not stop or start at the computer. It is not a single feature, like memory size, nor can it be guaranteed by a single feature or even a set of features. It comprises at a minimum computer hardware, software, networks, and other equipment to which the computers are connected, facilities in which the computer is housed, and persons who use or otherwise come into contact with the computer. Serious security exposures may result from any weak technical or human link in the entire complex. For this reason, security is only partly a technical problem: it has significant procedural, administrative, physical facility, and personnel components as well.

Technical measures alone cannot prevent violations of the trust people place in individuals, violations that have been the source of much of the computer security problem in industry to date . . . . Technical measures may prevent people from doing unauthorised things but cannot prevent them from doing things that their job functions entitle them to do. Thus, to prevent violations of trust rather than just repair the damage that results, one must depend primarily on human awareness of what other human beings in an organisation are doing.

But even a technically sound system with informed and watchful management and users cannot be free of all possible vulnerabilities. The residual risk must be managed by auditing, backup, and recovery procedures supported by general alertness and creative responses. Moreover, an organisation must have administrative procedures in place to bring peculiar actions to the attention of someone who can legitimately inquire into the appropriateness of such actions, and that person must actually make the inquiry. In many organisations, these administrative provisions are far less satisfactory than are the technical provisions for security.

It is important to balance technical and nontechnical approaches to enhancing system security and trust. Accordingly, the committee is concerned that the development of legislation and case law is being outpaced by the growth of technology and changes in our society. In particular, although law can be used to encourage good practice, it is difficult to match law to the circumstances of computer system use. Nevertheless, attacks on computer and communication systems are coming to be seen as punishable and often criminal acts . . . within countries, and there is a movement toward international coordination of investigation and prosecution. However, there is by no means a consensus about what uses of computers are legitimate and socially acceptable. Free speech questions have been raised in connection with recent criminal investigations into dissemination of certain computer-related information. There are also controversies surrounding the privacy impacts of new and proposed computer systems, including some proposed security safeguards.

## Potential of C4I

In US, C4I is a Department of Defence (DOD) acronym for command, control, communications, computers, and intelligence. While many of the information systems described in Realising the Potential of C4I: Fundamental Challenges are owned or operated by the Department of Defence, essentially all of the implications and lessons for DOD systems are valid for non-DOD government systems, and for systems in the private sector. Furthermore, the description of DOD practices in the field should not be taken as an exoneration of practices in non-DOD systems--indeed, it is highly likely that the same observations would apply to most such systems.

### *Functions of Effective Information Security*

Effective information systems security is based on a number of functions described below. This list of functions is not complete; nevertheless, evidence that all these functions are being performed in an effective and coordinated fashion will be evidence that information systems security is being taken seriously and conducted effectively. Some of these functions were also noted in the military context by the Defence Science Board, and some by the President's Commission on Critical Infrastructure Protection in its report. These functions are listed here because they are important, and because the committee believes that they have not yet been addressed by the DOD in an effective fashion.

*Function 1. Collect, analyse, and disseminate strategic intelligence about threats to systems.*

Any good defence attempts to learn as much as possible about the threats that it may face, both the tools that an adversary may use and the identity and motivations of likely attackers. In the information systems security world, it is difficult to collect information about attackers (though such intelligence information should be sought). It is, however, much easier to collect and analyse information on technical and procedural vulnerabilities, to characterise both the nature of these vulnerabilities and their frequency at different installations. Dissemination of information about these vulnerabilities enables administrators of the information systems that may be affected to take remedial action.

*Function 2. Monitor indications and warnings*

All defences—physical and cyber—rely to some extent on indications and warning of impending attack. The reason is that if it is known that attack is impending, the defence can take actions to reduce its vulnerability and to increase the effectiveness of its response. This function calls for:

— Monitoring of threat indicators. For example, near-simultaneous penetration attempts on hundreds of military information systems might reasonably be considered an indication of an orchestrated attack. Mobilisation of a foreign nation's key personnel known to have responsibility for information attacks might be another indicator. The notion of an "information condition" or "INFOCON," analogous to the defence condition (DEFCON) indicator, would be a useful summary device to indicate to commanders the state of the cyber-threat at any given time. This concept is being developed by various DOD elements but is yet immature.

— Assessment and characterisation of the information attack (if any). Knowledge of the techniques used in an attack on one information system may facilitate a judgment of the seriousness of the attack. For example, an attack that involves techniques that are not widely known may indicate that the perpetrators have a high degree of technical sophistication.

— Dissemination of information about the target(s) of threat. Knowledge of the techniques used in an attack on one information system may enable administrators responsible for other systems to take preventive actions tailored to that type of attack. This is true even if the first attack is unsuccessful, because security features that may have thwarted the first attack may not necessarily be installed or operational on other systems.

Note that dissemination of information about attacks and their targets is required on two distinct time scales. The first time scale is seconds or minutes after the attack is known; such knowledge enables operators of other systems not (yet) under attack to take immediate preventive action (such as severing some network connections). In this instance, alternative means of secure communication may be necessary to disseminate such information. The second time scale is days after the attack is understood; such knowledge allows operators throughout the entire system of systems to implement fixes and patches that they may not yet have fixed, and to request fixes that are needed but not yet developed.

*Function 3. Be able to identify intruders*

Electronic intruders into a system are admittedly hard to identify. Attacks are conducted remotely, and a chain of linkages from the attacker's system to an intermediate node to another and another to the attacked system can easily obscure the identity of the intruder. Nevertheless, certain types of information—if collected—may shed some light on the intruder's identity. For example, some attackers may preferentially use certain tools or techniques (e.g., the same dictionary to test for passwords), or use certain sites to gain access. Attacks that go on over an extended period of time may provide further opportunities to trace the origin of the attack.

*Function 4. Test for security weaknesses in fielded and operational systems.*

An essential part of a security program is searching for technical and operational or procedural vulnerabilities. Ongoing tests (conducted by groups often known as "red teams" or "tiger teams") are essential for several reasons:

— Recognised vulnerabilities are not always corrected, and known fixes are frequently found not to have been applied as a result of poor configuration management.

— Security features are often turned off in an effort to improve operational efficiency. Such actions may improve operational efficiency, but at the potentially high cost of compromising security, sometimes with the primary damage occurring in some distant part of the system.

— Some security measures rely on procedural measures and thus depend on proper training and ongoing vigilance on the part of commanders and system managers.

— Security flaws that are not apparent to the defender undergoing an inspection may be uncovered by a committed attacker (as they would be uncovered in an actual attack).

Thus, it is essential to use available tools and conduct red team or tiger team probes often and without warning to test security defences. In order to maximise the impact of these tests, reports should be disseminated widely. Release of such information may risk embarrassment of certain parties or possible release of information that can be used by adversaries to attack, but especially in the case of vulnerabilities uncovered for which fixes are available, the benefits of releasing such information—allowing others to learn from it and motivating fixes to be installed—outweigh these costs.

Tiger team attacks launched without the knowledge of the attacked systems also allow estimates to be made of the frequency of attacks. Specifically, the fraction of tiger team attacks that are detected is a reasonable estimate of the fraction of adversary attacks that are made. Thus, the frequency of adversary attacks can be estimated from the number of adversary attacks that are detected.

*Function 5. Plan a range of responses*

Any organisation relying on information systems should have a number of routine information systems security activities (e.g., security features that are turned on, security procedures that are followed). But when attack is imminent (or in process), an organisation could prudently adopt additional security measures that during times of non-attack might not be in effect because of their negative impact on operations. Tailoring in advance a range of information systems security actions to be taken under different threat conditions would help an organisation plan its response to any given attack.

For example, a common response under attack is to drop non-essential functions from a system connected to the network so as to reduce the number of routes for penetration. A determination in advance of what functions count as non-essential and under what circumstances such a determination is valid would help facilitate an orderly transition to different threat conditions, and would be much better than an approach that calls for dropping all functionality and restoring only those functions that people using the system at the time complain about losing. Note that such determinations can be made only from an operational perspective rather than a technical one, a fact that points to the essential need for an operational architecture in the design of C4I systems.

The principle underlying response planning should be that of "graceful degradation"; that is, the system or network should lose functionality gradually, as a function of the severity of the attack compared to its ability to defend against it. This principle stands in contrast to a different principle that might call for the maintenance of all functionality until the attack simply overwhelms the defence and the system or network collapses. The latter principle is tempting because reductions in functionality necessitated for security reasons may interfere with operational ease of use, but its adoption risks catastrophic failure.

It is particularly important to note that designing a system for graceful degradation depends on system architects who take into account the needs of security (and more generally, the needs of coping with possible component failures) from the start. For example, the principle of graceful degradation would forbid a system whose continued operation depended entirely on a single component remaining functional, or on the absence of a security threat. This principle is often violated in the development of prototypes. It is often said that "it is necessary for one to crawl before one can run," i.e., that it is acceptable to ignore security or reliability considerations when one is attempting to demonstrate the feasibility of a particular concept. This argument is superficially plausible, but in practice it does not hold water.

It is reasonable for a prototype to focus only on concept feasibility, ignoring considerations of reliability or security, only if the prototype will be thrown away and a new architecture is designed and developed from scratch to implement the concept. Budget and schedule constraints usually prevent such new beginnings, and so in practice the prototype's architecture is never abandoned, and security or reliability considerations must be addressed in the face of an architecture that was never designed or intended to support them.

*Function 6. Coordinate defensive activities throughout the enterprise*

Any large, distributed organisation has many information systems and subnetworks that must be defended. The activities taken to defend each of these systems and networks must be coordinated because the distributed parts have interconnections and the security of the whole organisation depends on the weakest link. Furthermore, it is important for different parts of organisations to be able to learn from each other about vulnerabilities, threats, and effective countermeasures.

*Function 7. Ensure the adequacy, availability, and functioning of public infrastructure used in systems*

Few networks are built entirely using systems controlled by the organisation that relies on them. Therefore organisations (including DOD) are required to work cooperatively with the owners of the infrastructure they rely on and relevant authorities to protect them.

*Function 8. Include security requirements in any specification of system or network requirements that is used in the acquisition process.*

Providing information systems security for a network or system that has not had security features built into it is enormously problematic. Retrofits of security features into systems not designed for security invariably leave security holes, and procedural fixes for inherent technical vulnerabilities only go so far. Perhaps more importantly, security requirements must be given prominence from the beginning in any system conceptualisation. The reason is that security considerations may affect the design of a system in quite fundamental ways, and a designer who decides on a design that works against security should at least be cognisant of the implications of such a choice. This function thus calls for information systems security expertise to be integrally represented on design teams, rather than added later.

*Function 9. Monitor, assess, and understand offensive and defensive information technologies.*

Good information systems security requires an understanding of the types of threats and defences that might be relevant. Thus, those responsible for information systems security need a vigorous ongoing program to monitor, assess, and understand offensive and defensive information technologies. Such a program would address the technical details of these technologies, their capability to threaten or protect friendly systems, and their availability.

*Function 10. Advance the state of the art in defensive information technology (and processes) with research.*

Although much can usually be done to improve information systems security simply through the use of known and available technologies, "bug fixes," and procedures, better tools to support the information systems security mission are always needed. In general, such improvements fall into two classes (which may overlap). One class consists of improvements so that tools can deal more effectively with a broader threat spectrum. A second class, equally important, provides tools that provide better automation and thus can solve problems at lower costs (costs that include direct outlays for personnel and equipment and operational burdens resulting from the hassle imposed by providing security). Similar considerations apply to processes for security as well. It is reasonable to conduct organisational research into better processes and organisations that provide more effective support against information attacks and/or reduce the impediments to using or implementing good security practices.

*Function 11. Promote information systems security awareness*

Just as it is dangerous to rely on a defensive system or network architecture that is hard on the outside and soft on the inside, it is also dangerous if any member of an organisation fails to take information systems security seriously. Because the carelessness of a single individual can seriously compromise the security of an entire organisation, education and training for information systems security must be required for all members of the organisation. Moreover, such education and training must be systematic, regarded as important by the organisation (and demonstrated with proper support for such education and training), and undertaken on a regular basis (both to remind people of its importance and to update their knowledge in light of new developments in the area).

*Function 12. Set security standards (both technical and procedural).*

Security standards should articulate in well-defined and actionable terms what an organisation expects to do in the area of security. They are therefore prescriptive. For example, a technical standard might be "all passwords must be eight or more characters long, contain both letters and numbers, be pronounceable, and not be contained in any dictionary," or "all electronic communications containing classified information must be encrypted with a certain algorithm and key length." A standard involving both technical and procedural measures might specify how to revoke cryptographic keys known to have been compromised. Furthermore, security standards should be expected to apply to all those within the organisation.

*Function 13. Develop and use criteria for assessing security status.*

Information security is not a one-shot problem, but a continuing one. Threats, technology, and organisations are constantly changing in a spiral of measures and countermeasures. Organisations must have ways of measuring and evaluating whether they have effective defensive measures in place. Thus, once standards are put in place, the organisation must periodically assess the extent to which members of the organisation comply with those standards, and characterise the nature of the compliance that does exist.

Metrics for security could include number of attacks of different types, fraction of attacks detected, fraction of attacks repelled, damage incurred, and time needed to detect and respond to attacks. Note that making measurements on such parameters depends on understanding the attacks that do occur--because many attacks are not detected today, continual penetration testing is required to establish such a baseline.

The security in today's fielded military systems is weak, and weaker than it need be, as illustrated by the following examples of behaviour and practices that the committee observed or heard:

— Individual nodes are running commercial software with many known security problems. Operators use little in the way of tools for finding these problems, to say nothing of fixing them.

— Computers attached to sensitive command and control systems are also used by personnel to surf Web sites worldwide, raising the possibility that rogue applets and the like could be introduced into the system.

— Units are being blinded by denial-of-service attacks, made possible because individual nodes were running commercial software with many known security problems.

— IP addresses and other important data about C2 [command and control] systems can be found on POST-IT notes attached to computers in unsecured areas, making denial of service and other attacks much easier.

— Some of the networks used by DOD to carry classified information are protected by a perimeter defence. As a result, they exhibit all of the vulnerabilities that characterise networks protected by perimeter defences.

Many field commanders told the committee that "cyberspace is part of the battlespace," and several organisations within the DOD assert that they are training "C2/cyber warriors." But good intentions have not been matched by serious attention to cyberspace protection. Soldiers in the field do not take the protection of their C4I systems nearly as seriously as they do other aspects of defence.

## Trustworthiness of Cyberspace

The trustworthiness of [a networked information system] encompasses correctness, reliability, security (conventionally including secrecy, confidentiality, integrity, and availability), privacy, safety, and survivability . . . . These dimensions are not independent, and care must be taken so that one is not obtained at the expense of another. For example, protection of confidentiality or integrity by denying all access trades one aspect of security—availability—for others. As another example, replication of components enhances reliability but may increase exposure to attack owing to the larger number of sites and the vulnerabilities implicit in the protocols to coordinate them. Integrating the diverse dimensions of trustworthiness and understanding how they interact are central challenges in building a trustworthy.

While catastrophic failure garners the most popular attention, there are many dimensions to trustworthiness and consequences may involve various subsets of them with varying degrees of severity. Understanding consequences is essential to forming baseline expectations of private action and what incentives may be effective for changing private action, but that understanding is often hampered by the difficulty of quantifying or otherwise specifying the costs and consequences associated with risks.

It is the nature of [a networked information system] that outages and disruptions of service in local areas may have very uneven consequences, even within the area of disruption. Failure of a single Internet service provider (ISP) may or may not affect transfer of information outside the area of disruption, depending on how the ISP has configured its communications. For example, caching practices intended to reduce network congestion problems helped to limit the scope of a Domain Name Service (DNS) outage. Corporations that manage their own interconnection (so-called intranets) may be wholly unaffected. Even widespread or catastrophic failures may not harm some users, if they have intentionally or unconsciously provided redundant storage or backup facilities. The inability to accurately predict consequences seriously complicates the process of calculating risk and makes it tempting to assume "best case" behaviour in response to failure.

Thus, risk mitigation is more typical and is generally encountered when many factors, including security and reliability, determine the success of a system. Risk mitigation is especially popular in market-driven environments where an attempt is made to provide "good enough" security or reliability or other qualities without severely affecting economic factors such as price and time to market. Risk mitigation should be interpreted not as a license to do a shoddy job in implementing trustworthiness, but instead as a pragmatic recognition that trade-offs between the dimensions of trustworthiness, economic realities, and other constraints will be the norm, not the exception. The risk mitigation strategies that are most relevant to trustworthiness can generally be characterised according to two similar models:

— *The insurance model.* In this model, the cost of countermeasures is viewed as an "insurance premium" paid to prevent (or at least mitigate) loss. The value of the information being protected, or the service being provided, is assessed and mechanisms and assurance steps are incorporated up to, but not exceeding, that value.

— *The work factor model.* A definition in cryptology for the term "work factor" is the amount of computation required to break a cipher through a brute-force search of all possible key values. Recently, the term has been broadened to mean the amount of effort required to locate and exploit a residual vulnerability. That effort may involve more efficient procedures rather than exhaustive searches. In the case of fault tolerance, the assumptions made about the types of failures (benign or arbitrary) that could arise are analogous to the concept of work factor.

The two models are subject to pitfalls distinctive to each and some that are common to both. In the insurance model, it is possible that the value of information (or disruption of service) to an outsider is substantially greater than the value of that information or service to its owners. Thus, a "high value" attack could be mounted, succeed, and the "insurance premium" lost along with the target data or service. Such circumstances often arise in an interconnected or networked world. For example, a local telephone switch might be protected against deliberate interruption of service to the degree that is justified by the revenue that might be lost from such an interruption. But such an analysis ignores the attacker whose aim is to prevent a physical alarm system from notifying the police that an intrusion has been detected into an area containing valuable items.

Another example is an instance in which a hacker expends great effort to take over an innocuous machine, not because it contains interesting data but because it provides computing resources and network connectivity that can be used to mount attacks on highervalue targets. In the case of the work factor model, it is notoriously difficult to assess the capabilities of a potential adversary in a field as unstructured as that of discovering vulnerabilities, which involves seeing aspects of a system that were overlooked by its designers.

## Vulnerabilities of the PTN and the Internet

The vulnerabilities of the PTN [public telephone network] and Internet are exacerbated by the dependence of each network on the other. Much of the Internet uses leased telephone lines as its physical transport medium. Conversely, telephone companies rely on networked computers to manage their own facilities, increasingly employing Internet technology, although not necessarily the Internet itself. Thus, vulnerabilities in the PTN can affect the Internet, and vulnerabilities in Internet technology can affect the telephone network.

Internet poses no new challenges—a system that can be accessed from outside only through a cryptographically protected channel on the Internet is at least as secure as the same system reached through a conventional leased line—new dangers arise precisely because of pervasive interconnectivity. The capability to interconnect networks gives the Internet much of its power; by the same token, it opens up serious new risks. An attacker who may be deflected by cryptographic protection of the front door can often attack a less protected administrative system and use its connectivity through internal networks to bypass the encryption unit protecting the real target. This often makes a mockery of firewall-based protection. The general accessibility of the Internet makes it a highly visible target and within easy reach of attackers. The widespread availability of documentation and actual implementations for Internet protocols means that devising attacks for this system can be viewed as an intellectual puzzle.

## Secure Systems and Networks

Laudable as a goal, ab initio building of trustworthiness into an NIS [networked information system] has proved to be impractical. It is neither technically nor economically feasible for designers and builders to manage the complexity of such large artifacts or to anticipate all of the problems that an NIS will confront over its lifetime. Experts now recognise steps that can be taken to enhance trustworthiness after a system has been deployed.

It is no accident that the market for virus detectors and firewalls is thriving. Virus detectors identify and eradicate attacks embedded in exchanged files, and firewalls hinder attacks by filtering messages between a trusted enclave of networked computers and its environment (from which attacks might originate). Both of these mechanisms work in specific contexts and address problems contemplated by their designers; but both are imperfect, with user expectations often exceeding what is prudent.

Networked information systems (NISs) integrate computing systems, communications systems, and people (both as users and operators). The defining elements are interfaces to other systems along with algorithms to coordinate those systems. Economics dictates the use of commercial off-the-shelf (COTS) components wherever possible, which means that developers of an NIS have neither control over nor detailed information about many system components. The use of system components whose functionality can be changed remotely and while the system is running is increasing. Users and designers of an NIS built from such extensible system components thus cannot know with any certainty what software has entered system components or what actions those components might take.

Today's climate of deregulation will further increase [networked information system] vulnerability in several ways. The most obvious is the new cost pressures on what had been regulated monopolies in the electric power and telecommunications industries. One easy way to cut costs is to reduce reserve capacity and eliminate rarely needed emergency systems; a related way is to reduce diversity (a potential contributor to trustworthiness) in the technology or facilities used. Producers in these sectors are now competing on the basis of features, too.

New features invariably lead to more complex systems, which are liable to behave in unexpected and undesirable ways. Finally, deregulation leads to new interconnections, as some services are more cost-effectively imported from other providers into what once were monolithic systems. Apart from the obvious dangers of the increased complexity, the interconnections themselves create new weak points and interdependencies. Problems could grow beyond the annoyance level that characterises infrastructure outages today, and the possibility of catastrophic incidents is growing.

To be labelled as trustworthy, a system not only must behave as expected but also must reinforce the belief that it will continue to produce expected behaviour and will not be susceptible to subversion. The question of how to achieve assurance has been the target of several research programs sponsored by the Department of Defence and others. Yet currently practiced and proposed approaches for establishing assurance are still imperfect and/ or impractical. Testing can demonstrate only that a flaw exists, not that all flaws have been found; deductive and analytical methods are practical only for certain small systems or specific properties.

Moreover, all existing assurance methods are predicated on an unrealistic assumption—that system designers and implementors know what it means for a system to be "correct" before and during development. Security research during the past few decades has been based on formal policy models that focus on protecting information from unauthorised access by specifying which users should have access to data or other system objects. It is time to challenge this paradigm of "absolute security" and move toward a model built on three axioms of insecurity:

— insecurity exists;

— insecurity cannot be destroyed; and

— insecurity can be moved around.

Improved trustworthiness may be achieved by the careful organisation of untrustworthy components. There are a number of promising ideas, but few have been vigorously pursued. "Trustworthiness from untrustworthy components" is a research area that deserves greater attention.

## Impact of Homogeneous System

The similarity intrinsic in the component systems of a homogeneous collection implies that these component systems share vulnerabilities. A successful attack on one system is then likely to succeed on other systems as well—the antithesis of what is desired for implementing trustworthiness. Moreover, today's dominant computing and communications environments are based on hardware and software that were not designed with security in mind; consequently, these systems are not difficult to compromise.

Technological convergence may also be realised through the market dominance of a few suppliers of key components, with monopoly as the limit case when technological homogeneity is dictated by the monopolist. However, the number of suppliers could grow as a result of the diffusion of computing into embedded, ubiquitous environments; the diversification and interoperability of communications services; and the continued integration of computing and communications into organisations within various market niches.

## Computer Program Security Flaws

Computer security flaws are any conditions or circumstances that can result in denial of service, unauthorised disclosure, unauthorised destruction of data, or unauthorised modification of data. Taxonomy of computer programme attempts to organise information about flaws so that, as new flaws are added, readers will gain a fuller understanding of which parts of systems and which parts of the system life cycle are generating more security flaws than others. This information should be useful not only to designers, but also to those faced with the difficult task of assessing the security of a system already built. To accurately assess the security of a computer system, an analyst must find its vulnerabilities. To do this, the analyst must understand the system thoroughly and recognise that computer security flaws that threaten system security may exist anywhere in the system.

There is a legitimate concern that this kind of information could assist those who would attack computer systems. This taxonomies are presently responsible for repelling attacks and correcting flaws. Their data, organised this way and abstracted, could be used to focus efforts to remove security flaws and prevent their introduction. Other taxonomies have recently been developed for organising data about software defects and anomalies of all kinds. These are primarily oriented toward collecting data during the software development process for the purpose of improving it. The security flaws that are detected only after the software has been released for operational use, while not incompatible with these efforts, reflects this perspective.

In fact, an inadvertently introduced security flaw in a programme is a bug. Generally, a security flaw is a part of a programme that can cause the system to violate its security requirements. Finding security flaws, then, demands some knowledge of system security requirements. Usually, they concern identification and authentication of users, authorisation of particular actions, and accountability for actions taken.

There are several kinds of security flaws. For example, if a system programmer inserts a Trojan horse1that exploits a covert channel to disclose sensitive information, both the Trojan horse and the co-vert channel are flaws in the operational system; the former will probably have been introduced maliciously, the latter inadvertently. Of course, any system that permits a user to invoke an uncertified programme is vulnerable to Trojan horses. Whether the fact that a system permits users to install programmes also represents a security flaw is an interesting question. The answer seems to depend on the context in which the question is asked. Permitting users of, say, an air traffic control system or, less threateningly, an airline reservation system, to install their own programmes seems intuitively unsafe; it is a flaw. On the other hand, preventing owners of PCs from installing their own programmes would seem ridiculously restrictive.

Different strategies can be used to avoid, detect, or compensate for accidental flaws as opposed to those intentionally inserted. For example, if most security flaws turn out to be accidentally introduced, increasing the resources devoted to code reviews and testing may be reasonably effective in reducing the number of flaws. But if most significant security flaws are introduced maliciously, these techniques are much less likely to help, and it may be more productive to take measures to hire more trustworthy programmers, devote more effort to penetration testing, and invest in virus detection packages.

Some features intentionally placed in programmes can at the same time inadvertently introduce security flaws (e.g., a feature that facilitates remote debugging or system maintenance may at the same time provide a trapdoor to a system). Where such cases can be distinguished, they are categorised as intentional but non-malicious. Although some malicious flaws could be disguised as inadvertent flaws, this distinction should be possible to make in practice-inadvertently created Trojan horse programmes are hardly likely! Inadvertent flaws in requirements or specifications ultimately manifest themselves in the implementation; flaws may also be introduced inadvertently during maintenance.Both malicious flaws and non-malicious flaws can be difficult to detect, the former because it has been intentionally hidden and the latter because residual flaws may be more likely to occur in rarely-invoked parts of the software. One may expect malicious code to attempt to cause significant damage to a system, but an inadvertent flaw that is exploited by a malicious intruder can be equally dangerous.

## Malicious Flaws

Malicious flaws have acquired colorful names, including Trojan horse, trapdoor, time-bomb, and logic-bomb. The term "Trojan horse" was introduced by Dan Edwards and recorded by James Anderson to characterise a particular computer security threat; it has been redefined many times. It generally refers to a programme that masquerades as a useful service but exploits rights of the programme's user-rights not possessed by the author of the Trojan horse-in a way the user does not intend.

Since the author of malicious code needs to disguise it somehow so that it will be invoked by a non-malicious user (unless the author means also to invoke the code, in which case he or she presumably already possesses the authorisation to perform the intended sabotage), almost any malicious code can be called a Trojan horse. A Trojan horse that replicates itself by copying its code into other programme files is commonly referred to as a virus One that replicates itself by creating new processes or files to contain its code, instead of modifying existing storage entities, is often called a worm.

A trapdoor is a hidden piece of code that responds to a special input, allowing its user access to resources without passing through the normal security enforcement mechanism. For example, a programmer of automated teller machines (ATMs) might be required to check a personal identification number (PIN) read from a card against the number keyed in by the user. If the numbers match, the user is to be permitted to enter transactions.

### Intentional, Non-Malicious Flaws

A Trojan horse programme may convey sensitive information to a penetrator over covert channels. A covert channel is simply a path used to transfer information in a way not intended by the system's designers. Since covert channels, by definition, are channels not placed there intentionally, they should perhaps appear in the category of inadvertent flaws.

Indeed, the most difficult ones to eliminate are those that arise in the fulfillment of essential system requirements. Unlike their creation, their exploitation is likely to be malicious. Exploitation of a covert channel usually involves a service programme, most likely a Trojan horse. This programme generally has access to confidential data and can encode that data for transmission over the covert channel. It also will contain a receiver programme that "listens" to the chosen covert channel and decodes the message for a penetrator. If the service programme could communicate confidential data directly to a penetrator without being monitored, of course, there would be no need for it to use a covert channel.

Covert channels are frequently classified as either storage or timing channels. A storage channel transfers information through the setting of bits by one programme and the reading of those bits by another. What distinguishes this case from that of ordinary operation is that the bits are used to convey encoded information. Examples would include using a file intended to hold only audit information to convey user passwords-using the name of a file or perhaps status bits associated with it that can be read by all users to signal the contents of the file.

Timing channels convey information by modulating some aspect of system behavior over time, so that the programme receiving the information can observe system behavior (e.g., the system's paging rate, the time a certain transaction requires to execute, the time it takes to gain access to a shared bus) and infer protected information. The distinction between storage and timing channels is not sharp. Exploitation of either kind of channel requires some degree of synchronisation between the sender and receiver. It also requires the ability to modulate the behavior of some shared resource.

In practice, covert channels are often distinguished on the basis of how they can be detected: those detectable by information flow analysis of specifications or code are considered storage channels. Other kinds of intentional but non-malicious security flaws are possible. Functional requirements that are written without regard to security requirements can lead to such flaws; one of the flaws exploited by the "Internet worm" could be placed in this category.

**Inadvertant Flaws**

Inadvertent flaws may occur in requirements; they may also find their way into software during specification and coding. Although many of these are detected and removed through testing, some flaws can remain undetected and later cause problems during operation and maintenance of the software system. For a software system composed of many modules and involving many programmers, flaws are often difficult to find and correct because module interfaces are inadequately documented and global variables are used. The lack of documentation is especially troublesome during maintenance when attempts to fix existing flaws often generate new flaws because maintainers lack understanding of the system as a whole. Although inadvertent flaws may not pose an immediate threat to the security of the system, the weakness resulting from a flaw may be exploited by an intruder.

There are many possible ways to organise flaws within this category. The taxonomy are primarily descriptive: the classification that provides a reasonable map of the terrain of computer programme security flaws, permitting us to group intuitively similar kinds of flaws and separate different ones. Providing secure operation of a computer often corresponds to building fences between different pieces of software (or different instantiations of the same piece of software), to building gates in those fences, and to building mechanisms to control and monitor traffic through the gates.

Inadvertent flaws can be classified as flaws related to:

— validation errors,
— domain errors,
— serialisation/aliasing errors,
— errors of inadequate identification/authentication,
— boundary condition errors, and
— other exploitable logic errors.

Validation flaws may be likened to a lazy gatekeeper-one who fails to check all the credentials of a traveler seeking to pass through a gate. They occur when a programme fails to check that the parameters supplied or returned to it conform to its assumptions about them, or when these checks are misplaced, so they are ineffectual. These assumptions may include the number of parameters provided, the type of each, the location or maximum length of a buffer, or the access permissions on a file.

Domain flaws, which correspond to holes in the fences, occur when the intended boundaries between protection environments are porous. For example, a user who creates a new file and discovers that it contains information from a file deleted by a different user has discovered a domain flaw.

A serialisation flaw permits the asynchronous behavior of different system components to be exploited to cause a security violation. In terms of the fences and gates metaphor, these reflect a forgetful gatekeeper-one who perhaps checks all credentials, but then gets distracted and forgets the result. These flaws can be particularly difficult to discover. A security-critical programme may appear to correctly validate all of its parameters, but the flaw permits the asynchronous behavior of another programme to change one of those parameters after it has been checked but before it is used. Many time-of-checkto-time-of-use (TOCTTOU) flaws will fall in this category, although some may be classed as validation errors if asynchrony is not involved.

An identification/authentication flaw is one that permits a protected operation to be invoked without sufficiently checking the identity and authority of the invoking agent. These flaws could perhaps be counted as validation flaws, since presumably some routine is failing to validate authorisations properly. However, a sufficiently large number of cases have occurred in which checking the identity and authority of the user initiating an operation has in fact been neglected to keep this as a separate category.

Boundary condition flaws typically reflect omission of checks to assure constraints (e.g., on table size, file allocation, or other resource consumption) are not exceeded. These flaws may lead to system crashes or degraded service, or they may cause unpredictable behavior. A gatekeeper who, when his queue becomes full, decides to lock the gate and go home, might represent this situation.

**Software Development Process**

Models of the system life cycle and the software development process have proliferated in recent years. Although iteration among the phases of software development is a recognised fact of life, the different phases still comprise distinguishable activities. Requirements are defined, specifications are developed based on new (or changed) requirements, source code is developed from specifications, and object code is generated from the source code. Even when iteration among phases is made explicit in software process models, these activities activities are recognised, separate categories of effort, so it seems appropriate to categorise flaws introduced during software development as originating in requirements and specifications, source code, or object code.

A major flaw in a requirement is not unusual in a large software system. If such a flaw affects security and its correction is not deemed cost-effective, the system and the flaw may remain. For example, an early multiprogramming operating system performed some I/O-related functions by having the supervisor programme execute code located in user memory while in supervisor state (i.e., with full system privileges). By the time this was recognised as a security flaw, its removal would have caused major incompatibilities with other software, and it was not fixed.

Requirements and specifications are relatively unlikely to contain maliciously introduced flaws. They are normally reviewed extensively, so a specification for a trapdoor or a Trojan horse would have to be well-disguised to avoid detection. More likely are flaws that arise because of competition between security requirements and other functional requirements. For example, security concerns might dictate that programmes never be modified at an operational site. But if the delay in repairing errors detected in system operation is perceived to be too great, there will be pressure to provide mechanisms in the specification to permit on-site reprogramming or testing. Such mechanisms can provide built-in security loopholes. Also possible are inadvertent flaws that arise because of missing requirements or undetected conflicts among requirements.

### Implementation of Source Code

The source code implements the design of the software system given by the specifications. Most flaws in source code, whether inadvertent or intentional, can be detected through a careful examination of it. Inadvertent flaws in source code are frequently a byproduct of inadequately defined module or process inter-faces. Programmers attempting to build a system to inadequate specifications are likely to misunderstand the meaning (if not the type) of parameters to be passed across an interface or the requirements for synchronising concurrent processes. These misunderstandings manifest themselves as source code flaws.

Intentional but non-malicious flaws can be introduced in source code for several reasons. A programmer may introduce mechanisms that are not included in the specification but that are intended to help in debugging and testing the normal operation of the code. However, if the test scaffolding circumvents security controls and is left in place in the operational system, it provides a security flaw. Efforts to be "efficient" can also lead to intentional but non-malicious source-code flaws, as in case DT1. Programmers may also decide to provide undocumented facilities that simplify maintenance but provide security loopholes-the inclusion of a “patch area” that facilitates reprogramming outside the scope of the configuration management system would fall in this category.

Technically sophisticated malicious flaws can be introduced at the source code level. A programmer working at the source code level, whether an authorised member of a development team or an intruder, can invoke specific operations that will compromise system security. Although malicious source code can be detected through manual review of software, much software is developed without any such review; source code is frequently not provided to purchasers of software packages (even if it is supplied, the purchaser is unlikely to have the resources necessary to review it for malicious code). A malicious source code flaw may be introduced directly by any individual who gains write access to source code files, but source code flaws can also be introduced indirectly.

### Object Code Programmes

Object code programmes are generated by compilers or assemblers and represent the machine-readable form of the source code. Because most compilers and assemblers are subjected to extensive testing and formal validation procedures before release, inadvertent flaws in object programmes that are not simply a translation of source code flaws are rare, particularly if the compiler or assembler is mature and has been widely used. When such errors do occur as a result of errors in a compiler or assembler, they typically show themselves through incorrect behavior of programmes in unusual cases, so they can be quite difficult to track down and remove. Because this kind of flaw is rare, the primary security concern at the object code level is with malicious flaws. Because object code is difficult for a human to make sense of (if it were not, software companies would not have different policies for selling source code and object code for their products), it is a good hiding place for malicious security flaws.

Lacking system and source code documentation, an intruder will have a hard time patching source code to introduce a security flaw without simultaneously altering the visible behavior of the programme. The insertion of a malicious object code module or replacement of an existing object module by a version of it that incorporates a Trojan horse is a more common threat. Writers of selfreplicating Trojan horses have typically taken this approach: a bogus object module is prepared and inserted in an initial target system. When it is invoked, perhaps during system boot or running as a substitute version of an existing utility, it can search the disks mounted on the system for a copy of itself and, if it finds none, insert one. If it finds a related, uninfected version of a programme, it can replace it with an infected copy .

When a user unwittingly moves an infected programme to a different system and executes it, the virus gets another chance to propagate itself. Instead of replacing an entire programme, a virus may append itself to an existing object programme, perhaps as a segment to be executed first. Creating a virus generally requires some knowledge of the operating system and programming conventions of the target system; viruses, especially those introduced as object code, typically cannot propagate to different host hardware or operating systems.

### Inadvertent flaws in Maintenance Programme

Inadvertent flaws introduced during maintenance are often attributable to the maintenance programmer's failure to understand the system as a whole. Since software production facilities often have a high personnel turnover rate, and because system documentation is often inadequate, maintenance actions can have unpredictable side effects. If a flaw is fixed on an ad hoc basis without performing a backtracking analysis to determine the origin of the flaw, it will tend to induce other flaws and this cycle will continue. Software modified during maintenance should be subjected to the same review as newly developed software; it is subject to the same kinds of flaws.

### Inadvertent flaws in Operational Modification

The well-publicised instances of virus programmes dramatise the need for the security analyst to consider the possibilities for unauthorised modification of operational software during its operational use. Viruses are not the only means by which modifications can occur: depending on the controls in place in a system, ordinary users may be able to modify system software or install replacements; with a stolen password, an intruder may be able to do the same thing. Furthermore, software brought into a host from a contaminated source (e.g., software from a public bulletin board that has, perhaps unknown to its author, been altered) may be able to modify other host software without authorisation.

### Location of Security flaws

A security flaw can be classified according to where in the system it is introduced or found. Most computer security flaws occur in software, but flaws affecting security may occur in hardware as well. Although this taxonomy principally addresses software flaws, programmes can with increasing facility be cast in hardware. This fact and the possibility that malicious software may exploit hardware flaws motivates a brief section addressing them. A flaw in a programme that has been frozen in silicon is still a programme flaw to us; it would be placed in the appropriate category under "Operating System" rather than under "Hardware."

### Software Flaws

In classifying the place a software flaw is introduced, we adopt the view of a security analyst who is searching for such flaws. Where should one look first? Because the operating system typically defines and enforces the basic security architecture of a system-the fences, gates, and gatekeepers-flaws in those security-critical portions of the operating system are likely to have the most far-reaching effects, so perhaps this is the best place to begin.

But the search needs to be focused. The taxonomy for this area suggests particular system functions that should be scrutinised closely. In some cases, implementation of these functions may extend outside the operating system perimeter into support and application software; in this case, that software must also be reviewed. Software flaws can occur in operating system programmes, support software, or application (user) software. This is a rather coarse division, but even so the boundaries are not always clear.

### Operating System Security flaws

Operating system functions normally include memory and processor allocation, process management, device handling, file management, and accounting, although there is no standard definition. The operating system determines how the underlying hardware is used to define and separate protection domains, authenticate users, control access, and coordinate the sharing of all system resources. In addition to functions that may be invoked by user calls, traps, or interrupts, operating systems often include programmes and processes that operate on behalf of all users.

These programmes provide network access and mail service, schedule invocation of user tasks, and perform other miscellaneous services. Systems often must grant privileges to these utilities that they deny to individual users. Finally, the operating system has a large role to play in system initialisation. Although in a strict sense initialisation may involve programmes and processes outside the operating system boundary, this software is usually intended to be run only under highly controlled circumstances and may have many special privileges, so it seems appropriate to include it in this category.

Operating system security flaws according to whether they occur in the functions for system initialisation, memory management, process management, device management (including networking), file management, or identification/authentication. System initialisation, although it may be handled routinely, is often complex. Flaws in this area can occur either because the operating system fails to establish the initial protection domains as specified (for example, it may set up ownership or access control information improperly) or because the system administrator has not specified a secure initial configuration for the system.

Memory management and process management are functions the operating system provides to control storage space and CPU time. Device management often includes complex programmes that operate in parallel with the CPU. These factors make the writing of device handling programmes both challenging and prone to subtle errors that can lead to security flaws. File systems typically use the process, memory, and device management functions to create long-term storage structures. With few exceptions, the operating system boundary includes the file system, which often implements access controls to permit users to share and protect their files. Errors in these controls, or in the management of the underlying files, can easily result in security flaws.

The identification and authentication functions of the operating system usually maintain special files for user IDs and passwords and provide functions to check and update those files as appropriate. It is important to scrutinise not only these functions, but also all of the possible ports of entry into a system to ensure that these functions are invoked before a user is permitted to consume or control other system resources.

**Support Software**

Support software comprises compilers, editors, debuggers, subroutine or macro libraries, database management systems, and any other programmes not properly within the operating system boundary that many users share. The operating system may grant special privileges to some such programmes; these are privileged utilities. In Unix, for example, any "setuid" programme owned by "root" effectively runs with access-checking controls disabled. This means that any such programme will need to be scrutinised for security flaws, since during its execution one of the fundamental security-checking mechanisms is disabled.

Privileged utilities are often complex and sometimes provide functions that were not anticipated when the operating system was built. These characteristics make them difficult to develop and likely to have flaws that, because they are also granted privileges, can compromise security. For example, daemons, which may act on behalf of a sequence of users and on behalf of the system as well, may have privileges for reading and writing special system files or devices (e.g., communication lines, device queues, mail queues) as well as for files belonging to individual users (e.g., mailboxes). They frequently make heavy use of operating system facilities, and their privileges may turn a simple programming error into a penetration path. Flaws in daemons providing remote access to restricted system capabilities have been exploited to permit unauthenticated users to execute arbitrary system commands and to gain system privileges by writing the system authorisation file.

Even unprivileged software can represent a significant vulnerability because these programmes are widely shared, and users tend to rely on them implicitly. The damage inflicted by flawed, unprivileged support software (e.g., by an embedded Trojan horse) is normally limited to the user who invokes that software. In some cases, however, since it may be used to compile a new release of a system, support software can even sabotage operating system integrity. Inadvertent flaws in support software can also cause security flaws; intentional but non-malicious flaws in support software have also been recorded.

**Application Software**

Programmes that have no special system privileges and are not widely shared as application software. Damage caused by inadvertent software flaws at the application level is usually restricted to the executing process, since most operating systems can prevent one process from damaging another. This does not mean that application software cannot do significant damage to a user's own stored files, however, as many victims of Trojan horse and virus programmes have become painfully aware. An application programme generally executes with all the privileges of the user who invokes it, including the ability to modify permissions, read, write, or delete any files that user owns. In the context of most personal computers now in use, this means that an errant or malicious application programme can, in fact, destroy all the information on an attached hard disk or writeable floppy disk.

Malicious intrusion at the application software level usually requires access to the source code (although a virus could conceivably attach itself to application object code) and can be accomplished in various ways. Inadvertent flaws at the hardware level can cause problems such as improper synchronisation and execution, bit loss during data transfer, or incorrect results after execution of arithmetic or logical instructions. Intentional but non-malicious flaws can occur in hardware, particularly if the manufacturer includes undocumented features (for example, to assist in testing or quality control). Hardware mechanisms for resolving resource contention efficiently can introduce covert channels. Malicious modification of installed hardware (e.g., installing a bogus replacement chip or board) generally requires physical access to the hardware components, but microcode flaws can be exploited without physical access. An intrusion at the hardware level may result in improper execution of programmes, system shutdown, or, conceivably, the introduction of subtle flaws exploitable by software.

## Network Security Management

Network Security Management (NSM) is the collections, analysis, and escalation of indications and warnings to detect and respond to intrusions. Therefore, NSM, and IDS products, focus on threats. In contrast, vulnerability assessment products are concerned with vulnerabilities. Some vulnerability-oriented products and security information management suites incorporate "threat correlation" modules that simply apply known vulnerabilities to assets. There are plenty of references to threats but no mention of parties with capabilities and intentions to exploit those vulnerabilities. In the world of NSM, indicators are outputs from products. They are the conclusions formed by the product, as programmed by its developer. Indicators generated by IDSs are typically called alerts.

IDS products lack context. Context is the ability to understand the nature of an event with respect to all other aspects of an organisation's environment. As a simple example, imagine a no-notice penetration test performed by a consulting firm against a client. If the assessment company successfully compromises a server, an IDS might report the event as an intrusion. For all intents and purposes, it is an intrusion. However, from the perspective of the manager who hired the consulting firm, the event is not an intrusion.

The IDS could be configured to detect the use of the PsExec tool and report it as a "hacking incident."PsExec allows remote command execution on Windows systems, provided the user has appropriate credentials and access. The use of such a tool by an unauthorised party could indicate an attack. Simultaneously, authorised system administrators could use PsExec to gain remote access to their servers. The granularity of policy required to differentiate between illegitimate and legitimate use of such a tool is beyond the capabilities of most institutions and probably not worth the effort! As a result, humans must make the call.

All indicators have value, but some have greater value. An alert stating a mail server has initiated an outbound FTP session to a host in Russia is an indicator. A spike in the amount of Internet Control Message Protocol (ICMP) traffic at 2 a.m. is another indicator. Generally speaking, the first indicator has more value than the second, unless the organisation has never used ICMP before.

Warnings are the results of an analyst's interpretation of indicators. Warnings represent human judgments. Analysts scrutinise the indicators generated by their products and forward warnings to decision makers. If indicators are similar to information, warnings are analogous to finished intelligence. Evidence of reconnaissance, exploitation, reinforcement, consolidation, and pillage are indicators.

**Collection, Analysis, and Escalation**

In the NSM world, distinct components are responsible for these actions.

— *Products perform collection.* A product is a piece of software or an appliance whose purpose is to analyse packets on the network. Products are needed on high-speed networks because people cannot interpret traffic without assistance.

— *People perform analysis.* While products can form conclusions about the traffic they see, people are required to provide context. Acquiring context requires placing the output of the product in the proper perspective, given the nature of the environment in which the product operates. Because few products are perfectly customised for the networks they monitor, people increasingly complement deficiencies in software. This is not the fault of the developer, who cannot possibly code his product to meet all of the diverse needs of potential customers. On the other hand, it is an endorsement of open source software. Being free to accept modifications by end users, open source software is best suited for customisation. Just as products must be tuned for the local environment, people must be trained to understand the information generated by their products.

— *Processes guide escalation.* Escalation is the act of bringing information to the attention of decision makers. Decision makers are people who have the authority, responsibility, and capability to respond to potential incidents. Without escalation, detection is virtually worthless.

**Detection and Response**

Detection and response are the two most important of the four elements of the security process. Since prevention eventually fails, organisations must maintain the capability to quickly determine how an intruder compromised a victim and what the intruder did after gaining unauthorised access. This response process is called scoping an incident. "Compromise" doesn't always mean "obtain root access." An intruder who leverages the privileges given to him or her by a flawed database is just as deadly as the attacker who obtains administrator access on a Windows host. Anyone who has performed incident response on a regular basis quickly learns the priorities of decision makers. Managers, chief information officers, and legal staff don't care how an intruder penetrated their defenses. They typically ask the following questions.

— What did the intruder do?

— When did he or she do it?

— Does the intruder still have access?

— How bad could the compromise be?

Answers to these questions guide the decision makers' responses. If executives don't care how an intrusion was detected, it doesn't matter how the compromise is first discovered. No one asks, "Did our intrusion detection system catch this?" NSM analysts turn this fact to their advantage, using the full range of information sources available to detect intrusions. It doesn't matter if the hint came from a firewall log, a router utilisation graph, an odd NetFlow record, or an IDS alarm. Smart analysts use all of these indicators to detect intrusions.

Although executives don't care about the method of intrusion, it means the world to the incident responders who must clean up the attacker's mess. Only by identifying the method of access and shutting it down can responders be confident in their remediation duties. Beyond disabling the means by which the intruder gained illegitimate access, incident responders must ensure their enterprise doesn't offer other easy paths to compromise.

When determining a postincident course of action, the work of vulnerability assessment products becomes important. Assessment tools can identify "low-hanging fruit" and guide remediation actions once evidence necessary to "patch and proceed" or "pursue and prosecute" is gathered. The three parties can contribute expertise in the following manner. The prevention team should share the security posture of the organisation with the detection and response teams. This knowledge helps guide the detection and response processes, which in return verifies the effectiveness of the prevention strategy. Remember that intrusions are policy violations. Outsiders or insiders can be responsible for these transgressions. Although NSM data is helpful for identifying network misconfigurations, determining resource use, and tracking employee Web surfing habits, its legitimate focus is identifying intrusions.

### Failure of IDS Deployments

It seems the number of disgruntled IDS owners exceeds the number of satisfied customers. The must-have security product of the mid-1990s was the firewall. A properly configured firewall implements access control (i.e., the limitation of access to systems and services based on a security policy). Once deployed, a firewall provides a minimal level of protection. If told to block traffic from the Internet to port 111 TCP, no one need ever check that it is doing its job. (The only exception involves unauthorised parties changing the firewall's access control rules.) This is a technical manager's dream: buy the box, turn the right knobs, and push it out the door. It does its job with a minimum amount of attention.

After the firewall, security managers learned of IDSs. In the late 1990s the IDS became the must-have product. Technical managers treated IDS deployments as firewall deployments: buy, configure, push out the door. This model does not work for IDSs. A firewall performs prevention, and an IDS performs detection. A firewall will prevent some attacks without any outside supervision. An IDS will detect some attacks, but a human must interpret, escalate, and respond to its warnings. If you deploy an IDS but never review its logs, the system serves no purpose. Successful IDS deployments require sound products, trained people, and clear processes for handling incidents.

It is possible to configure most IDSs as access control devices. Features for implementing "shunning" or "TCP resets" turn the IDS from a passive observer into an active network participant. Short-term incident containment may merit activating an IDS's access control features, but the IDS should be returned to its network audit role as soon as the defined access control device (e.g., a filtering router or firewall) is configured to limit or deny intruder activity.

One of the urban myths of the computer security field holds that 80% of all attacks originate from the inside. This "statistic" is quoted by anyone trying to sell a product that focuses on detecting attacks by insiders.

**Security Principles**

Detection lies at the heart of the NSM operation, but it is not the ultimate goal of the NSM process. Ideally, the NSM operation will detect an intrusion and guide incident response activities prior to incident discovery by outside means. Although it is embarrassing for an organisation to learn of compromise by getting a call from a downstream victim or customer whose credit card number was stolen, these are still legitimate means of detecting intrusions.

Many intruders are smart and unpredictable. This means that people, processes, and products designed to detect intrusions are bound to fail, just as prevention inevitably fails. NSM's key insight is the need to collect data that describes the network environment to the greatest extent possible. By keeping a record of the maximum amount of network activity allowed by policy and collection hardware, analysts buy themselves the greatest likelihood of understanding the extent of intrusions. Consider a connectionless back door that uses packets with PSH and ACK flags and certain other header elements to transmit information. Detecting this sort of covert channel can be extremely difficult until you know what to monitor. When an organisation implements NSM principles, it has a higher chance of not only detecting that back door but also keeping a record of its activities should detection happen later in the incident scenario. The following principles augment this key NSM insight.

### *Detection of Intruder Activities*

Intrusions are not magic, although it is wise to remember Arthur C. Clarke's Third Law: "Any sufficiently advanced technology is indistinguishable from magic." Despite media portrayals of hackers as wizards, their ways can be analysed and understood. Certain phases may be more observable than others. The sophistication of the intruder and the vulnerability of the target set the parameters for the detection process. Because intruders introduce traffic that would not ordinarily exist on a network, their presence can ultimately be detected. This leads to the idea that the closer to normal intruders appear, the more difficult detection will be.

This tenet relates to one of Marcus Ranum's "laws of intrusion detection." Ranum states, "The number of times an uninteresting thing happens is an interesting thing."Consider the number of times per day that an organisation resolves the host name "www.google.com." This is an utterly unimpressive activity, given that it relates to the frequency of searches using the Google search engine. For fun, you might log the frequency of these requests. If suddenly the number of requests for www.google.com doubled, the seemingly uninteresting act of resolving a host name takes on a new significance.

Perhaps an intruder has installed a back door that communicates using domain name server (DNS) traffic. Alternatively, someone may have discovered a new trick to play with Google, such as a Googlewhack or a Googlefight.DSIBTNDSecurity professionals tend to have an all-or-nothing attitude toward security. It may be the result of their ties to computer science, where answers are expressed in binary terms of on or off, 1 or 0. This attitude takes operational form when these people make monitoring decisions. If they can't figure out a way to see everything, they choose to see nothing.

This attitude is self-defeating. Sampling can and should be used in environments where seeing everything is not possible. In each of the scenarios above, analysing a sample of the traffic gives a higher probability of proactive intrusion detection than ignoring the problem does. Some products explicitly support this idea.

### *Detection through Sampling*

Related to the idea of sampling is the concept of traffic analysis. Traffic analysis is the examination of communications to identify parties, timing characteristics, and other meta-data, without access to the content of those communications. At its most basic, traffic analysis is concerned with who's talking, for how long, and when.Traffic analysis has been a mainstay of the SIGINT community throughout the last century and continues to be used today. (SIGINT is intelligence based on the collection and analysis of adversary communications to discover patterns, content, and parties of interest.) Traffic analysis is the answer to those who claim encryption has rendered intrusion detection obsolete.

**Limitations**

NSM is not a panacea; it suffers limitations that affect the ways in which NSM can be performed. This may have been possible for a majority of Internet-enabled sites in the mid-1990s, but it's becoming increasingly difficult (or impossible) in the mid-2000s. It is possible to buy or build robust servers with fast hard drives and well-engineered network interface cards. Collecting all the traffic creates its own problems, however. The difficulty shifts from traffic collection to traffic analysis. If you can store hundreds of gigabytes of traffic per day, how do you make sense of it?

Despite these problems, NSM principles recommend collecting as much as you can, regardless of your ability to analyse it. Because intruders are smart and unpredictable, you never know what piece of data hidden on a logging server will reveal the compromise of your most critical server. You should record as much data as you possibly can, up to the limits created by bandwidth, disk storage, CPU processing power, and local policies, laws, and regulations. You should archive that information for as long as you can because you never know when a skilled intruder's presence will be unearthed. Organisations that perceive a high level of risk, such as financial institutions, frequently pay hundreds of thousands of dollars to deploy multi-terabyte collection and storage equipment. While this is overkill for most organisations, it's still wise to put dedicated hardware to work storing network data. Remember that all network traffic collection constitutes wiretapping of one form or another.

The advantage of collecting as much data as possible is the creation of options. Collecting full content data gives the ultimate set of options, like replaying traffic through an enhanced IDS signature set to discover previously overlooked incidents. Rich data collections provide material for testing people, policies, and products. Network-based data may provide the evidence to put a criminal behind bars.

NSM's answer to the data collection issue is to not rely on a single tool to detect and escalate intrusions. While a protocol analyser like Ethereal is well suited to interpret a dozen individual packets, it's not the best tool to understand millions of packets. Turning to session data or statistics on the sorts of ports and addresses is a better way to identify suspicious activity. No scientist studies an elephant by first using an electron microscope! Similarly, while NSM encourages collection of enormous amounts of data, it also recommends the best tool for the job of interpretation and escalation.

***Real-time Intrusion Detection***

Most forms of real-time intrusion detection rely on signature matching, which is largely backward looking. Signature matching is a detection method that relies on observing telltale patterns of characters in packets or sessions. Most signatures look for attacks known to the signature writers. While it's possible to write signatures that apply to more general events, such as an outbound TCP session initiated from an organisation's Web server, the majority of signatures are attack-oriented. They concentrate on matching patterns in inbound traffic indicative of exploitation.

The majority of high-end intrusions are caught using batch analysis. Batch analysis is the process of interpreting traffic well after it has traversed the network. Batch analysts may also examine alerts, sessions, and statistical data to discover truly stealthy attackers. This requires people who can step back to see the big picture, tying individual events together into a cohesive representation of a high-end intruder's master plan. Batch analysis is the primary way to identify "low-and-slow" intruders; these attackers use time and diversity to their advantage. By spacing out their activities and using multiple independent source addresses, low-and-slow attackers make it difficult for real-time analysts to recognise malicious activity.

Despite the limitations of real-time detection, NSM relies on an event-driven analysis model. Event-driven analysis has two components. First, emphasis is placed on individual events, which serve as indicators of suspicious activity. Explaining the difference between an event and an alert is important. An event is the action of interest. It includes the steps taken by intruders to compromise systems. An alert is a judgment made by a product describing an event. For example, the steps taken by an intruder to perform reconnaissance constitute an event. The IDS product's assessment of that event might be its report of a "port scan." That message is an alert.

Alert data from intrusion detection engines like Snort usually provides the first indication of malicious events. While other detection methods also use alert data to discover compromises, many products concentrate on alerts in the aggregate and present summarised results. For example, some IDS products categorise a source address causing 10,000 alerts as more "harmful" than a source address causing 10 events. Frequently these counts bear no resemblance to the actual risk posed by the event.

Many commercial IDS products give you an alert and that's all. The analyst is expected to make all validation and escalation decisions based on the skimpy information the vendor chose to provide. Event-driven NSM analysis, however, offers much more than the individual alert. As mentioned earlier, NSM relies on alert, session, full content, and statistical data to detect and validate events. This approach could be called holistic intrusion detection because it relies on more than raw alert data, incorporating host-based information with network-based data to describe an event.

IDS interface designers have a history of ignoring the needs of analysts. They bury the contents of suspicious packets under dozens of mouse clicks or perhaps completely hide the offending packets from analyst inspection. They require users to copy and paste IP addresses into new windows to perform IP-to-host-name resolution or to look up IP ownership at the American Registry for Internet Numbers. They give clunky options to create reports and force analysis to be performed through Web browsers. The bottom line is this: Every extra mouse click costs time, and time is the enemy of intrusion detection. Every minute spent navigating a poorly designed graphical user interface is a minute less spent doing real work-identifying intrusions. NSM analysts use tools that offer the maximum functionality with the minimum fuss.

Open source tools are unusually suited to this approach; many are single-purpose applications and can be selected as best-of-breed data sources. NSM tools are usually customised to meet the needs of the local user, unlike commercial tools, which offer features that vendors deem most important. Sguil is an example of an NSM tool designed to minimise analyst mouse clicks. The drawback of relying on multiple open source tools is the lack of a consistent framework integrating all products. Currently most NSM operators treat open source tools as stand-alone applications.

Many managed security service providers (MSSPs) offer the ability to monitor and administer firewalls, routers, and IDSs. The vast majority of these vendors neither understand nor perform NSM as defined in this book. Such vendors are more concerned with maintaining the uptime of the systems they manage than the indicators these devices provide. Any vendor that relies on standard commercial intrusion detection products is most assuredly not performing true NSM. Any vendor that subscribes to NSM principles is more likely to deploy a customised appliance that collects the sorts of information the NSM vendor believes to be important. Customers are more likely to receive useful information from a vendor that insists on deploying its own appliance. Vendors that offer to monitor everything do so to satisfy a popular notion that monitoring more equals greater detection success.

Other vendors sell products that aggregate information from diverse network devices into a single console. This capability may be a necessary but insufficient condition for performing NSM. It certainly helps to have lots of information at the analyst's fingertips. In reality, the GIGO principle-"garbage in, garbage out"-applies. A product for security event management or security incident management that correlates thousands of worthless alerts into a single worthless alert offers no real service. It may have reduced the analyst's workload, but he or she is still left with a worthless alert. Some of the best NSM analysts in the business rely on one or two trusted tools to get their first indicators of compromise. Once they have a "pointer" into the data, either via time frame, IP address, or port, they manually search other sources of information to corroborate their findings.

Digital forensics is an immature field, despite the fact that investigators have performed autopsies of computer corpses for several decades. Digital forensics is typically divided into host-based forensics and network-based forensics. While many think forensics means searching a hard drive for illicit images, others believe forensics involves discovering evidence of compromise. Until digital forensics professionals agree on common definitions, tools, and tactics, it's premature to refer to NSM, or any other network-based evidence collection process, as network-based forensics. Incident response is a computer security term; digital forensics is a legal one. Legal terms carry the burden of chains of custody, meeting numerous court-derived tests and other hurdles ignored by some incident responders. While NSM should respect laws and seek to gather evidence worthy of prosecuting criminals, the field is not yet ready to be labeled as network-based forensics.Beginning in 2002, the term intrusion prevention system (IPS) assumed a place of important in the minds of security managers.

Somewhere some smart marketers decided it would be useful to replace the d in IDS with the p of prevention. "After all," they probably wondered, "if we can detect it, why can't we prevent it?" Thus started the most recent theological debate to hit the security community. An intrusion prevention system is an access control device, like a firewall. An intrusion detection system is a detection device, designed to audit activity and report failures in prevention. NSM operators believe the prevention and detection roles should be separated. If the two tasks take place on a single platform, what outside party is available to validate effectiveness?

Intrusion prevention products will eventually migrate into commercial firewalls. Whereas traditional firewalls made access control decisions at layer 3 (IP address) and layer 4 (port), modern firewalls will pass or deny traffic after inspecting layer 7 (application data). Poor technological choices are forcing firewall vendors to take these steps. As application vendors run ever more services over Hypertext Transfer Protocol (HTTP, port 80 TCP), they continue to erode the model that allowed layer 4 firewalls to function. Microsoft's decision to operate multiple services on a single set of ports (particularly 135 and 139 TCP) has made it difficult to separate legitimate from illegitimate traffic. The problems will haunt port 80 until access control vendors compensate for the application vendor's poor choices.

***Use of NSM Principles***

Analysts using NSM tools and techniques interpret integrated sources of network data to identify indications and form warnings, escalating them as actionable intelligence to decision makers, who respond to incidents. NSM analysts would first check their statistical data sources to confirm the findings of the network administrators. Depending on the tools used, the analysts might discover an unusual amount of traffic flowing over an unrecognised port to a server on a laboratory network. The NSM analysts might next query for all alert data involving the lab server over the last 24 hours, in an effort to identify potentially hostile events. Assuming no obviously malicious alerts were seen, the analysts would then query for all session data for the same period. The session data could show numerous conversations between the lab server and a variety of machines across the Internet, with all of the sessions initiated outbound by the lab server. Finally, by taking a sample of full content data, the analysts could recognise the footprint of a new file-sharing protocol on a previously unseen port.These steps might seem self-evident at first, but the work needed to implement this level of analysis is not trivial. Such preparation requires appreciation for the principles already mentioned, along with the selection and deployment of tools and techniques yielding high-fidelity data. Far too often security personnel spend thousands of dollars on equipment that produces little valuable information in the face of uncertainty. Having the right data on hand means faster and more accurate incident response, thereby preserving the assets that security professionals are bound to protect.

Hopefully you accept that a prevention-oriented security strategy is doomed to fail. If not, consider whether or not you agree with these four statements.

1. Most existing systems have security flaws that render them susceptible to intrusions, penetrations, and other forms of abuse. Finding and fixing all these deficiencies is not feasible for technical and economic reasons.
2. Existing systems with known flaws are not easily replaced by systems that are more secure-mainly because the systems have attractive features that are missing in the more secure systems, or else they cannot be replaced for economic reasons.
3. Developing systems that are absolutely secure is extremely difficult, if not generally impossible.
4. Even the most secure systems are vulnerable to abuses by insiders who misuse their privileges.

## References

Aceituno, V., (2005). "On Information Security Paradigms", *ISSA Journal*, September.

Anderson, K., (2006)."IT Security Professionals Must Evolve for Changing Market", *SC Magazine*, October 12.

Dhillon, G., (2007). *Principles of Information Systems Security: text and cases*, John Wiley & Sons.

Easttom, C., (2011).*Computer Security Fundamentals*. Pearson Press.

Lambo, T., (2006)."ISO/IEC 27001: The future of infosec certification", *ISSA Journal,* November.

McNab, Chris (2004). *Network Security Assessment*. Sebastopol, CA: O'Reilly.

White, Gregory (2003). *All-in-one Security+ Certification Exam Guide*. Emeryville, CA: McGraw-Hill/Osborne.

# 8

# Fair Use on the Internet

In its most general sense, a fair use is any copying of copyrighted material done for a limited and "transformative" purpose, such as to comment upon, criticize, or parody a copyrighted work. Such uses can be done without permission from the copyright owner. In other words, fair use is a defense against a claim of copyright infringement. If your use qualifies as a fair use, then it would not be considered an illegal infringement.

So what is a "transformative" use? If this definition seems ambiguous or vague, be aware that millions of dollars in legal fees have been spent attempting to define what qualifies as a fair use. There are no hard-and-fast rules, only general rules and varied court decisions, because the judges and lawmakers who created the fair use exception did not want to limit its definition. Like free speech, they wanted it to have an expansive meaning that could be open to interpretation.

## Fair Use Analysis

Most fair use analysis falls into two categories:

- commentary and criticism, or
- parody.

### Commentary and Criticism

If you are commenting upon or critiquing a copyrighted work — for instance, writing a book review — fair use principles allow you to reproduce some of the work to achieve your purposes. Some examples of commentary and criticism include:

- quoting a few lines from a Bob Dylan song in a music review
- summarizing and quoting from a medical article on prostate cancer in a news report
- copying a few paragraphs from a news article for use by a teacher or student in a lesson, or
- copying a portion of a Sports Illustrated magazine article for use in a related court case.

The underlying rationale of this rule is that the public reaps benefits from your review, which is enhanced by including some of the copyrighted material. Additional examples of commentary or criticism are provided in the examples of fair use cases.

### Parody

A parody is a work that ridicules another, usually well-known work, by imitating it in a comic way. Judges understand that, by its nature, parody demands some taking from the original work being parodied. Unlike other forms of fair use, a fairly extensive use of the original work is permitted in a parody in order to "conjure up" the original.

## Measuring Fair Use

Unfortunately, the only way to get a definitive answer on whether a particular use is a fair use is to have it resolved in federal court. Judges use four factors to resolve fair use disputes, as discussed in detail below. It's important to understand that these factors are only guidelines that courts are free to adapt to particular situations on a casebycase basis. In other words, a judge has a great deal of freedom when making a fair use determination, so the outcome in any given case can be hard to predict.

The four factors judges consider are:

- the purpose and character of your use
- the nature of the copyrighted work
- the amount and substantiality of the portion taken, and
- the effect of the use upon the potential market.

Fair use is an affirmative defence to a claim of copyright infringement. It is a privilege, not a right. More specifically, it is "an equitable rule of reason, which permits courts to avoid rigid application of the copyright statute when, on occasion, it would" undermine the purpose of copyright." The primary objective of copyright is not to reward the labour of authors, but 'to promote the Progress of Science and useful Arts.' . . . To this end, copyright assures authors the right to their original expression, but encourages others to build freely upon the ideas and information conveyed by a work." Courts apply the four fair use factors with this over arching purpose in mind.

The first factor in the fair-use analysis, the purpose and character of the infringing work, has two primary facets, whether the use serves a commercial purpose, and whether the new use is transformative.

### Commercial Use

Commercial use of copyrighted material cuts against a finding of fair use. According to the Supreme Court "the crux of the profit/non-profit distinction is not whether the sole motive of the use is monetary gain, but whether the user stands to profit from the exploitation of the copyrighted material without paying the customary price." This standard does not require courts to make a clear-cut choice between two absolute choices—i.e., making a dispositive decision of whether a use is a "commercial" or "non-profit" per se. Rather, "the commercial nature of a use is a matter of degree, not absolute." This places the question of commercial use on a continuum between two extremes:

1) a use that serves a non-commercial purpose by a non-commercial entity charging no fee whatsoever, and
2) a use that serves a commercial purpose by a commercial entity deriving its revenue directly from a fee charged for the copyrighted material.

### Transformative Use

"The goal of copyright, to promote science and the useful arts, is generally furthered by the creation of transformative works." For this reason, "the more transformative the new work, the less will be the significance of other factors, like commercialism, that may weigh against a finding of fair use." What constitutes a "transformative work" is not subject to exacting definition. However, as a general rule, if the new work "merely supersedes the objects of the original creation," it is not transformative, but if it "adds something new, with a further purpose or different character, altering the first with new expression, meaning, or message," it is transformative.

Transformative uses add new information, new aesthetics, new insights and new understandings. Such uses may include criticising the copyrighted work, "exposing the character of the original author, proving a fact," or representing the original work in order to defend or rebut it.

The second factor, the nature of the copyrighted work, recognises that there is a hierarchy of copyright protection in which original, creative works are afforded greater protection than derivative works or factual compilations. Also, the fact that a work is published or unpublished is a critical element of this factor. The use of published works is more likely to qualify as fair use because the first appearance of the artist's expression has already occurred. Thus, a finding of fair use will be couched between two extremes. Use of an unpublished, creative work weighs against fair use, while use of a published work relating factual material weighs in favour of fair use.

The third fair-use factor considers the amount and substantiality of the portion used in relation to the copyrighted work as a whole. "There are no absolute rules as to how much of a copyrighted work may be copied and still be considered a fair use." Rather, this factor has both quantitative and qualitative components, under which courts have found a use to be unfair where the material used formed a "substantial percentage" of the copyrighted work or where the material was "essentially the heart of" the copyrighted work. In applying this standard, the Supreme Court has held that this factor "must be examined in context," focusing on whether the extent of copying is "consistent with or more than necessary to further the purpose and character of the use."

While courts frequently identify this as the most important element of a fair use analysis, the legislative history cautions that it "must almost always be judged in conjunction with the other three criteria." In addressing this factor, courts "consider not only the extent of market harm caused by the particular actions of the alleged infringer, but also whether unrestricted and widespread conduct of the sort engaged in by the defendant . . . would result in a substantially adverse impact on the potential market." The Supreme Court has stated, "the only harm to derivatives that need concern us . . . is the harm of market substitution." While a "work that merely supplants or supersedes another is likely to cause a substantially adverse impact on the potential market of the original," courts have held that "a transformative work is less likely to do so."

## Functions of Fair Use Doctrine

Application of the fair use doctrine is one way courts endeavour to strike the proper balance. Merely browsing a web site containing copyrighted material may, theoretically, constitute copyright infringement. As one court has stated, "when a person browses a web site, a copy of the website is made in the computer's random access memory (RAM), to permit the viewing of the website's material. And in making a copy, even a temporary one," copyright's reproduction, distribution, and public display rights are potentially violated.

However, courts have acknowledged that while browsing may, on its face, infringe on copyright, it will, in most foreseeable cases, be a fair use. Courts have held web sites and other Internet service providers liable for infringements conducted through various Internet-related functions such as linking, media streaming, file sharing and storage, the maintenance of electronic bulletin boards, and posting. Fair use, however, was successfully invoked in a case involving the use of low resolution, "thumbnail" copies of photographic images. Notwithstanding the low number of successful fair use claims, courts appear to be applying the fair use factors in a technologically neutral manner. That is, the new digital environment has not caused the courts to abandon or significantly deviate from traditional fair use analysis.

### Linking

"Linking," a ubiquitous Internet function, comes in two varieties: outline links and inline links. When a user clicks on an outline link, the browser displays a new web site. When a user clicks on an inline link, the browser pulls content - e.g., an image file, textual material, or audio stream - from another web site into the linking site for performance or display. "Framing" is substantially similar to inline linking and occurs when material from a link is displayed within a "frame" or window border of a page on the linking web site. The use of these technologies to appropriate copyrighted material raises a number of issues.

*Outline links*: An outline link that connects a user to a site containing infringing material may further infringing reproductions, performances, distributions, and displays by others. If a linked site contains infringing material, the link may give rise to secondary liability for contributory or vicarious infringement on the part of the linking site, particularly if the linking site is promoting the copying, transmission, public display or public performance of material at the linked site. To the extent that the linked material is not infringing in itself, the reproduction, distribution, performance, or display that results from the link may not be authorised, and therefore may constitute an infringement in its own right. The fair use doctrine may apply to many outline links, because it is likely the case that many site owners will want their material disseminated as widely as possible.

However, where a link causes harm, fair use may not be appropriate. For example, unauthorised links may burden the linked site's server by increasing traffic to the web site. To the extent that the links pull in users that the linked site is not targeting, the owner of the linked site could argue that such traffic is unwanted and prevents the distribution of copyrighted material to its desired audience. Specific kinds of outline links, such as deep linking, may raise other issues.

*Deep linking*: Most web sites have a "home" page to which all subsidiary pages are linked. A home page is akin to a front door that users open to gain access to the web site's contents. Often, a web site's commercial applications, such as advertising and other commercial solicitations, are displayed as the user enters the site's front door and proceeds through the first few subsidiary pages. A deep link can bypass a web site's introductory pages, and therefore its commercial applications, sending a user directly to the site's content or particular service.

*Inline links and frames*: Inline links and frames appear more problematic than outline links, in general, and deep links, in particular. As this technology allows a web site to appropriate copyrighted material by pulling content from another site into its own, an unauthorised inline link or frame may infringe on the right of reproduction, display, or performance, or may constitute the creation of an unauthorised derivative work.

Kelly v. Arriba Soft Corp, involved inline linking and framing by a visual search engine of copyrighted photographs. In response to a user's query, Arriba, the search engine, displayed the results of its search as a series of "thumbnail" images. Arriba would then deep link its users to the full sized images. However, before Arriba had initiated this practice, a user could click on the thumbnail and view the full version within the context of the Arriba's web site. The Ninth Circuit parsed the case into two distinct issues. The second involved the use of inline links and frames to display those images within the context of the search engine's web site. The search engine's display of the full-sized images was held not to be a fair use.

Under the first analytical factor, the court stated that pulling the images into the search engine's web site did not serve a different purpose or add new expressive elements to the photographs. The practice harmed the photographer's existing market by discouraging traffic to his web site, where he sold advertising space as well as books and travel packages. In addition, the use harmed the photographer's derivative markets. For instance, he could sell or license his photographs to other web sites or to a stock photo database, which then could offer the images to its customers. Accordingly, the court held that the unauthorised inline linking to or framing of copyrighted photographic images was not a fair use, but constituted an infringement of a copyright holder's public display right.

**Thumbnail Images**

"Thumbnails," imprecise copies of low resolution, scaled down images, are widely exploited by web sites. Generally, a website will use a thumbnail as a reference device, and embed a link in the image, which will, in turn, send a user to a high resolution, full scale version of the image. When used for this purpose, a thumbnail of an image may potentially infringe on a number of exclusive rights, including the reproduction, distribution, public display rights, and, arguably, the right to make derivative works.

In Kelly, the court found that the use of thumbnail images implicated the photographer's reproduction right, but was, nonetheless, a fair use. While the use of the images served a commercial purpose, the search engine neither used the images to directly promote its web site nor tried to profit by selling them. As the search engine did not directly benefit from the images and did not use them in a "highly exploitative way, the commercial nature of the use only slightly weighed against a finding of fair use." The thumbnails also served a transformative use, since they "were much smaller, lower-resolution images that served an entirely different purpose than [the] original images, [functioning] as a tool to help index and improve access to images on the Internet ... ."For similar reasons, the court found that the thumbnails did not have an adverse impact on the photographer's market, but would enhance his market by creating a demand for the larger images.

### Streaming

Streaming provides access to a wide variety of visual and musical works, allowing users to listen to re-transmissions of radio programs, concerts and other musical events and services, as well as view music videos, television shows, movies, cartoons, and other transmissions of visual content. A single transmission of music or video can simultaneously infringe on a copyright holder's reproduction, distribution, public display and performance rights, in addition to the right to make derivative works. In Video Pipeline v. Buena Vista Home Entertainment, the defendant, Video Pipeline, created and streamed movie trailers to its clients, video retailers, for exhibition to their customers. The court held that this practice infringed on the plaintiff's reproduction, public performance, and distribution rights, as well as its right to make derivative works.

The streams were not defensible under the fair use doctrine. The court found that the use furthered a commercial purpose, since the service derived a direct financial benefit from the streams - its sole purpose was to advertise and promote video rentals. Moreover, the use was not transformative, since no new "creative ingenuity" was involved in preparing the previews, aside from "snipping and clipping." Even though the length of the previews were usually less than two minutes, whereas the length of the motion pictures was over one and a half hours, the small amount used did not sway the court to find in favour of fair use. From a qualitative perspective, the court found the previews relied too heavily upon the "expressive value" of copyrighted works—e.g., their themes, plots, character, and overall premise. In doing so, the clips went to the heart of the copyrighted works, co-opting their essence.

### File Sharing

File sharing refers to a process in which devices controlled by end users, known as peers, interact directly with each other to transfer files between them, rather than using an intermediary, such as a central server, to transfer files. Music, literature, motion pictures, photographs, and other examples of copyrightable content can be traded over a file sharing, or "peer-to-peer" network. These networks are architecturally diverse. The design of some file-sharing networks employs a central server to house a publicly accessible and searchable index of files available over the network.

Other designs eliminate centralised servers altogether. In these systems, a user joins an immediate community of peers and searches within that community. The user's query goes through the immediate community first, and if it is not satisfied, the query then goes to another community of peers. When peers engage in the unauthorised trade of copyrighted material, the copyright holder's reproduction and distribution rights are implicated. The Internet service that provides for the functionality of these networks may be held secondarily liable for the infringing acts of its users, even though it does not reproduce, store, or directly distribute copies of the infringing files on its servers.

In A&M Records v. Napster, various record companies brought an infringement action against Napster, an Internet service that facilitated the sharing of digital music files among its users. The files themselves-the infringing material-always remained on user systems and never passed through Napster's system. However, Napster maintained a central server that indexed the contents of the network. This feature allowed users to search for particular files of interest and to initiate a peer-to-peer transfer of those files. This functionality was the basis for holding Napster secondarily liable for the infringing acts of its users.

Rejecting Napster's argument that the users were making fair use of the record companies' copyrighted material, the court emphasised that the use was commercial because the users of the network received for free what they normally would have to buy, namely, compact discs. It was not transformative, since the service added no new creative or expressive elements to the copyrighted material. Moreover, the court held that the service not only harmed the copyright owner's existing market for the sale of musical compact discs, but also raised barriers to the copyright owner's entry into the same market.

## Price Discrimination on Internet

Price discrimination is one of the basic concepts in microeconomics. Some instances of price discrimination are not visible to the public, except through indirect effects. For example, gasoline wholesalers in the U.S. charge gas stations prices that depend on the "zones" where the stations are located, zones that often contain just a single station. The price differences within a single state approach 15%, far exceeding differences in distribution costs. They help explain why the car-owning inhabitants of New York City (who are on average more affluent than those in the rest of the country) pay far more for gas than those in rural areas of New York State.

While it is not known publicly how prices for different zones are derived, one can expect that they are based on prior experience, presence of competition, and demographics of a zone, the last provided in great detail by U.S. Census Bureau. At an extreme, income tax relies on taxpayers providing detailed financial information, and is enforced by the coercive power of the government. A very interesting example is that of U.S. private colleges. These educational institutions have high tuition and fees, typically around $25,000 per year in 2001 among the more selective schools.

However, all these schools offer financial aid to students, and in some of them, the amount spent on aid (which is determined overwhelmingly on need) comes to about half of the tuition revenues. In essence these institutions are practicing price discrimination on a massive scale, charging according to their estimates of what the students' parents can afford. Parents can preserve their full financial privacy, but at the cost of paying the full tuition. There are several important features to this system. One is that competing colleges are all driven by the incentives to price discriminate towards very similar pricing policies.

Another important factor is that the massive privacy violation involved in allocating student aid is abetted by the government. Parents usually have to fill out federal forms to obtain aid for their children. Fraudulent filings are subject to federal criminal penalties, and are not just a matter of a civil dispute between the college and the parents. Thus the government assists educational institutions in price discrimination. This is, of course, done in the interests of social welfare. However, much of the price discrimination by private institutions furthers social welfare. That is why we can expect governments' role to be ambiguous. They will be trying to respond to citizens' demands for privacy protection, and at the same time trying to facilitate sellers' price discrimination.

Public universities are also being drawn towards greater price discrimination. Incentives to price discriminate are just one element that goes into price setting, and it is often hard to determine their role. In economic analyses of price discrimination, a particularly sticky issue is that of "joint costs." Space constraints prevent a thorough treatment here, but it should be noted that joint costs can be used to explain many instances of what seems to be price discrimination. However, as differential pricing intensifies, it becomes clearer that price discrimination is usually the main motive.

Price discrimination is extremely tempting, and increasingly feasible, but it is like playing with fire. The practical problem is how to price discriminate effectively. Buyers are naturally reluctant to say how much they are willing to pay. In the past, technology for price discrimination was very limited, as purchasers had effective privacy. The standard way of overcoming this problem is through versioning, as is done with books.

Hardcover books sell for more than paperbacks, far more than the cost difference justifies, and are usually available a year or so earlier. This induces the readers who are impatient or who care about nice hardcover volumes to pay more. Such versioning has been going on for ages, but it became much more noticeable and was first studied systematically in the middle of the 19th century, in connection with railroads. The incentive to price discriminate leads even to extreme versions of versioning, in which extra costs are incurred in order to make a product less serviceable. This is known as the "damaged goods" approach, and appears to be used with increasing frequency.

A classic example is provided by the IBM Laser Printer and Laser Printer E of 1990. The latter cost less, printed at half the speed of the former, and differed from it in having an extra chip that slowed down processing. Versioning, and especially "damaged goods" practices, incurs costs for buyers, or sellers, or both. One of the big gains from price discrimination would be the reduction of such waste. Instead of being cruel, mean, or lavish to various customers, sellers could just charge them what they are willing to pay.

Price discrimination is likely to play an increasing role in the future, for two main reasons. One is that an increasing fraction of the costs of producing goods and services consists of fixed one-time charges, with low marginal costs. The other reason is that modern technology is making it possible to price discriminate. For example, Coca Cola was discovered in 2000 to be experimenting with soda vending machines that would raise prices when temperatures were high. It might have wanted to do this in the past, but the technology was not available. The incentives to price discriminate are likely to overcome the trend towards the type of dynamic pricing that is normally associated with claims of the "New Economy."

The standard predictions there are of widespread use of auctions, shopping agents, and related techniques. Priceline.com, eBay, and the myriad of B2B and B2C exchanges were supposed to be the forerunners of the new future. They were expected to bring back the art of haggling, and by better matching of supply and demand, as well as by lower transaction costs, to produce a significantly more efficient economy. They are growing, but their progress has been disappointing to their early proponents. The drive for price discrimination offers a partial explanation. If transactions are conducted anonymously, it is hard to tell how much a buyer is willing to pay.

One can try to set up auction mechanisms to do that, but it is hard. It is easier and more productive to just charge more to those able to pay more, if one can. Note that governments do not collect taxes by sending their software agents to negotiate with those of the taxpayers. Instead, tax agencies use their coercive power to find out how much people earn, and then extract a large share.

That privacy-reducing measures are induced by the drive to price discriminate does not imply that the people designing or implementing those measures think of their work this way. Enterprises generally try to optimise their state by making small incremental changes within the confines of their technological, economic, and legal environment. It is usually only when we step back that we can say it was the social and economic advantages of price discrimination that shaped the choices faced by the decision makers. 19th century railroad managers who set freight rates and late 20th century American college administrators who decided on tuition fees were not aiming to price discriminate. They did what seemed best for their institutions, it's just that their decisions led to increasing price discrimination. The managers who today invest in privacy eroding data collection systems are likely also often not thinking consciously about price discrimination.

Instead, they are acting on the hope that the information they gather can be used to increase their enterprises' profits. Usually what they have in mind for early applications are relatively mild departures from traditional business practices. As they gain experience, better tools are developed, and general business practices change, their methods will evolve. The logic of price discrimination is likely to lead them eventually to techniques that will be much more overtly discriminatory.

The "New Economy" visions of represent fairly small departures from the usual practices in the current "Old Economy." Auctions and automated shopping bots are well known, and fit well the standard economic models. Their spread does not require any major revisions of the economic canon. On the other hand, spread and intensification of price discrimination are likely to lead to major changes in thinking about economics, law, and public policy. "First degree" price discrimination, in which the buyer is charged his maximal willingness to pay, has long been treated in the literature as an unattainable ideal.

Erosion of privacy and improved IT systems will enable a close approximation to this ideal to be achieved. Further, the presence of price discrimination in a market traditionally has been seen as a sign of monopoly power on the part of sellers. More competition has been regarded almost universally as a cure. However, there have always been some contrary examples, in which intensification of competition led to an increase in differential charging. Public's concerns about privacy are well-founded, since current and historical precedents strongly suggest such a future would be resented. In practice, we are not likely to see this future any time soon. However, we will be catching an increasing number of glimpses of it, as enterprises move to exploit the opportunities that differential pricing offers.

The notion of a market price is very powerful, and underlies much of the theoretical framework of economics. Prices that depend on the buyer would require a complete rethinking of that framework. All those nice intersecting supply and demand curves would have to be replaced by more complicated constructs. While the incentives to price discriminate are likely to be among the most powerful forces shaping our economy, the extreme Orwellian forms outlined above are not likely to appear, at least not soon.

There are strong countervailing factors which are likely to slow the spread of overt price discrimination and push it into concealed forms. One such factor is arbitrage, in which buyers who secure low prices sell to those who are faced with high prices. For effective price discrimination, that method has to be circumvented. Airline yield management is as effective as it is because a ticket is a contract for carriage of a specific person, and is not transferable.

In other areas, accepted practices and often laws have to be changed. That, however, requires time. Another, even more important factor slowing the spread of price discrimination comes from behavioural economics. People do not like being subjected to dynamic pricing. There is abundant evidence of this, as shown, for example, in reactions to airline yield management and the moves to extend such practices to other areas. Yet more evidence can be found in the reactions to 19th century railroad pricing, reactions that dominated politics at the end of that century in the U.S..

Even in the days when racial, age, gender, and other types of discrimination were not just widely practiced, but respectable, price discrimination aroused strong opposition. Such reactions are still common. The public's dislike of price discrimination will be combined with new tools for detecting price discrimination. These tools are products of the same technologies that enable sellers to practice differential pricing. The result is likely to be that price discrimination will grow, but in a concealed form.

Stress will be on tactics such as bundling and loyalty programmes, which tend to disguise the actual price that is charged. This means that auction mechanisms and micropayments are likely to be used in very limited situations. On the other hand, there will be continued pressure to erode privacy in order to find out just what the willingness to pay is, as well as to control how products and services are used. Thus privacy will continue to erode. Price discrimination is often just one of many factors that lead to deployment of new technologies or business models. Thus it is often hard to tell just how important differential pricing is in various situations.

However, it is likely to be among the most important motives in the growth in Digital Rights Management (DRM) schemes, as well as in the spread of licensing as opposed to outright sales, and in tying arrangements, such as security techniques that enable a printer to work effectively only with cartridges from that printer's manufacturer. Price discrimination is clearly the main (although usually hidden) issue in the discussions of the future of the Internet, including the prospects for retaining the "end-to-end" principle.

The debates about open access and peering are really about the extent to which differential pricings should be allowed. Governments are often expected and pressured to act to preserve privacy. Of course, governments are among the main privacy violators, in pursuit of either tax revenues or criminals. Still, those incentives are well understood, and at least in democratic societies can be controlled by the public. Thus there is still widespread hope that governments can be persuaded to limit privacy intrusions by the private sector.

However, government roles in this area have been and likely will continue to be ambiguous. The problem is that price discrimination often

to an intensive dose of differential pricing by looking at how their ancestors reacted.

We can also hope to learn how price discrimination might develop by observing how it developed on railroads. Researchers in economics and marketing have come up with models which show that even when price discrimination is feasible, it might not be to the advantage of the sellers to engage in it, since it could lead to more intense competition. However, those are the usual theoretical models, and so one has to worry about their applicability. As it turns out, railroads did not want to engage in price discrimination, but could not help getting drawn into it. That is likely to happen again in our future. The impact of the Internet on the economy has been compared to that of railroads in the 19th century.

There are certainly many intriguing analogies. There are also noticeable differences. Perhaps the most important was that railroads were far larger (in comparison to the whole economy) than the Internet. Therefore in looking at the impact on society, it is better to compare railroads to all of IT. Railroads were the dominant industry in the second half of the 19th century. By 1880, about $4.6 billion had been invested in American railroads. This investment (accumulated over decades) came to about 40% of that year's GDP. (The comparable percentage of today's GDP would come to $4 trillion.) The railroad revolution led to a pricing revolution.

The stimulus came from the incentives for price discrimination that railroad economics generated. Railroads required investments that were huge for that time. On the other hand, marginal costs were comparatively small. Even most of the operational costs (such as track maintenance) were largely independent of traffic volumes. Hence it was inexpensive to run extra trains or longer trains, with most of the additional revenue dropping straight to the bottom line. A major innovation that railroads introduced was to provide not just the basic network of rails, but a complete transportation service, involving their own stations, locomotives, and cars. This allowed them to price discriminate effectively. Because of the scale of investment that was required, they had enough market power to do this.

Interestingly enough, the early expectations for railroads were that they would operate the way turnpikes did, with customers providing their own cars and locomotives. There were technical reasons for such a change, as was predicted by some early observers. However, it appears that the possibilities for price discrimination were also very important in inducing this transition. Certainly price discrimination became one of the most noticeable features of railroad pricing. 19th century railroads did not have the information technologies that would allow for "frequent rider" programmes. Neither did they have a "positive passenger identification" system, complete with government-issued identification cards, that would allow them to sell non-transferable advance purchase tickets with Saturday night stay-over restrictions. What they did have were a variety of other tools for price discrimination, and they used them with abandon.

Versioning was one of the main ones. There was also extensive personal discrimination. Passenger tickets in the U.S. were commonly bought from brokers, and varied widely in price. While versioning worked reasonably well for passengers, it could not work for freight. Hence explicit price discrimination was the rule for freight from early days. This was carried out through complicated freight classifications, leading to confusion and complaints. There was plenty of scope for discriminatory dealing, with special deals for particular shippers. Charging more for short haul than long haul along the same line was prevalent.

The pricing revolution that accompanied the railroad era generated a counterrevolution. This counterrevolution appears to have been most intense in the United States, although there was a similar movement in Britain. Railroads were initially welcomed very warmly. However, with time they became probably the most hated institutions in the country. The pervasive price discrimination by railroads was undermining the moral legitimacy of capitalism. Unequal treatment in an opaque environment raised questions whether success was being achieved by one's merit, or through corrupt deals (as in the "crony capitalism" that many countries are accused of harbouring today).

Congress did eventually respond to these concerns. The initial (and most important) sections of the Interstate Commerce Act of 1887 can be summarised as follows:

(1) Rates to be just and reasonable'

(2) Personal discrimination forbidden

(3) "Undue or unreasonable preference" forbidden

(4) Charging more for short than long haul on same line forbidden

(5) Pooling forbidden

(6) Rates to be published

(7) Impediments to continuous travel of freight forbidden

The remaining dozen or so sections were concerned primarily with administrative matters (setting up the ICC, determining procedures and penalties, and so on). There are several remarkable features to the above summary of the Interstate Commerce Act. Only one section deals with the level of pricing. Moreover, it is vague, and basically just restates what was already an obligation of railroads as common carriers under common law, ordinary statutes, as well as the railroad charters.

Of the other 6 main sections, all but one limit discrimination and "dynamic pricing." It is now widely accepted that the passage of the Interstate Commerce Act of 1887 was not a pure triumph of the populist movement and its allies in the anti-railroad camp. The railway industry largely decided that regulation was in its best interests and acquiesed in and even encouraged government involvement. This is often portrayed as the insidious capture of the regulators by the industry they regulate. There is certainly much evidence to support this view.

For example, a modern description of the Elkins Act of 1903 says that, "By 1903 it had become apparent that the law relating to personal discrimination and rebating needed strengthening. The carriers themselves sponsored legislation of this sort because they were losing revenue as a result of the widespread discrimination and departure from published rates. Yet they were unable to stop the practice without the aid of the government." The railroads were clearly using regulation to limit competition. Before, even while they were exploiting their customers, they were also engaged in cutthroat competition that brought many of them to ruin.

Government intervention stabilised the industry. Yet this was not a simple subversion of the regulatory process. Railroads' customers did get something they cared deeply about. To be more precise, those customers got much of half of what they had been asking for, namely reasonably simple, predictable, and seemingly fair prices. What they did not get was their other demand, namely lower prices.

**Regulation of Transportation**

Regulation did not reduce average prices, and may even have served to raise them. On the other hand, it did lead to simpler pricing. However, it was not truly simple pricing. The economic logic of price discrimination was too powerful to overcome. Some 19th century reformers argued that it might be acceptable to allow railroads to gouge passengers any way they wished, but that freight fares should be simple and fair, since those were crucial to the smooth functioning of the economy. Yet, ironically, it was only passenger fares that were truly simplified. Most countries settled on a fixed rate per mile (or kilometer,...), different for each class, with some special excursion, weekend, commuter, and other fares.

While simple passenger pricing did emerge from the protest movements, price discrimination for freight remained. Personal discrimination (charging different prices for the same service to different customers) was greatly reduced, although there remained various vestiges of it, for example in different charges for different localities. However, the incentives to charge more for transport of more valuable cargo were apparently too strong to be ignored. The difference was that this practice was codified, and was subject to extensive government regulation. Political attacks on railroads were replaced by regulatory and judicial hearings, with millions of pages of filings.

The rigidities and inefficiencies of the railroad regulatory regime (which was extended to truck transportation in the U.S.) grew to an absurd extent. By one estimate there were over 43 trillion rates on file with the Interstate Commerce Commission in the 1960s. It was almost a miracle when two rate clerks would come up with the same prices for any complicated quotes. A large body of experts in setting, verifying, and challenging transportation rates developed, and they found plenty of jobs at carriers, customers, and specialised consulting firms.

The inefficiencies of the system (which included fleets of trucks running empty half of the time, and transportation companies whose only substantial assets were federal trucking licenses) led to push for reform, and a freeing of the markets. The deregulation of the late 1970s and early 1980s swept most of the regulatory system away. The government, prodded by reformers, decided that there was enough competition between railroads, trucks, airlines, pipelines, barge lines, and other carriers to let a relatively free market operate. There is still some government oversight (through the Surface Transportation Board) to prevent extreme cases of carriers exercising market power, but it is far more limited than before. The general assessment among experts who have studied the effects of deregulation is that it has been a great success.

Average prices have fallen in all industries. For example, inflation-adjusted rail rates are down 45% since 1984. Yet not everybody is happy. The public sense of fairness is offended by findings such as that on railroads, "captive shippers commonly pay rates 20% higher than shippers with competitive alternatives". Railroad freight rates are invisible to the general population. On the other hand, airline fares are a frequent topic for conversation and complaints. There is extensive statistical evidence that deregulation has been a success.

Even though technological progress is slow, average fares are down, planes are flying fuller than before, and seats are usually available even at the last minute. However, what the public talks about is unhappiness with the bewildering variety of constantly changing fares, travel restrictions, fares to an intermediate city costing more than to a more distant one (even when one flies on the same plane), and so on. Airline yield management is spreading to trains, hotels, and even golf courses. This is not applauded by the public.

The incentives to price discriminate are growing, while the means to price discriminate are exploding, as technologies erode privacy and enable more sophisticated controls. Therefore enterprises will likely be pulled towards differential pricing. It may not lead to greater profits, but the experience of the railroads in the 19th century suggests that the competitive dynamic of the marketplace will not allow them to refrain from trying. Will their customers accept overt price discrimination? The business world operates that way, with extensive use of differential pricing. Perhaps individuals in their private lives will also learn to live with it. As the economy evolves, our discretionary incomes grow, and people may accept that purchasing is a game.

## Protection of Internet Integrity

The Internet society is not restricted to geographical, legal, or corporate boundaries. The physical distribution of services, processes, and data, is no longer necessarily the same as the perceived location Agent technology is a key enabling technology in this Internet society; software agents are autonomous and pro-active, can autonomously roam the Internet, perform transactions, and gather information. A number of issues need to be clarified before software agents and related technology can be used on a large (world-wide) scale in open systems such as the Internet. The possible legal challenges and problems arise in relation to the use of agents, such as: liability, security, privacy and contractual implications. These and other legal challenges facing users and producers of agent technology as well as regulators are compounded by the fact that intelligent agents are marked out by various unprecedented features.

Traditional legal paradigms do not suffice. The well-known paradigms have all developed along the lines of intervention by natural or legal persons within local bounds of space and time. However, these confines have lost their meaning in a world that is characterised by a society in which autonomous and anonymous communication and interaction by machines is flourishing. The complex issue of agent technology thus introduces a variety of challenges and opportunities that span the domains of agent systems applications on the one hand and law on the other hand. Within the individual domains of technology and law, the implications are known to some extent.

For example, in the context of e-commerce: issues such as liability and contract formation. Yet experiences, needs and requirements from novel applications (such as mobile agents) have not yet been dealt with from a legal perspective. Moreover, what is missing is a thorough and overall evaluation of the relation between technical perspectives and interests on the one hand and legal perspectives and interests on the other hand. The interaction between agent development and legal dimensions is mostly unknown, yet technical progress warrants the need for legal clarification, and legal implications may require resolution of technical issues. Agent technology comprises not only software agents, but also agent platforms: supportive middleware which enables the functioning of software agents.

## Agent Technology

Agents are used in a wide variety of applications: process control, manufacturing, air traffic control, information management, electronic commerce, business process management, patient monitoring, health care, games, and interactive theatre and cinema. The role of agent technology is expected to grow in the foreseeable future. Currently, software agents are used in restricted applications involving no outside parties or agents, with the expectation that in five years time agents may be involved in cross-boundary systems, leading to the use of agents in fully open systems in ten years time. It is important to note that agent technology involves agents and agent platforms. Agents are usually envisioned as 'active entities', while agent platforms constitute a technical (software) infrastructure to support agents. Their responsibilities differ: agents pursue goals for user applications, while agent platforms need to manage agents and their needs for resources.

A number of different parties are involved in the use of software agents and agent platforms, including users, owners, distributors, developers, and designers. The word 'owner' is thus not used in its legal meaning when used with respect to agents or agent processes. The marketplace is created so that multiple companies can cooperate to provide a single place for buyers to buy books. For ease of explanation, participants are either sellers or buyers, but not both. Each seller has his or her own booth to display books, advertisements, engage in conversation and negotiation with potential buyers, etc. A seller may represent a specific company and/or a theme: thriller, fantasy, computer, law, comics, etc.

A company may use multiple seller agents. A central cashier is present for buyers to buy books for the agreed price and conditions, possibly including book transportation arrangements. Floor plans and catalogues are present so that buyers can navigate the marketplace and browse titles to find books to their liking. An important contribution of agent technology is the following metaphor: the 'agent' concept facilitates modelling inherently distributed processes and systems as autonomous pro-active processes.

Pro-activeness and autonomy are related to an agent's ability to reason about its own processes, goals and plans. The ability to communicate and co-operate with other agents and to interact with the outside world often relies on an agent's ability to acquire and maintain its own knowledge of the world and other agents. Agents often work for a human user, directly or indirectly via other agents. In some definitions, humans are also considered to be 'agents', thereby unifying and anthromorphising the notion of agency. A rationale for this modelling perspective is that each pro-active autonomous (and possibly intelligent) entity is modelled as an agent and takes part in the multi-agent system by means of the defined communication and interaction protocols. A 'human' agent is often 'implemented' as a software programme with graphical (web) interfaces, through which a human can participate in a multi-agent system.

When humans wish to communicate with an agent, they can employ, e.g., facilities such as e-mail or instant messaging. In the example of the marketplace, participants can be modelled as agents: each participant is autonomous, and can start, continue and/or stop a transaction with other participants. A participant is able to interact with the environment, e.g. to consult a floor plan to locate specific booths at the marketplace. The participant may move to a booth to inspect and trade in locally available books, an action which was not possible from another location outside of the booth. The only way to influence a participant is by communication or interacting in the environment.

Agent communication languages (ACLs) describe "speech acts" in the form of message exchanges, e.g. KQML and FIPA-ACL. The semantics of a message in an ACL is generally left open to the extent that it is associated with an ontology, e.g. the Semantic Web effort develops ontologies by which machines may understand information and overcome an interoperability problem. An ontology is, generally stated, a description of the concepts and relations that can be used to represent (part of) a domain. In the example marketplace, languages, protocols and ontologies can be standardised by the marketplace organisation, forcing compliance of seller agents and buyer agents and facilitating inter-agent communication and object/service interaction.

A buyer agent can interact with a book-catalogue object to select a book to be bought. The buyer agent then asks the associated seller agent for the book's price. The seller agent, in turn, replies with information necessary to complete a book sale. Finally, the buyer agent interacts with the cash register to buy the book. This rather simple protocol does not include more realistic aspects such as negotiation on price and delivery conditions and avoids issues such as security, privacy and copyright.

In the example marketplace, a book-catalogue is modelled as an object: it can be inspected by agents, but the catalogue itself is not actively contacting agents. The floor plan in the example, however, is capable of alerting buyers to potentially interesting nearby sellers, based on the current position of a buyer. The floor plan is considered a service: an active element supporting the functioning of agents without itself being an agent, as the floor plan cannot buy or sell books. The cash register's functionality is a web-service, one that can e.g. initiate credit card payments for the associated book-selling companies. A software agent does not differ in this respect from other software on a computer: when it 'runs', it is considered to be a process with code (programming instructions), data (comparable to a human' s 'long-term memory' ) and execution state (comparable to a human' s 'working memory' ). An agent is hosted by an agent platform. An agent platform is middleware: software which runs on computer(s) and provides a uniform environment to other software.

In the marketplace example, one organisation may provide computers to host the marketplace application, including cash register, agent-registration, etc., while other companies may provide one or more computers to host their own seller-agents and book-catalogues. Companies can thus easily update their seller agents and catalogues. A user can host his or her own buyer agent on his or her own home computer, or have a buyer agent migrate to the marketplace's computers. Middleware in general, and agent platforms in specific, provide the means to hide differences in underlying computers (and, e.g., their operating systems such as Unix, Windows XP, Mac OS X, Linux, Palm OS, etc.) by offering a more standardised interface to agents (and their developers). Examples of agent platforms include FIPA, Jade, ZEUS, and AOS.

The FIPA interface is currently being standardised as a 'de facto' standard in the form of prevalent Jade implementations. However, interoperability between different types of agent platforms is not simple, even with the FIPA / Jade grassroots standardisation. A number of issues still need to be addressed, e.g. concerning inter-agentplatform security, migration, communication, interoperability, agent identity management, etc. When discussing agent platforms, a number of aspects need to be addressed. First of all, an agent platform typically manages agents, provides communication and interaction services and offers migration services.

Finally, deployment of an agent platform in the real world needs to be addressed. An agent platform manages the allocation of resources to agents, e.g. such as which agent 'runs' on which computer (if a choice exists) with what speed and which services (e.g., httpaccess to remote web-sites, or access to a local database). In addition to hosting agents, an agent platform creates agents, deletes agents, searches for agents, etc. An agent platform provides mechanisms for security, including access control for migrating agents as well as defence against possible malicious, or faulty, agents.

In the example marketplace, seller agents commonly reside on companies' agent platforms, and buyer agents are more dynamic; they can enter the marketplace, and possibly migrate to and from a company's agent platform. This implies that the marketplace agent platform needs to manage migration of buyer agents together with access policies for buyer agents entering the marketplace, manage address information of buyer and seller agents (for inter-agent communication purposes), providing needed resources to buyer agents, etc. Policies for access control, i.e. deciding whether an agent is to be hosted by a specific agent platform, are usually based on the agent's identity, its owner, or other characteristics. In addition, information on reputation or gossip, and observations of the (expected) load of the agent platform itself may influence these policies.

Trust, a multi-facetted concept, is often based on reputation and gossip information. Trust plays an important role in agent systems, involving trust between and among agents and agent platforms. Access control for agents may involve the exchange of credentials; for example, the Trustbuilder system is used to negotiate which resources agents may access, based on both specific agent's and Trustbuilder systems' policies and credentials. In the example marketplace, access policies for entering the marketplace for the first time can be based on a buyer agent's credentials including producer of the agent, and the human user's reputation for payment and rebates.

In addition, the marketplace may use experiences of another marketplace, e.g. in which CD's are sold, about trustworthiness and (mis)behaviour of users. Additional policies are needed, for example to govern agent creation: can an agent create another agent or clone itself. Issues concerning ownership, identification and authentication as well as liability still need to be addressed. Anonymity is another issue: are anonymous agents allowed? Complete anonymity may hamper communication facilities (no addressee or recipient are known, bulletin-board communication approaches may be an alternative option) and pseudonyms may be confusing when agents migrate to other agent platforms where different pseudonyms are used.

The subject of anonymity and software agents is discussed in more detail elsewhere in this special issue, based on. In the example marketplace, anonymity is not an option: buyer and seller agents in the marketplace need to be identifiable for communication, management and migration purposes. However, the identity of the human user is only needed (if at all) when completing a transaction at the cashier service. A user can choose to reuse their buyer agent, or have new buyer agents (with different identities) enter the marketplace. An agent platform provides services to agents, including communication, interaction, and directory services.

Communication services may differ in their 'quality of service'. For example, Email, as used by humans, is an unreliable service as messages may get lost or delivered late, because a guarantee of delivery is missing. Similarly, communication protocols for agents may have different costs (in terms of bandwidth, number of messages sent, time taken, etc.) and characteristics such as reliability and security. In a similar vein, interaction protocols are defined with which agents can interact with objects and (web-)services. Protocols may include message-based protocols and streamingprotocols (e.g., a continuous flow of information from a sensor or audio station).

Standardisation is currently not widely researched. In the example marketplace, a service offered to buyer agents may consist of an information stream of advertisements (similar to stock-tickers, e.g. via RSS) for a buyer agent. Likewise, seller agents may wish to have a continuous update of which buyer agents are currently interested in specific issues, e.g., by monitoring the behaviour of buyer agents browsing through book catalogues. Agents and services can be found with directory services.

Directory services couple names of agents and services to characteristics, such as abilities to perform certain tasks. In the example marketplace, yellow pages can be used to find seller agents with specific abilities, such as a seller agent specialised in literature on agent technology and law. A directory service can be used to provide such yellow page functionality. Note that directory services in large distributed systems in which many information updates occur, is currently a topic of research.

Agent platforms need to extend communication services to agents on other agent platforms, as communication is usually an inter-agent-platform service. For this to work, agent platforms also need inter-agent-platform protocols and languages. FIPA provides some standardisation but additional standardisation is required. Whether agents can interact with objects and services which are hosted on different agent platforms, usually depends on the configuration of both the local agent platform and remote agent platforms. If no remote access is allowed, and agent may migrate to the other agent platform, or have other agents migrate (as 'helper' agents). In the example marketplace, the agent platforms involved in supporting agents participating in the marketplace facilitate inter-agent communication. This is similar to humans using cell-phones: cell-phone usage is (usually) transparent with respect to the specific telecommunication companies involved as they resolve the underlying connections for relaying speech.

Agents, objects and services may be distributed over a large number of agent platforms. Agents may migrate from one agent platform to another: they are mobile. A common reason for mobility involves the quality of access to resources such as large volumes of data and security constraints. An agent may gain faster access to data when an agent resides on the same agent platform as the data, instead of a remote agent platform with restricted (inter) network capacity (e.g., a modem connection offers less bandwidth than an Ethernet or DSL connection).

In the example marketplace, a compelling reason for buyer agents to migrate to the marketplace's agent platform is security: the migration policy involves stringent checks of, e.g., owner reputation, agent software reliability, and protocol compatibility. Agents which successfully entered the marketplace, can then more easily migrate to a company's agent platform, as all stringent checks have been performed earlier. A reason to migrate to a company's agent platform may be to do a full text search on books for sale at that company.

A full text search is an expensive operation, especially if the buyer's agent contains specific evaluation criteria or algorithms to assess a book's usefulness. By migrating this buyer's agent to the company's agent platform, digitally encoded books need not leave the company's computers and network, thereby preventing possible misappropriation and reducing the amount of data shared over the Internet. There are number of the steps involved in migrating an agent. Suppose a user has acquired a buyer agent on his or her mobile phone. This buyer agent is instructed to enter the book marketplace and to buy a specific book. The user's mobile phone contains a (small) agent platform, which starts negotiations with the marketplace's agent platform. These negotiations may include checking of credentials and authentication steps. When all is in order, the user's agent platform suspends the user's buyer agent, and places the transportable format of the agent in an 'agent container': this basically is a data-structure (such as a ZIP-file) containing relevant files for an agent and its associated process(es).

The buyer's agent is currently not functioning; policies may be provided, e.g., to store messages for this agent until the agent is 're-activated'. The user's agent platform transports the suspended buyer agent's container to the marketplace's agent platform. The marketplace's agent platform is responsible for resuming ('awakening') the buyer agent on the basis of information in its agent container. The buyer agent is now hosted by the marketplace agent platform and resumes its functioning. Both the user's agent platform and the marketplace's agent platform have to make certain that the buyer agent is also registered as being hosted at the marketplace's agent platform, e.g. with respect to routing communication messages. After completion of the migration protocol it is not any longer necessary to maintain a connection between the marketplace's agent platform and the user's agent platform.

Migrating an agent entails migrating its process involving code, data and execution state. A number of options exist. In one approach, an agent may not need to be aware of migration, e.g., to store important information in its agent container. The agent may continue with its functioning and it typically does not need to be 'restarted' at its destination. This type of migration, transparent to the agent, is termed strong mobility; the agent' s code, data and execution state are migrated. Strong mobility as found in NOMADS, Ara, and D'Agents, requires that an entire agent, including its execution state and other details, is saved before an agent is migrated to a new location: this requires homogeneity of operating systems, agent platforms and programming languages.

The opposite is weak mobility, in which only an agent's code and data are migrated, but its execution state is discarded. In this alternative, an agent is always 'restarted' at its destination, and it needs to store important information from its execution state in its data to be able to resume its functioning from the moment it migrated. Many agent systems support weak mobility and Aglets. Most of the agent systems are implemented using the Java programming language and the Java Virtual Machine (JVM), which provides object serialisation as a basic mechanism to store execution state information as data.

Security is of key importance in deployed agent systems. Agents need to be protected during migration and execution. Agent platforms, however, also need to be protected from malicious and malfunctioning agents. Current research on secure agent systems concentrates mainly on protecting agent platforms (and the computers on which they run) against hostile mobile agents. Only very few systems also provide facilities for protecting mobile agents against hostile agent platforms. The example marketplace spans agent platforms from multiple companies and possible users.

Their underlying computers, operating systems and other resources may be heterogeneous, yet security and reliability needs to be assured otherwise companies and users will not participate. An agent platform may support agents from different multi-agent systems, although this is currently not commonplace. Existing agent platforms such as ZEUS, NOMADS, Sensible Agents, RETSINA, JADE, OAA, MASIF and Ajanta are approaches in which tools for developing agents are combined with agent platforms. Basic facilities such as communication, creation and deletion of agents are provided by most agent platforms; mobility is often limited. AgentScape is a mobile agent platform designed to support large numbers of heterogeneous agents and locations, securely and reliably.

Aspects such as interoperability, efficiency and performance, but also security, are part of the current research to which the OpenNet project (formerly the AgentCities project) contributes by providing an overarching infrastructure for testing agent systems. An open collection of FIPA compliant agent platforms is created on which multiple multi-agent systems can reside. An agent platform thus needs to manage multiple concerns, e.g. from local agents (and their users) as well as unknown external agents (and their users). Successful deployment of agent systems requires scalability: very large numbers of agents, services and resources require adequate support by agent platforms.

Large-scale agent systems are often heterogeneous systems: heterogeneous with respect to the computer hardware (e.g., Sun SPARC, Intel x86/i64), the computer operating system supported (e.g., Solaris, Linux, Windows XP), the agent programming languages support (e.g., C++, Java, Python, and Prolog) and the communication infrastructure (e.g., available qualities of service). An agent platform should provide a homogeneous, transparent interface to agents. A major technological challenge is to build scalable, secure, and fault tolerant agent platforms, that support multiple distributed applications, heterogeneity, and multiple qualities of services. Application of any technology has consequences, some of which are foreseen and wanted, others may be unwanted.

Agent technology is not different in this respect: its application may involve certain risks. Below, first risks of using agents are described, then risks of using agent platforms. Agents are expected to function 'autonomously', without a user's constant supervision. Agents run on an agent platform, communicate with multiple agents on the Internet and interact with numerous objects and (web) services. It is most often unknown to the user which agents, objects and services are involved. Mobility increases the risks an agent faces: agents may be hosted by a potentially malicious agent platform, outside the control of their user and thus become more vulnerable.

The underlying problem is that other parties, such as agent platforms, other software agents, humans, virus applications, etc., can change or copy the code and/or data of an agent, either intentionally or accidentally. This may have far-reaching consequences and entail large risks to users. For example, an unwanted modification of an agent's code and/or data may influence an agent's behaviour significantly. Changing data especially confidential information (e.g., bank saldo, bank accounts) or data with an economic value may be sufficient to cause significant damage. In addition, instructions and goals of an agent can be modified.

The agent may then exhibit unwanted behaviour, for example by buying goods for exorbitant prices, buying multiple items, engaging in malicious behaviour, etc In the marketplace example, a buyer agent may be modified, e.g., by a book-selling company, by raising the buyer's agent maximum price increasing the likeliness of the agent purchasing one or more books. Similarly, a seller agent may be modified to provide large discounts to specific buyer agents. Catalogues may be tampered with to display higher prices for competitor seller agents, thereby stealing their (potential) business. More severe consequences for the entire marketplace can, e.g., be caused by a change in the code of a buyer agent which may cause the agent to engage in many bogus interactions to the cashier service, frustrating the functioning of the marketplace for other agents by means a kind of 'denial of service' attack.

Another issue is stealing information, including private information such as addresses, bank accounts, credit card numbers, and an agent's internal (strategic) aims and instructions. This information can then be used for malicious purposes not necessarily related to the agent's application. For example, electronic banking information in buyer agents may be used to acquire cash advances or goods for third parties in a different country, thereby causing financial losses to users. Alternatively, a seller agent may make use of knowing the instructions of a buyer agent, to predict the buyer agent's behaviour and attempt to steer the buyer agent in certain directions.

For example, by knowing the criteria for establishing the maximum acceptable price, the seller agent knows the 'optimal' price to aim for. In addition, an agent may disappear temporarily or permanently, possibly representing a loss of investments in training and acquisition of the agent as well as frustrating the acquisition of results from the agent. Dependent on the severity of the damages caused by a misbehaving agent, the agent's reputation may be jeopardised, as well as their user's or owner's reputation. In addition, a user or owner may face litigation. The extent of possible damages depends on the agent and the specifics of the context.

For example, corruption of a single agent in a swarm application (i.e. an application with large numbers relatively simple agents used to examine emergent behaviour) may have a negligible effect. In the example marketplace, the user of a corrupted, misbehaving, buyer agent may be banned, although the user was not (directly) responsible for the agent's misbehaviour. The functioning of the marketplace is not frustrated when one user and associated buyer agents are removed. Whether such policies are fair to users and constitute viable business practices remains to be seen. Using agent platforms is also not without risk. An agent platform hosts an agent: the code and data of which validity, reliability and trustworthiness cannot be easily determined automatically.

Agents compete for an agent platform' s resources (such as processor cycles, bandwidth, disk space) and services (such as (reliable and secure) communication, mobility, automated updates, streaming connections). Malicious agents may succeed in migrating to a trustworthy system. Code and/or data of an agent platform can be modified or stolen, by mistake or by design. Possible consequences include modifying or stealing information on agents or conditions for (dis)allowing access to migrating agents, or management policies, etc.

An agent platform may then exhibit unwanted behaviour, e.g. by allowing unknown agents to enter, assign or remove resources to agents, or delete agents. In the example marketplace, stealing information on buyer agents, as well information about buyer agents such as their human users, characteristics, etc., can be used to corrupt the marketplace by modifying internal data of agent platforms, e.g. causing buyer agents to appear as seller agents, etc. In addition, stolen information can be used for other malicious purposes, including attacking related multi-agent applications which trust the bookmarketplace or trust specific human users.

By changing information in agent platforms in the marketplace also rather different behaviour may appear. For example, specific agents may be killed entirely, or migrated to non-trustworthy, non-affiliated systems of companies out to gain access to the actual buyer agents and their private information. An agent platform may also cease to function, with possible financial losses. Damages to agents of users, as well as incorrect function of users' applications, can be extensive and difficult to determine. Depending on the severity of misbehaviour, the reputation of the agent platform, and its users and/or owners, can be jeopardised.

**Platforms for Agent**

From a technical perspective, integrity is strongly related to preventing improper alteration of a system (and its assets), where an alteration should be detectable and recoverable, whereas availability is strongly related to fault-tolerance and reliability. In looking at it from a legal perspective, the integrity of a computer system is protected under both criminal law and civil law. Civil ownership provides a basis to act against infractions of integrity. Criminally, a computer system is considered as a physical object, the damaging of which is a criminal offence if it is done intentionally and without right. For an object to be damaged, it is sufficient that it has ceased to function; it need not be physically damaged.

For example, erasing relevant parts of a computer's operating system damages the system; it may no longer function properly. Erasing a single Word-document from a computer's hard disk does not. The foregoing suggests it is possible to affect the integrity of data without affecting the integrity of the physical carrier of the data. This raises the question how the integrity of data as such is protected in law. The integrity of data is protected separately in both criminal and civil law. In civil law the affection of the integrity of data may constitute an unlawful act.

In criminal law the integrity of data as such is the subject of specific criminal offences. The Cyber crime Convention of the Council of Europe provides an example of the statutory provision that is representative of the national legal provisions protecting availability and integrity of data. Article 4.1 Convention of Cyber crime (CoC) deals with data interference: Both an agent's and an agent platform's integrity need to be protected from other agents and agent platforms. The integrity of users, owners and system administrators is not dealt with in this article. The availability of agents and agent platforms needs to be (realistically) guaranteed. In the marketplace example, it is obvious that the availability and integrity of the code of agents and agent platforms is of major importance. Deficiencies in the availability and integrity of the code of an agent or agent platform may lead to many different problems.

Messages may not be received or they may be received multiple times. Deadlines - e.g. for accepting an offer - may not be met. Potential buyers or sellers may not be visible to other participants in the marketplace. The list of potential problems is almost innumerable. It is also clear that both agents and agent platforms are in this respect interdependent. The owner of an agent may go a long way to ensure integrity of his agent, but this is to no avail if the agent must function on an agent platform that suffers from deficiencies. The reverse also holds for ensuring integrity of agent platforms and potentially deficient agents.

Apart from the integrity of code also integrity of data is relevant. This may regard both data as part of a message being sent between different entities as well as information stored in databases. Since data are directly relevant for the contents of the transactions that take place on the marketplace, it is not difficult to envisage damages that could result from deficiencies in the integrity and availability of data. When considering the relevant technical issues, two issues are of importance: integrity and availability of both agents and agent platforms. An agent must be protected from unwanted alterations, caused by system malfunctions or malicious entities, e.g. other agents or agent platforms.

From a legal perspective it is desirable that the facts can be reconstructed 'afterwards' , i.e. after something has happened that influenced the availability and integrity of an agent. For this purpose, an agent may be obliged to keep a trace of information (including orders) received from users and possibly from other agents, together with its responses. Fortunately, possible (counter)measures exist against integrity violations. From a technical perspective, encryption can be used to secure information, although transportation of encryption keys by migrating agents still poses a dilemma to researchers. Another technique is to use secure change logs in agents: digitally signed entries in a log file containing the signatures of all involved parties. Such change logs can be used to determine what happened to an agent; an important aspect of litigation cases.

Techniques to detect improper modifications are mainly based on tracing alterations to an agent. A mobile agent may need to carry these traces during its life span if agent platforms 'en route' cannot be trusted. One technique is to use an encrypted agent container as the unit for transportation of an agent and its associated information, as alterations are securely logged. Alternatively, an agent may regularly visit a trusted third party for an integrity check or frequently send messages back to its owner reporting on its status. This may ensure continuing a user's trust in agents. Trust and reputation play an important role for agents, with respect to both other agents and agent platforms.

Techniques to manage trust in large open multi-agent systems are being researched. With respect to availability, techniques to recover from improper alterations are usually based on restoring information from a copy (a 'backup') at a secure location. Techniques differ in their guarantees with respect to the relevance of the back-upped information (e.g., the more recent, the better) and whether other agents may notice that a specific agent is recovering.

The agent container, mentioned before, is one means for an agent to frequently backup its data (and code if changed). In other techniques, agents may have fault-tolerance (e.g., via backups) built-in which may better guarantee their availability as they may recover more easily albeit at a significantly higher cost in resource consumption. If no (recent) backup is available, then information may possibly be restored by replaying past behaviour (and consulting relevant agents and agent platforms). This may be unfeasible as vast amounts of information may need to be shared and highly dynamic environments may prevent retrieval of past behaviours; it also is a possible means for denial-of-service attacks. An agent also needs protection from an agent platform.

Unfortunately, an agent platform has enormous power over an agent which cannot easily be restrained. Some solutions advocate special purpose hardware, others have developed cryptographic techniques. Protocols requiring agent platforms to provide a rationale for their modifications to agents may also be needed. In addition, standards for protocols and auditing logs concerning agent integrity need to be developed. Clearly in all these areas more research is required, in particular with respect to heterogeneous large-scale open systems.

To preserve the availability and integrity of an agent platform, it needs to provide mechanisms for access control, prevention, monitoring and corrective action. Usually these mechanisms are provided by a system administrator. Existing agent platforms have started to address these and other security issues. Below a number of such possible measures are discussed, including examples of corrective measures. To limit possible damages, preventive measures may be taken involving access policies and restricting the possible actions of agents.

Access policies, for agents, can be based on reputation of owner, user and/or producer of an agent, combined with experiences from other, trusted, agent platforms. An agent platform may assign different levels of 'trust' to agents it hosts. One preventive measure is to check an agent's code for known viruses and other malignant behaviour: a costly endeavour if possible at all. A safer approach is to have an agent only use code which is known to be valid, by accepting or downloading the code from known, trusted sites or parties. Another measure is to place the agent in a restricted execution environment, known as a 'sandbox', e.g. the Java Virtual Machine, with which unwanted code commands can be intercepted. A third measure is, when deciding to host an agent, to impose constraints, including permissions (read/write to specific information, execution of other programmes) and resource consumption constraints. Information in both agents and agent platforms, including code and data, can be protected by encryption techniques, of which a number exist.

A complex aspect is whether mobile agents can safely carry their own decryption keys, while traversing potentially malicious agent platforms. To provide a reliable environment for each of its agents, an agent platform needs to monitor itself to detect unwanted behaviour. Often, unexpected behaviour, however, is caused by correctly functioning agents: e.g. when all buyer agents in the example marketplace access the same catalogue congestion and overloading may occur. Monitoring resource consumption on agent platforms for management purposes to limit the resources allocated to each agent is a possible preventive measure.

It is technically possible to digitally and securely record all actions of an agent platform together with its agreements with agents, for the purpose of furnishing proof in litigation cases. Unfortunately, this leads to extremely large volumes of recorded data, with associated costs, problems of storage and retrieval as well as legal questions as regards the lawfulness of keeping the data. Another source of information is from outside entities such as system administrators, agents, trusted third parties, and other agent platforms. This information needs to be assigned a level of trust, before subsequent action is taken. An agent platform requires guidelines on which automated corrective actions it can take in which situation, as too many potential situations may emerge to involve a human system administrator.

A misbehaving system administrator's agent may be treated differently than someone else's misbehaving untrusted agent. An agent platform may be required to maintain a trace of its corrective actions possibly with a rationale, and may be required to employ a standard protocol for notifying agents or their users on corrective actions. In analysing the issue of removal or modification of agent processes, two situations must be distinguished. On the one hand, as stated earlier, it is possible that a system administrator and an owner of a software agent have a contractual agreement detailing the specifics and conditions of the use of the platform by an agent. In this case, their mutual relation is governed by their individual contract as well as the general terms and conditions.

With respect to the issue of removal or modification of agent processes, the relevant question here is whether the contract contains a provision on a possible removal or modification. When such a provision is included, the parties have to act according to what has been agreed upon. It is, however, possible that no contractual agreement exists. In this case, the applicable legal regime must provide the answer. Data are however not processes, but it seems reasonable to assume that processes cannot be terminated without removing or altering data and that comparable considerations apply with respect to processes. This stance is also grounded on the insight that a 'process' on a computer constitutes information in memory chips and CPU's (central processor unit), which interpret and modify this information (involving both code, data and execution state of a process). From the provision of article 4 CoC, it becomes clear that breaching the integrity of data is only a criminal offence if it is done 'without right'. It is thus relevant to determine whether a system administrator acts without right (or not) if he removes an agent's process from his platform or modifies it.

On the one hand, the system administrator is the owner of his platform, or he acts on behalf of the owner. An owner may, in general, remove or alter data and processes that reside or run on his platform. On the other hand, the system administrator has allowed the software agent to commence running on his platform at some point in the past. Therewith he may or may not have raised certain expectations. Furthermore, it is the question whether he may exercise his rights as an owner without regard for the interests of other people, viz. the 'owner' of an agent's process running on his platform.

To illustrate the above in more detail and to identify relevant circumstances two court cases appear relevant. Both cases, one from Dutch law and one from American law, are analysed below to illustrate the types of circumstances that play a role in dealing with integrity problems of software agents. Each case is analysed from a legal and a technical perspective. The first case, XS4all vs. ABFAB is used to introduce issues concerning the rights and obligations of system administrators. The second case, Bidder's Edge vs. eBay, concerns the rights of (non-mobile) software agents. The analyses of both cases offer indications for several concluding remarks. The direct marketing company ABFAB sent commercial e-mails (spam) to the subscribers of XS4all, a famous Dutch ISP.

In order to protect its subscribers from spam sent by ABFAB and in order to protect its system integrity, XS4all wanted to forbid ABFAB to send spam to its system. XS4all founded its claim inter alia on its property right in its system. Basically XS4all' s reasoning is sound. As the proprietor of an object one can freely enjoy his or her property and fend off third parties that interfere with ones unencumbered enjoyment of the property. There may, however, be circumstances in which an appeal to once property right alone is not enough to fend off others that interfere. This may, e.g., be the case with very unsubstantial interferences with a property right or if the object is used for purposes that reflect a certain public interest (such as an e-mail service) and the interference involves this public interest. The question then becomes: under what circumstances can a proprietor fend off interferers?

In Dutch legal doctrine two schools of thought exist. According to the first school a proprietor can fend off third parties if he or she can show that he or she has a good reason to do so, justifying his actions. According to the second theory he ore she can only act if the third party acts unlawfully towards him or her. The Dutch Supreme Court has chosen the former theory. It is clear that this school leaves more room for 'enforcement' by the proprietor. After all, it is for XS4all much easier to indicate that it has good reasons to fend off spam from ABFAB (protection against spam, protection of system integrity) than is to indicate that ABFAB acts unlawfully when it sends commercial e-mail (it is after all questionable whether sending commercial mail is unlawful per se).

eBay is an Internet-based, person-to-person trading site. eBay offers sellers the ability to list items for sale and prospective buyers the ability to search those listings and bid on items. Bidder's Edge (BE) is an auction aggregation site designed to offer on-line auction buyers the ability to search for items across numerous on-line auctions without having to search each auction individually. The information that is made available on the BE site is stored in a database of information that BE compiles through access to auction sites such as eBay. eBay demanded that BE ceased accessing the eBay site, because BE's queries for filling its database compromised the capacity of eBay's system. The Court found that BE's access to the site constituted a trespass to chattels. A trespass to chattels is defined by the Court as an intentional interference with the possession of personal property has proximately caused injury.

With respect to the first requirement, the Court concluded that BE's activity is sufficiently outside the range of the use permitted by eBay that it is unauthorised for the purposes of establishing a trespass. Although the website is publicly accessible, eBay does not grant the public unconditional access and does not generally permit the type of automated access made by BE. In fact, eBay explicitly notifies automated visitors that their access is not permitted. BE continued however to "crawl" eBay's web site even after eBay demanded BE to terminate this activity. The Court decided that even if BE's web crawlers were authorised to make individual queries of eBay's system, BE's web crawlers exceeded the scope of any such consent when they begin acting like robots by making repeated queries. With respect to the second requirement the Court held that eBay suffered damage by the mere fact that BE's use is appropriating eBay's personal property by using valuable bandwidth and capacity, and necessarily compromising eBay's ability to use that capacity for its own purposes.

The XS4all / ABFAB case indicates that a system administrator intending to modify an agent must first refer to his (employer's) ownership of the system. Apart from that he or she must balance his or her own interests against those of the agentowner and such balancing must not be unfair. The BE/eBay case identifies issues in the case of a system administrator removing unwanted agent processes. In the first place, the conditions under which the system administrator has allowed a software agent to use his or her system are of importance. In this respect, it is relevant that the software agent or its user can recognise conditions and the nature of these conditions imposed by a system administrator. In the second place, it is relevant to what extent the software agent uses the capacity of the system administrator's system. In the above case, it wasn't necessary that alternative uses were frustrated by the fact that BE used the system. It was sufficient that capacity was consumed that could have been used by eBay or its customers. Finally, the eBay/BE case shows that problems with software agents are already a reality. In general the owner of an agent platform has some leeway in dealing with software agents.

Nonetheless the agent platform owner will always have to adduce a good reason for acting against software agents and the balancing if his or her own interests against those of the owner of the software agent must not be unfair. In this respect it is helpful if the agent platform owner has communicated beforehand what the conditions are under which a software agent may make use of the platform.

**Future Challenges**

The worldwide deployment of (open and closed) agent systems, however, hinges on social and commercial acceptance, which is fostered by meeting explicit legal standards. Guidelines are needed to describe standard techniques to employ in agent systems, and standard measures to take in specific situations. Development of guidelines is a time-consuming endeavour, as understanding of the interplay between technological aspects of agents and agent platforms is still developing. Important technical aspects of agents and agent platforms, interoperability, scalability and security, are being researched, the results of which may influence legal possibilities.

In an earlier stage the system administrator is, for example, in a much stronger position to impose conditions of use upon software agents and their users, for example by means of a contractual provision. If during an earlier stage protocols are made to request or to force an agent to migrate, then the system administrator's problem seems more manageable and may even not be perceived as a 'problem': (standardised) and well-thought protocols minimise integrity and availability problems. The conditions under which access to a computer system is granted are relevant.

Nevertheless, a number of outstanding questions with respect to these conditions remain. The conditions for use of an agent platform must, e.g., be clearly communicated to the software agent (and possibly its user) by the system administrator. The current practice with which website maintainers can constrain automated access by providing a file with conditions, can easily be ignored by external parties: an explicit agreement is not reached. A straightforward way to enforce agreement on conditions may be a mechanism that is able to 'physically' prohibit any use of an agent platform when the usage violates conditions. Tools and techniques need to be developed for an agent platform to monitor usage and check for violation (and agreement) of conditions. Technical measures may have an all or nothing character: allowing either too much or too little. In the eBay v. BE case, the former blocked at one point the latter's IP-addresses in an attempt to prohibit the acts that violated the conditions. This measure did not, however, differentiate between acts in compliance or violation of the conditions. This case also highlights a second drawback of physical measures: BE easily robbed the measure of its effectiveness by using a proxy-server, thus hiding her IP-address and nullifying the effect of eBay's IP-blocking.

In addition, technical measures may, on their own, make the precise conditions for use insufficiently explicit: was e.g. BE's access through the proxy-server allowed since it was not blocked or must IP-blocking be understood to be a general denial of access? It is indispensable to have a protocol that facilitates communication of the conditions of use much more clearly and explicitly than is the case with 'coercive technical measures'. A distinction needs to be made with respect to the recipient of the conditions of use. If they are to be communicated to the software agent, a protocol is required that can express that conditions are being communicated and specify these conditions, in such a way that this is meaningful for the software agent, e.g., by using an annotation language such as XrML.

In addition, it is desirable for communication of conditions to guarantee non-repudiation of receipt, i.e. it must be provable that the software agent has undeniably received and understood the conditions. An appropriate protocol could, e.g., require a software agent to acknowledge receipt of the conditions. If the conditions are to be communicated to the owner of the software agent, the owner must be identifiable and have a contact address. Again, a protocol is necessary, including non-repudiation of receipt. Not only usage and access conditions needs to be specified, but also rights, obligations and sanctions need to be explicitly agreed upon by the involved parties, which can include terms of notification, number of warnings issued and possible normative deliberations.

Both an agent platform and a software agent have obligations to each other, e.g. to respect their respective (private) data, accommodate fair usage, etc. Such an explicit agreement alleviates potential (legal) problems when, e.g., a system administrator employs certain measures affecting the performance and functioning of software agents. Especially when agent platforms automatically act according to policies and take these agreements into account, without involving a system administrator in every decision. A predictable agent platform may be better trusted and valued by software agents and their human users. In the XS4all vs. ABFAB case, a system administrator has a number of options.

For a system administrator to regulate message volume, management policies may be a used, e.g., to dynamically constrain resource usage, i.e. the number of messages to be send per time-unit. A rationale may have been to grant every user the opportunity to send and receive email and at the same time-constrain large-scale senders. Additionally, security (and access control) policies may have been put into place whereby anti-virus and anti-spam measures temporarily block sources of vast amounts of emails (or other messages). To stop distributed denial of service attacks, in which multiple computers (e.g., more than 100,000) are involved in sending messages to a target computer, a system administrator may enlist the help of other system administrators, ISPs and network administrators, who together may stench the message flood. In the eBay vs. Bidder's Edge case the agent platform could consider isolating the suspicious Bidder's Edge agents in such a way that is not harmful to eBay's system, possibly while storing enough data in order to allow the agents to resume on another system (this was not an option for eBay).

A more drastic option which eBay's system administrator could consider is killing Bidder's Edge agents. In all situations eBay's system administrator could consider notifying the owner of the agents (Bidder's Edge) of their illegal presence and their potential termination. Unique identities of agents facilitate notification of stakeholders. Software robots were used to search, amongst others, eBay's database to update the Bidder's Edge database. eBay's system administrator could identify software agents such as the Bidder's Edge robots, e.g. by analysis of the IP-addresses from which these agents originated or their co-ordinated behaviour.

In the case of eBay, preventive measures were not of relevance, as far as can be deduced from the case. Possible preventive measures include constraining resource usage when an agent is accepted. In case of eBay for example, it was technically possible for Bidder's Edge agents to extensively access eBay, far more than is 'normally' required by clients. As technology progresses, guidelines need to be frequently updated to reflect current state-of the-art technologies and measures. This is increasingly important in a world in which security patches are frequently issued (e.g., cf. Microsoft Windows Update) and new hardware is developed (e.g., optical computing, quantum computing).

Mechanisms may need to be developed to automatically update existing agent systems to current legal, technical and security requirements. In sum, the system administrator, as the owner of a computer system, allows software agents to use his or her agent platform. The system administrator may or may not bind the use by the software agents to certain conditions. At a later point in time the system administrator may want to disallow the use of his agent platform.

## Practical Effect of Fair Use Defense

The practical effect of this law and the court decisions following it is that it is usually possible to quote from a copyrighted work in order to criticize or comment upon it, teach students about it, and possibly for other uses. Certain well-established uses cause few problems. A teacher who prints a few copies of a poem to illustrate a technique will have no problem on all four of the above factors (except possibly on amount and substantiality), but some cases are not so clear. All the factors are considered and balanced in each case: a book reviewer who quotes a paragraph as an example of the author's style will probably fall under fair use even though he may sell his review commercially; but a non-profit educational website that reproduces whole articles from technical magazines will probably be found to infringe if the publisher can demonstrate that the website affects the market for the magazine, even though the website itself is non-commercial.

Free Republic, LLC, owner of the political website freerepublic.com, was found liable for copyright infringement in L.A. Times v. Free Republic for reproducing and archiving full-text versions of plaintiffs' news articles even though the judge found the website minimally commercial. She held that "while defendants' do not necessarily 'exploit' the articles for commercial gain, their posting to the Free Republic site allows defendants and other visitors to avoid paying the 'customary price' charged for the works."

The April 2000 opinion ruled concerning the four factors of fair use that:

1) defendants' use of plaintiffs' articles is minimally, if at all, transformative,
2) the factual content of the articles copied "weighs in favour of finding of fair use of the news articles by defendants in this case", though it didn't "provide strong support"
3) concerning the amount and substantiality prong, "the wholesale copying of plaintiffs' articles weighs against the finding of fair use", and
4) the plaintiffs showed that they were trying to exploit the market for viewing their articles online and defendants did not rebut their showing by proving an absence of usurpation harm to plaintiffs.

Ultimately the court found "that the defendants may not assert a fair use defense to plaintiffs' copyright infringement claim".

### Fair Use as a Defense

The Supreme Court of the United States described fair use as an affirmative defense in Campbell v. Acuff-Rose Music, Inc. This means that, in litigation on copyright infringement, the defendant bears the burden of raising and proving that the use was fair and not an infringement. Thus, fair use need not even be raised as a defense unless the plaintiff first shows (or the defendant concedes) a "prima facie" case of copyright infringement. If the work was not copyrightable, the term had expired, or the defendant's work borrowed only a small amount, for instance, then the plaintiff cannot make out a prima facie case of infringement, and the defendant need not even raise the fair use defense.

Since the defendant has the burden of proof, some copyright owners frequently make claims of infringement even in circumstances where the fair use defense would likely succeed in hopes that the user will refrain from the use rather than spending resources in his defense. This type of lawsuit is part of a much larger problem in First Amendment law.

Since paying a royalty fee may be much less expensive than having a potential copyright suit threaten the publication of a completed work in which a publisher has invested significant resources, many authors may seek a license even for uses that copyright law ostensibly permits without liability.

The frequent argument over whether fair use is a "right" or a "defense" is generated by confusion over the use of the term "affirmative defense." "Affirmative defense" is simply a term of art from litigation reflecting the timing in which the defense is raised. It does not distinguish between "rights" and "defenses", and so it does not characterize the substance of the defendant's actions as "not a right but a defense".

In response to perceived over-expansion of copyrights, several electronic civil liberties and free expression organizations began in the 1990s to add fair use cases to their dockets and concerns. These include the Electronic Frontier Foundation ("EFF"), the American Civil Liberties Union, the National Coalition Against Censorship, the American Library Association, numerous clinical programs at law schools, and others. The "Chilling Effects" archive was established in 2002 as a coalition of several law school clinics and the EFF to document the use of cease and desist letters. Most recently, in 2006, Stanford University began an initiative called "The Fair Use Project" (FUP) to help artists, particularly filmmakers, fight lawsuits brought against them by large corporations.

In 2009, fair use appeared as a defense in lawsuits against filesharing. Charles Nesson argued that file-sharing qualifies as fair use in his defense of alleged filesharer Joel Tenenbaum. Kiwi Camara, defending alleged filesharer Jammie Thomas, announced a similar defense.

On September 2, 2009 Israeli District court ruled out a detailed decision not allowing disclosure of "John Doe"'s details for the request of the FA Premier League based on several reasons, but the most interesting were that "fair use" under the new Israeli law of 2007 (which is based on the US 4 factors test) is a right and not merely a defense. The court specifically states that the public may have base for a legal cause of action if its fair use right is infringed by the copyright holder. Other important decision in said judgment is the fact that the court finds streaming Internet filesharing site of live soccer games not infringing copyright as this use is fair use (mainly due to the importance of certain sport events and the public's right). The court analyzes the 4 factors and decides that due to such importance of sporting games (and other less important factors), such use is fair.

## Economic Benefit of Fair Use

A balanced copyright law provides an economic benefit to many high-tech businesses such as search engines and software developers. Fair Use is also crucial to non-technology industries such as insurance, legal services, and newspaper publishers. On September 12, 2007, the Computer and Communications Industry Association (CCIA), a group representing companies including Google Inc., Microsoft Inc., Oracle Corporation, Sun Microsystems, Yahoo! and other high-tech companies, released a study that found that Fair Use exceptions to US copyright laws were responsible for more than $4,500 billion dollars in annual revenue for the United States economy representing one-sixth of the total US GDP. The study was conducted using a methodology developed by the World Intellectual Property Organization. The study found that fair use dependent industries are directly responsible for more than eighteen percent of US economic growth and nearly eleven million American jobs. "As the United States economy becomes increasingly knowledge-based, the concept of fair use can no longer be discussed and legislated in the abstract. It is the very foundation of the digital age and a cornerstone of our economy," said Ed Black, President and CEO of CCIA. "Much of the unprecedented economic growth of the past ten years can actually be credited to the doctrine of fair use, as the Internet itself depends on the ability to use content in a limited and unlicenced manner."

## References

Depoorter, Ben; Parisi, Francesco (2002). "Fair Use and Copyright Protection: A Price Theory Explanation".*International Review of Law and Economics* 21 (4): 453–473.

Gordon, Wendy J. (1982). "Fair Use as Market Failure: A Structural and Economic Analysis of the 'Betamax' Case and Its Predecessors". *Columbia Law Review* 82 (8): 1600–1657.

Paterson, Kenneth G.; Yau, Arnold K.L. (2006). "Cryptography in theory and practice: The case of encryption in IPsec" (PDF). *Eurocrypt 2006, Lecture Notes in Computer Science Vol. 4004*. Berlin. pp. 12–29.

Samuelson, Pamela (1995). "Copyright's fair use doctrine and digital data". *Publishing Research Quarterly* 11 (1): 27–39.

# Bibliography

Aceituno, V., (2005). "On Information Security Paradigms", *ISSA Journal*, September.

Alistair Duff (2000) *Information Society Studies.* London: Routledge.

Allen, Julia H. (2001). *The CERT Guide to System and Network Security Practices.* Boston, MA: Addison-Wesley.

Anderson, K., (2006)."IT Security Professionals Must Evolve for Changing Market", *SC Magazine*, October 12.

Bhagwati, Jagdish N. (2005). *In defense of Globalization.* New York: Oxford University Press

Cooke, Sandra D. (2003). "Information Technology Workers in the Digital Economy", in Digital Economy 2003. 2003: Economics and Statistics Administration, Department of Commerce.

Depoorter, Ben; Parisi, Francesco (2002). "Fair Use and Copyright Protection: A Price Theory Explanation".*International Review of Law and Economics* 21 (4): 453–473.

Dhillon, G., (2007). *Principles of Information Systems Security: text and cases*, John Wiley & Sons.

Easttom, C., (2011).*Computer Security Fundamentals.* Pearson Press.

Esther Dyson/George Gilder/George Keyworth/Alvin Toffler (1994) Cyberspace and the American Dream: A Magna Carta for the Knowledge Age. In: *Future Insight 1.2.* The Progress & Freedom Foundation.

Frank Webster (2002) *Theories of the Information Society.* London: Routledge.

Gordon, Wendy J. (1982). "Fair Use as Market Failure: A Structural and Economic Analysis of the 'Betamax' Case and Its Predecessors". *Columbia Law Review* 82 (8): 1600–1657.

Harkins, D.; Carrel, D. (November 1998). *The Internet Key Exchange (IKE).* IETF. RFC 2409.

Hoffman, P. (December 2005). *Cryptographic Suites for IPsec.* IETF. RFC 4308.

Jan Van Dijk (2006) *The Network Society.* London: Sage. Second Edition.

Kent, S.; Atkinson, R. (November 1998). *IP Encapsulating Security Payload (ESP).* IETF. RFC 2406.

Krutz, Ronald L.; Russell Dean Vines (2003). *The CISSP Prep Guide* (Gold Edition ed.). Indianapolis, IN: Wiley.

Lambo, T., (2006)."ISO/IEC 27001: The future of infosec certification", *ISSA Journal,* November.

Layton, Timothy P. (2007). *Information Security: Design, Implementation, Measurement, and Compliance.* Boca Raton, FL: Auerbach publications.

Manuel Castells (2000) *The Rise of the Network Society. The Information Age: Economy, Society and Culture*. Volume 1. Malden: Blackwell. Second Edition.

McNab, Chris (2004). *Network Security Assessment*. Sebastopol, CA: O'Reilly.

McQuade, S. (ed) (2009) *The Encyclopedia of Cybercrime,* Westport, CT: Greenwood Press.

Michael Dawson/John Bellamy Foster (1998) Virtual Capitalism. In: Robert W. McChesney/Ellen Meiksins Wood/John Bellamy Foster (Eds.) (1998) *Capitalism and the Information Age.* New York: Monthly Review Press. pp. 51–67.

Nico Stehr (2002) *Knowledge & Economic Conduct.* Toronto: University of Toronto Press.

Parker D (1983) *Fighting Computer Crime,* U.S.: Charles Scribner's Sons.

Paterson, Kenneth G.; Yau, Arnold K.L. (2006). "Cryptography in theory and practice: The case of encryption in IPsec" (PDF). *Eurocrypt 2006, Lecture Notes in Computer Science Vol. 4004*. Berlin. pp. 12–29.

Pattavina, A. (ed) *Information Technology and the Criminal Justice System,* Thousand Oaks, CA: Sage.

Peltier, Thomas R. (2001). *Information Security Risk Analysis*. Boca Raton, FL: Auerbach publications.

Rider (1944). *The Scholar and the Future of the Research Library.* New York City: Hadham Press.

Sakane, S.; Kamada, K.; Thomas, M.; Vilhuber, J. (November 1998). *Kerberized Internet Negotiation of Keys (KINK).*IETF. RFC 4430.

Samuelson, Pamela (1995). "Copyright's fair use doctrine and digital data". *Publishing Research Quarterly* 11 (1): 27–39.

Seely Brown, John; Duguid, Paul (2000). *The Social Life of Information.* Harvard Business School Press.

Walden, I. (2007) *Computer Crimes and Digital Investigations,* Oxford: Oxford University Press.

Wall, D.S. (2007) *Cybercrimes: The transformation of crime in the information age,* Cambridge: Polity.

White, Gregory (2003). *All-in-one Security+ Certification Exam Guide*. Emeryville, CA: McGraw-Hill/Osborne.

Yannis Veneris (1984) *The Informational Revolution, Cybernetics and Urban Modelling,* PhD Thesis, University of Newcastle upon Tyne, UK.